Shree Swaminarayan Gadi

The Divine Heritage of the Supreme Lord Shree Swaminarayan

Acharya Swamishree Purushottampriyadasji Maharaj

ISBN 81-89189-20-4

First Edition 1978
Second Edition (Revised) 1991
Third Edition (Revised) 2004

Graphics
Shree Mukta Graphics
Shree Swaminarayan Mandir
Maninagar Ahmedabad Gujarat India 380 008

Printing
King Image Ltd.
Mahakant Complex Ashram Road
Ahmedabad Gujarat India 380 006

Maninagar@SwaminarayanGadi.com
SwaminarayanGadi.com

Shreejibapa

Swamibapa

Victory to Lord Shree Swaminarayan

Shree Swaminarayan Gadi
The Divine Heritage of the Supreme Lord Shree Swaminarayan

Translation by
His Divine Holiness Acharya Swamishree
Purushottampriyadasji Maharaj
Sants and Devotees

Published by
Maninagar Shree Swaminarayan Gadi Sansthan
Shreeji-sankalp-murti Adya Acharya-pravar Dharma-dhurandar 1008
Shree Muktajeevan Swamibapa Suvarna Jayanti Mahotsav Smarak Trust

Shree Swaminarayan Mandir
Maninagar Ahmedabad 380 008 Gujarat India

In celebration of
Shree Muktajeevan Swamibapa Shatabdi (Centenary)
1907 - 2007 CE

Page Structure

Reference

Transliteration of verse

Chapter number and title

Sanskrut or Gujarati verse

Main text

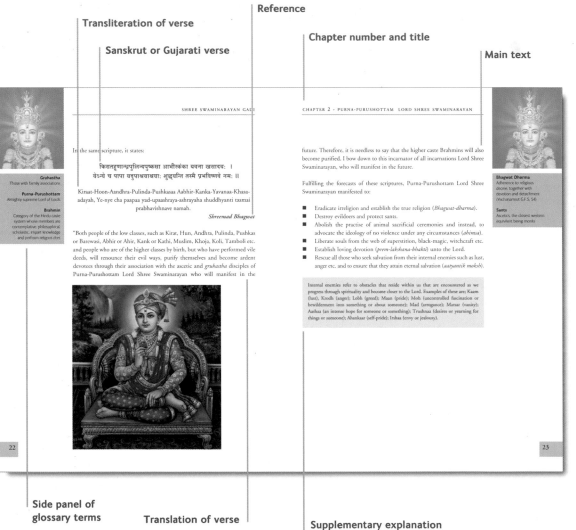

Gruhastha
Those with family associations

Purna-Purushottam
Almighty supreme Lord of Lords

Brahmin
Category of the Hindu caste system whose members are contemplative, philosophical, scholastic, impart knowledge and perform religious rites

CHAPTER 2 - PURNA-PURUSHOTTAM LORD SHREE SWAMINARAYAN

future. Therefore, it is needless to say that the higher caste Brahmins will also
become purified. I bow down to this incarnator of all incarnations Lord Shree
Swaminarayan, who will manifest in the future.

Fulfilling the forecasts of these scriptures, Purna-Purushottam Lord Shree
Swaminarayan manifested to:

- Eradicate irreligion and establish the true religion (*Bhagwat-dharma*).
- Destroy evildoers and protect sants.
- Abolish the practise of animal sacrificial ceremonies and instead, to advocate the ideology of no violence under any circumstances (*ahimsa*).
- Liberate souls from the web of superstition, black-magic, witchcraft etc.
- Establish loving devotion (*prem-lakshana-bhakti*) unto the Lord.
- Rescue all those who seek salvation from their internal enemies such as lust, anger etc. and to ensure that they attain eternal salvation (*aatyantik moksh*).

Internal enemies refer to obstacles that reside within us that are encountered as we
progress through spirituality and become closer to the Lord. Examples of these are; Kaam
(lust), Krodh (anger); Lobh (greed); Maan (pride); Moh (uncontrolled fascination or
bewilderment into something or about someone); Mad (arrogance); Matsar (vanity);
Aashaa (an intense hope for someone or something); Trushnaa (desires or yearning for
things or someone); Ahankaar (self-pride); Irshaa (envy or jealousy).

Bhagwat Dharma
Adherence to religious decree, together with devotion and detachment (Vachanamrut G.F.S. 54)

Sants
Ascetics, the closest western equivalent being monks

22

23

Side panel of glossary terms

Translation of verse

Supplementary explanation
Clarification of religious and philosophical points.
These are additional to the original text

This English translation of the holy scripture, Shree Swaminarayan Gadi, is dedicated to our beloved Gurudev Adya Acharya-pravar Jeevanpran Shree Muktajeevan Swamibapa. May his divine grace and benevolence shower upon us all so that the true supremacy of Lord Shree Swaminarayan and His divine heritage are understood by all and their teachings of spirituality and morality are spread throughout the world.

Swami Purushottampriyadasji
Acharya of Shree Swaminarayan Gadi

સ્વામી. પુરુષોત્તમપ્રિયદાસજી

In the Vachanamrut, Gadhada Middle Section 21, Lord Shree Swaminarayan states that those who aspire for spirituality should know the glory of the ever-present Lord and His sants. Once this is thoroughly understood, a firm determination regarding their supremacy is evoked and such individuals never stray from the path of spiritual welfare and eternal salvation.

By creating this translation of the scripture, Shree Swaminarayan Gadi, His Divine Holiness Acharya Swamishree Purushottampriyadasji Maharaj has ensured that the glory of the supreme Lord Shree Swaminarayan and His divine hierarchy of spiritual successors can be easily assimilated by sincere aspirants of the almighty Lord.

May his divine benevolence and spiritual strength remain with us all.

Sants and devotees of Shree Swaminarayan Gadi.

Introduction

The divine Gadi, upon which Lord Swaminarayan presides in His divine abode Akshardham, is Shree Swaminarayan Gadi.

Shree Swaminarayan Gadi is the supreme and eternal Gadi.

Shree Swaminarayan Gadi embodies the infinite power, supremacy and sovereignty of Lord Swaminarayan.

Just as the glory of Lord Swaminarayan is boundless, unique and unparalleled, the glory of Shree Swaminarayan Gadi is also boundless, unique and without equal. Shree Swaminarayan Gadi represents the divine office of Lord Swaminarayan.

In the year 1781 CE, the ever-merciful Lord Swaminarayan came onto this Earth, and established His supreme divine heritage, Shree Swaminarayan Gadi.

Lord Swaminarayan chose Sadguru Shree Gopalanand Swamibapa as His heir and entrusted him with the helm of the entire religion, the sovereignty of Shree Swaminarayan Gadi and gave him the key to eternal salvation.

In this divine lineage, then came Sadguru Shree Nirgundasji Swamibapa, Sadguru Shree Ishwarcharandasji Swamibapa and Jeevanpran Shree Muktajeevan Swamibapa, who gave Shree Swaminarayan Gadi a physical embodiment upon this earth.

Jeevanpran Swamibapa travelled all over the world, propagating the supreme tenets of Lord Shree Swaminarayan and Jeevanpran Shree Abji Bapashree.

Jeevanpran Shree Muktajeevan Swamibapa enthroned His Divine Holiness Acharya Swamishree Purushottampriyadasji Maharaj as the heir of Shree Swaminarayan Gadi.

Today, Acharya Swamishree Purushottampriyadasji Maharaj is continuing in the divine footsteps of Gurudev Jeevanpran Swamibapa, personifying the supreme sovereignty of Lord Shree Swaminarayan.

Shree Swaminarayan Gadi is

- The only resort at which the true and divine principles of Lord Shree Swaminarayan can be understood.
- Where the Lord will always preside, in the form of His Sankalp-swaroops.
- Where the Lord will be ever-present upon this earth, through the Acharya of this supreme, eternal Gadi.
- The Gadi whose true disciples will attain the Lord's eternal bliss.
- The very same Gadi that the Lord presides upon in His divine abode Akshardham.
- The Gadi that, by the Lord's express command, was given a physical embodiment by Shree Muktajeevan Swamibapa.

The glory of Shree Swaminarayan Gadi is epitomised in this scripture. It was first published in Gujarati, and released in 1977 CE (Samvat 2033) during the Shree Muktajeevan Swamibapa Amrut Mahotsav, when Jeevanpran Swamibapa succumbed to the humble wishes of his devotees and allowed them to celebrate his 70th manifestation day with great pomp and ceremony. As part of this Mahotsav, the Tula ceremony was performed during which Jeevanpran Swamibapa was weighed with gold, silver, platinum and the five precious gems; diamonds, emeralds, rubies, sapphires and pearls. This was a great historical occasion because no-one had ever been honoured in this manner.

The glorious text of this scripture contains a narrative describing the supreme heritage of Shree Swaminarayan Gadi. By reading about the divine episodes of Lord Shree Swaminarayan and His spiritual descendants, one is able to gain an understanding of the supreme philosophy and teachings of Lord Shree Swaminarayan, Jeevanpran Abji Bapashree and Adya Acharya-pravar Jeevanpran Shree Muktajeevan Swamibapa.

The first official recital of the scripture, Shree Swaminarayan Gadi was also held as part of the Amrut Mahotsav. The narrator of this divine scripture was none other than Swamibapa's choicest sant and subsequent heir, Shree Purushottampriyadasji Swamishree.

His Divine Holiness Acharya Swamishree Purushottampriyadasji Maharaj has created this English translation of the Shree Swaminarayan Gadi scripture, so that those who are not fluent readers of Gujarati can understand the true and unadulterated principles of Lord Shree Swaminarayan.

The text of the original scripture has been augmented with additional photographs, accompanying text, glossary terms and appendices to enable those who are foreign to the complexities of the Swaminarayan theology to gain an appreciation for the grandeur of Lord Shree Swaminarayan's supreme heritage, Shree Swaminarayan Gadi.

This English translation has been released in celebration of the Muktajeevan Swamibapa Shatabdi Mahotsav, the ten year long celebrations in commemoration of Jeevanpran Swamibapa's centenary.

May we humbly pray to Lord Swaminarayan, Jeevanpran Shree Abji Bapashree, Jeevanpran Swamibapa and His Divine Holiness Acharya Swamishree that we are given the strength and wisdom to remain adherent to the commands of the merciful Lord Swaminarayanbapa Swamibapa and understand the glory of Shree Swaminarayan Gadi. May we always remain at the supreme shelter of Shree Swaminarayan Gadi.

Jay Shree Swaminarayan

His Divine Holiness Acharya Swamishree Purushottampriyadasji Maharaj

Creator of this English translation

His Divine Holiness Acharya Swamishree Purushottampriyadasji Maharaj manifested in Samvat 1998 Adhik Jeth Sud 13, Thursday 28th of May 1942, in Bharasar - Kutch, India, at the home of father Shamjibhai Naran Madhani and mother Rambai. Jeevanpran Swamibapa gave him the name Hirji.

In his infant years, Acharya Swamishree had a stomach ailment that meant that he remained frail. Many types of medical treatments were tried but nothing was effective in curing the illness. Eventually, Shamjibhai took his son to Swamibapa and placed him at Swamibapa's feet. Jeevanpran Swamibapa said, "You have come to surrender him to me. Do not worry, he is mine and will always be mine. You will not understand my words now, but at the right time, everyone will understand what I am saying." From that day, Acharya Swamishree's health improved.

At the age of 11, Acharya Swamishree went to live in the boarding school in Maninagar to continue his education. Together with his studies, he remained alert to serve Swamibapa and the temple whenever he could. Very quickly, he became a favourite student of the boarding school. All the sants had a sincere affection for him. On one occasion, Jeevanpran Swamibapa said to him, "It is my wish that you become a sant." Immediately Acharya Swamishree replied, "Bapa, I am ready."

At the tender age of 19 years, 9 months and 23 days, in Samvat 2018 Fagan Sud 15 (Sunday 21st March 1962), Gurudev Jeevanpran Shree Muktajeevan Swamibapa initiated Acharya Swamishree as a sant and named him Swami Purushottampriyadasji.

Acharya Swamishree receiving initiation into the sant fraternity

This name reveals the identity of Acharya Swamishree – the Swami who is beloved to Purushottam, i.e. beloved to the supreme Lord. Purushottam was also Jeevanpran Swamibapa's name before he was initiated as a sant. Therefore, the name denotes the immense love that Jeevanpran Swamibapa has for Acharya Swamishree.

On one occasion, Jeevanpran Swamibapa took Acharya Swamishree to Bharasar, to the home of Shamjibhai Madhani. Jeevanpran Swamibapa pointed to Acharya Swamishree and said to Shamjibhai, "By giving your son to me, you have done a great service to the entire religion. He will personify the great virtues of renouncement, asceticism, spiritual knowledge and devotion. He will explain the supreme philosophy all around the world. His faith and dedication to me will become an example for all those who want to lead a disciplined, spiritual and moral life."

According to Jeevanpran Swamibapa's wishes, Acharya Swamishree studied Sanskrut, classical music and dance. Very quickly, he became a highly respected sant. From his early years as a sant, Jeevanpran Swamibapa kept Acharya Swamishree in his personal service.

In 1965, Jeevanpran Swamibapa officially took Acharya Swamishree to be his personal secretary and entrusted him with all his administrative responsibilities. From then onwards, Acharya Swamishree accompanied Jeevanpran Swamibapa wherever he went. Acharya Swamishree wrote down all the discourses and divine episodes of Jeevanpran Swamibapa that he heard about or experienced in person. He subsequently collated all the discourses and published them as Jeevanpran Swamibapa ni Vato Parts 1 and 2. He also compiled a three part biography of Jeevanpran Swamibapa's divine life upon the Earth, titled Shree Muktajeevan Swamibapa Charitramrut-sukh-sagar.

In Samvat 2035 Fagan Sud 2, Wednesday 28th February 1979, Jeevanpran Shree Muktajeevan Swamibapa appointed Acharya Swamishree to be his heir and subsequent Acharya of Shree Swaminarayan Gadi. Jeevanpran Swamibapa said, "I handover the helm of the Karan Satsang - Shree Swaminarayan Gadi to Shree Purushottampriyadasji Swami. In every respect, Lord Swaminarayan, Jeevanpran Bapashree and I, will work through him, and will always remain with him."

Jeevanpran Swamibapa entrusting Acharya Swamishree with the sovereignty of Shree Swaminarayan Gadi

Shortly after this investiture Jeevanpran Swamibapa visited the United Kingdom. This was to be his third tour of the country. It was during this tour, in Samvat 2035 Bhadarva Sud 7, Thursday 30th August 1979, that Jeevanpran Swamibapa withdrew his divine darshan from this world. He was presiding in Bolton at that time. Jeevanpran Swamibapa's final words were to His beloved heir, "Now, I will only eat if you feed me with your own hands." Through these words, Jeevanpran Swamibapa revealed that he gives darshan today through Acharya Swamishree.

Acharya Swamishree exemplified his absolute devotion to Jeevanpran Swamibapa by inspiring the creation of Shree Muktajeevan Swamibapa Smruti Mandir (Memorial Temple) in Ghodasar, Ahmedabad, India - at the exact site of Jeevanpran Swamibapa's cremation ceremony. This magnificent marble Temple contains unique architecture, art and sculpture, all indicating Jeevanpran Swamibapa's service to society.

Due to Acharya Swamishree's relentless efforts, the supreme principles and benevolent practices taught by Lord Swaminarayan and propagated throughout the world by Jeevanpran Swamibapa are flourishing more and more with each day at Shree Swaminarayan Gadi.

Shree Muktajeevan
Swamibapa Smruti Mandir

His Divine Holiness Acharya Swamishree:

- Has provided spiritual enlightenment and character reformation to thousands of people, both young and old and of all castes, creeds and races.
- Is actively involved in initiating the preservation of moral and cultural values.
- Has inspired the inauguration of numerous religious scriptures.
- Is a renowned social reformer and absolute pacifist promoting world peace, tolerance and understanding of all faiths and nations.
- Embarks on tours around the world to raise awareness of the fundamentals of humanity.
- Has established many social, educational, health, cultural and spiritual centres.
- Instigates campaigns, to offer free medical assistance, distribute vital medicines, and provide assistance in educating the poor and disadvantaged.
- Arranges the distribution of clothes and food for the poor and needy in society.
- Encourages his disciples to donate blood and enrol on organ donor schemes.
- Encourages water conservation and initiates projects to construct reservoirs.
- Has a personal interest in the preservation of the environment and ecology in general.
- During times of drought, famine and earthquake, has visited the afflicted regions and assisted in saving the lives of thousands through providing a multitude of aid.

Recognising the great qualities of His Divine Holiness Acharya Swamishree, leading scholars, priests and religious workers have bestowed many honorary titles upon him. These have included the following:

- Saddharma-ratnakar   The ocean of true religiosity.
- Saddharma-jyotirdhar   The beacon, torch of true religiosity.
- Seva-murti-param-tap   The incarnation of service of the highest austerity.
- Darshanik-sarva-bhaum   The leader of all six categories of the ancient Hindu spiritual philosophy.
- Siddhant-vagish   The personification of principles, at their most elite.
- Sanatan-dharma-sanrakshak   The protector of the eternal religion.
- Sat-siddhant-divakar   The greatest illuminator of true religion.

In this manner, His Divine Holiness Acharya Swamishree, has magnificently led Shree Swaminarayan Gadi Sansthan, the worldwide centre for spiritual, cultural and social welfare, into the 21st Century.

Jeevanpran Swamibapa lovingly embraces Acharya Swamishree at Lake Windermere, UK on the final day that Jeevanpran Swamibapa gave darshan in his human form upon this earth

Jeevanpran Swamibapa presides on Shree Swaminarayan Gadi,
with his beloved sants Acharya Swamishree and Shree Bhaktavatsaldasji Swami

**Purna Purushottam
Lord Shree Swaminarayan**

**Shreeji-sankalp-murti
Sadguru Shree
Gopalanand Swami**

**Shreeji-sankalp-murti
Sadguru Shree
Nirgundasji Swami**

**Shreeji-sankalp-murti
Jeevanpran Shree
Abji Bapashree**

**Shreeji-sankalp-murti
Sadguru Shree
Ishwarcharandasji Swami**

**Shreeji-sankalp-murti
Jeevanpran Shree
Muktajeevandasji Swamibapa**

Chapter 1

Shree Swaminarayan Gadi

Above all, in the divine abode Akshardham, is a great mass of light. It is immeasurable and infinite. It pervades into all four directions, above and below. In the midst of this lustre is a large Gadi. The divine Murti of Lord Purushottam presides upon that Gadi with all His infinite Muktas seated around Him.

Lord Shree Swaminarayan, Vachanamrut Loya 14

Shree Purushottam is the sovereign Lord. He is the eternal Murti who eternally presides upon His majestic throne, in the form of Akshardham.

Lord Shree Swaminarayan, Vachanamrut Gadhada Middle Section 64

This divine, majestic, lustrous throne, is Shree Swaminarayan Gadi.

SHREE SWAMINARAYAN GADI

Unparalleled, Unique, Ageless, Eternal, Supreme, Paramount

Shree Swaminarayan Gadi is:

- Karan Satsang.
- The Gadi that Purna Purushottam Lord Shree Swaminarayan Himself established.
- The gateway to attain the ever-present (*pragat*) Lord Shree Swaminarayan.
- The Gadi entrusted by the incarnator of all incarnations (Sarvavtari) Lord Shree Swaminarayan to Yogivarya Sadguru Shree Gopalanand Swami and which was handed down through His spiritual successors to Jeevanpran Swamibapa, who gave it a physical embodiment.
- The Gadi through which one can attain the status of *Anadi-mukta* whilst still in a physical body and thus enjoy the ultimate bliss of Lord Swaminarayan by becoming unified with His *Murti*.
- The Gadi at the resort of which one can obey the commands of Lord Shree Swaminarayan and implicitly surrender oneself unto Him through the practice of chaste devotion (*pativrata-bhakti*) with supreme *upasana*.

Gadi
Throne

Akshardham
The divine abode of
Lord Shree Swaminarayan

Murti
Divine image or form of the Lord

Muktas
Liberated souls

Vachanamrut
The words of Lord Shree
Swaminarayan compiled as a
scripture. See Appendix

Purna Purushottam
Almighty supreme Lord of Lords

Yogivarya
One who has accomplished the
virtues of the Yog philosophy

Sadguru
Status of eminent ascetic (sant)

Upasana
Correct understanding
of the Lord. See Appendix

Sankalp-swaroop
The physical embodiment of
the thoughts of Lord Shree
Swaminarayan i.e. those who
give darshan upon this earth by
the will of the Lord; they are
synonymous to the Lord Himself
Bapashree ni Vato Part 1 Varta 7
Bapashree ni Vato Part 2 Varta 165

Jeevanpran
Life and soul

Acharya
Preceptor

Karan Satsang: *Karan* means cause, and *Satsang* means true (*sat*) association (*sang*). Hence it means establishing a true association with Lord Swaminarayan and His Sankalp-swaroops. Only in the Karan Satsang, Shree Swaminarayan Gadi Sansthan, can one achieve eternal salvation (*aatyantik-moksh*), by forming a true rapport with Lord Swaminarayan. Lord Swaminarayan Himself re-manifested as Jeevanpran Abji Bapashree and reaffirmed the true tenets of the Karan Satsang:

- Supreme worship of Lord Swaminarayan.
- The state of the *Anadi-mukta*.
- Chaste devotion unto Lord Swaminarayan.
- The omnipresence of Lord Swaminarayan.
- The trinity of the divine forms of Lord Swaminarayan, are each one and the same. There is not an iota of difference between the divine form residing in Akshardham (*dham-nu-swaroop*), the human personification on this earth (*manushya-swaroop*) and the idols installed in the temples (*pratima-swaroop*).

The true and direct association with the supreme Lord Swaminarayan, can be achieved at Shree Swaminarayan Gadi, through the Acharya of Swaminarayan Gadi.

For further details refer to *Bapashree ni Vato Part 1 Varta 4*

Anadi-mukta: This is the highest state of the liberated soul.

- *Ekantik-muktas* have the obstacle of their material bodies to overcome before they can become as one with Lord Swaminarayan.
- *Param-ekantik-muktas* dwell in the vicinity of the Lord in His Akshardham.
- *Anadi-muktas* dwell within the *Murti* of Lord Swaminarayan in His Akshardham. However they are two distinct entities; the Lord - the master, and the *Anadi-mukta* - the mastered (eternally devoted soul).

For further details refer to Bapashree ni Vato Part 2 Varta 3

Bapashree ni Vato
The discourses of Jeevanpran Abji Bapashree

Darshan
The visualisation of the Lord. Also the act of looking with reverence and devotion at the image or deity in the shrine. sometimes of seeing a holy person

Bhakti
Devotion

Aarti
Ritual ceremony. See Appendix

In the Vachanamrut, Lord Swaminarayan says that the ultimate type of *bhakti* is chaste devotion (*pativrata-bhakti*). This encompasses the following nine types of *bhakti*. A virtuous woman will have a deep respect and infallible chaste devotion towards her husband. When these virtues are directed towards God, *pativrata-bhakti* has been achieved. This is the goal that everyone should strive for.

The nine-fold bhakti comprises of: *shravan-bhakti* - listening to the discourses of the Lord; *kirtan-bhakti* - singing the praises of God; *smaran-bhakti* - reminiscing about the Lord; *padsevan-bhakti* - physically serving the Lord; *archan-bhakti* - performing devotional ceremonies, (e.g. *aarti*, applying sandalwood paste (*chandan*) to the Lord's forehead, adoration); *vandan-bhakti* - bowing and prostrating before the Lord; *dasya-bhakti* - always remaining the Lord's devout servant; *sakhya-bhakti* - having a rapport with the Lord so that there remains a total faith in His commands and His wishes are implicitly obeyed; *samarpan-bhakti* - offering all, wealth, body and soul to the Lord.

Shree Swaminarayan Gadi is:

- The Gadi that bestows eternal salvation upon those who become its disciples.
- The spiritual Gadi that is protected by the Shreeji-sankalp-swaroop through whom the incarnator of all incarnations, Lord Shree Swaminarayan Himself acts.
- The glory of Shree Swaminarayan Gadi is boundless, infinite and beyond description.

Therefore, those who seek salvation and take shelter at Shree Swaminarayan Gadi:

- Will accomplish supreme *upasana* with chaste devotion unto Purna Purushottam Lord Shree Swaminarayan.
- Shall understand and experience the omnipresence and ever-presence of Lord Shree Swaminarayan.
- Will recognise and understand the supremacy of Lord Shree Swaminarayan and attain a divine life by remaining adherent to His commands.
- Will realise and experience that the master of all, Lord Shree Swaminarayan - Shree Ghanshyam Maharaj, who gives *darshan* in the form of idols within temples, is truly divine.
- Will understand that the Shreeji-sankalp-swaroop, i.e. those who are equivalent to the ever present Lord Shree Swaminarayan, have no human characteristics within them, and are truly divine.
- Shall attain the status of *Anadi-mukta* whilst still having a material body and will enjoy the bliss of the Lord's *Murti*.

Therefore, in every respect, Shree Swaminarayan Gadi is the essential resort for those who seek salvation. There are many *gadis*, but Shree Swaminarayan Gadi is supreme and is the quintessential Gadi.

The motive for which a *gadi* has been established, can only be fulfilled by that *gadi*. The *gadi* established for temporal motives can only fulfil such worldly objectives.

Purna Purushottam Lord Shree Swaminarayan handed over the helm of the entire Swaminarayan religion to Sadguru Shree Gopalanand Swami, thereby entrusting him with the key to eternal salvation. Through this spiritual heritage, the key to eternal salvation remains only in the hands of the Acharya of Shree Swaminarayan Gadi. Therefore, one's objective to attain true salvation can only be fulfilled at Shree Swaminarayan Gadi.

It is with the divine grace and strength of the incarnator of all incarnations (Sarvavtari) Lord Shree Swaminarayan, Shreeji-sankalp-murti Jeevanpran Bapashree, Yogindra Shreeji-sankalp-murti Shree Gopalanand Swami, Sadguru Shree Nirgundasji Swami, Nidar Siddhantvadi Sadguru Shree Ishwarcharandasji Swami and the Adya Acharya-pravar of Shree Swaminarayan

Gadi, His Divine Holiness Jeevanpran Swamibapa, that the glory of Shree Swaminarayan Gadi has been epitomised in this divine scripture.

Just as birds sing in ecstasy after drinking the water of a sweet stream, seekers of salvation (*mumukshu*) who read and contemplate the philosophy of this divine scripture, will be quenched of their thirst for the divine nectars of religious decree (*dharma*), spiritual knowledge (*gnan*), asceticism (*vairagya*) and devotion (*bhakti*). Having become devotees of Shree Swaminarayan Gadi, they will enjoy the bliss that exists in the Lord's *Murti*. Such are the divine blessings of Lord Shree Swaminarayan.

Chapter 2

Purna Purushottam Lord Shree Swaminarayan

All the incarnations originate from the very Lord that presides in this Satsang. This Lord is the cause of all the incarnations. He immanently resides within them.

Lord Shree Swaminarayan, Vachanamrut Ahmedabad 6

I travelled to the abode of Shree Purushottam Narayan (the supreme Lord), which transcends everything. I saw that it is I who is the Purushottam. There is no-one else as eminent as Me. I am the creator, sustainer and destroyer of all the cosmoses. Within all the cosmoses, it is with My divine lustre that the countless deities and their abodes are radiant.

Lord Shree Swaminarayan, Vachanamrut Ahmedabad 7

The ancient Hindu scripture, the Brahmand-Puran, forecast:

दत्तात्रेयः कृतयुगे त्रेतायां रघुनन्दनः ।
द्वापरे वासुदेवः स्यात् कलौ स्वामी वृषात्मजः ।।

Dattatreyah Krutayuge, Tretayaam Raghunandanah;
Dwapare Vasudevah syaat, Kalau Swami Vrushatmajah.

"In the age of Sat-yug, Lord Dattatreya will manifest. In Treta-yug, Lord Raghunandan, alias Ramchandraji, will manifest. Vasudev, alias Lord Shree Krishna, will manifest in Dwapar-yug, and in the age of Kali-yug, the son of Dharmadev, Lord Shree Swaminarayan will manifest."

In the Holy Scripture, the Padma-Puran, it is said:

पाखण्डबहुले लोके स्वामिनाम्ना हरिः स्वयम् ।
पापपङ्कनिमग्नं तज्जगदुद्धारयिष्यति ।।

Paakhanda-bahule loke Swami-naamnaa Harih swayam,
Paap-pank-nimagnam taj-jagad-uddhaarayishyati.

"When dishonesty has spread throughout society and the world has become immersed in a mire of sin, Lord Shree Swaminarayan will manifest in order to liberate all."

The Vishnu-Dharmottar scripture states:

महाधर्मात्यये पुण्ये नाम्ना पापविनाशके ।
हरिप्रसादविप्रस्य स्वामिनाम्ना हरिः स्वयम् ।।

Mahaa-dharmaatyaye punye naamnaa paap-vinaashake,
Hariprasad-viprasya Swami-naamnaa Harih swayam.

"When the principles of the elite religion are being destroyed, Lord Swaminarayan will manifest at the home of the *Brahmin* Hariprasad. By the mere utterance of His name, sinners will be purified."

Purna Purushottam
Almighty supreme Lord of Lords

Satsang
Fellowship associated with the Swaminarayan religion

Vachanamrut
The words of Lord Shree Swaminarayan compiled as a scripture. See Appendix

Yug
Era

Sat-yug, Treta-yug, Dwapar-yug, Kali-yug
See Appendix

Lord Dattatreya
One of the 24 incarnations of the Lord

Lord Raghunandan / Ramchandraji
One of the 24 incarnations of the Lord

Vasudev / Shree Krishna
One of the 24 incarnations of the Lord

Dharmadev
Lord Swaminarayan's father when He manifested on this world. He was the embodiment of religion

Brahmin
Category of the Hindu caste system whose members are contemplative, philosophical, scholastic, impart knowledge and perform religious rites

Hariprasad
Another name for Dharmadev, the Lord's father

Sahajanand
Another name of Lord Swaminarayan given by Shree Ramanand Swami

Satpurush
Saintly person

Caste System: Manu, the Vedic sage, formulated the caste system with four main categories differentiating people according to their characteristics; the *Shudras* - those serving society; the *Vaishyas* - those with skills and abilities which enabled them to be engaged in trade, commerce and business; the *Kshatriyas* - those who administrate and execute projects to protect the community at large; and the *Brahmins* - those who are contemplative, philosophical, impart knowledge and perform religious rites.

By merit, a person could rise from a lower group to a higher group; and through criminal and anti-social behaviour, descend groups. Manu said, "Neither birth nor sacraments, study nor ancestry can decide whether a person is a *Brahmin* or not. Character and conduct alone can decide."

Lord Swaminarayan manifested as a *Brahmin*. However He refuted the idea of segregation and discrimination and had followers from all aspects of society from the poor to the kings.

In the Vishwaksen-Sanhita scripture, it is said:

भूम्यां कृतावतारो वै सर्वानेताञ्जनानहम् ।
प्रापयिष्यामि वैकुण्ठं सहजानन्दनामतः ।।

Bhoomyaam krutaavataaro vai sarvaan-etaan-janaan-aham,
Praapayishyami Vaikuntham Sahajanand-naamatah.

"I will assume the name Sahajanand and will manifest upon this earth. I will ensure that souls attain My divine abode."

In the eleventh chapter of the Shreemad Bhagwat, it is written:

कृतादिषु प्रजा राजन् कलाविच्छन्ति सम्भवम् ।
कलौ खलु भविष्यन्ति नारायणपरायणाः ।।

Krutaadishu prajaa raajan Kalaa-vichchhanti sambhavam,
Kalau khalu bhavishyanti Narayan-paraayanaahaa.

"The people of Sat-yug, Treta-yug and Dwapar-yug wish to be born in Kali-yug, because it is in this age that the supreme Lord Shree Swaminarayan and His Satpurush will manifest."

In the same scripture, it states:

किरातहूणान्ध्रपुलिन्दपुष्कसा आभीरकंका यवना खसादयः ।
येऽन्ये च पापा यदुपाश्रयाश्रयाः शुद्ध्यन्ति तस्मै प्रभविष्णवे नमः ॥

Kiraat-Hoon-Aandhra-Pulinda-Pushkasaa Aabhir-Kankaa-Yavanaa-Khasa-adayah,
Ye-nye cha paapaa yad-upaashraya-ashrayaha shuddhyanti tasmai prabhavishnave namah.

"Both people of the low classes, such as *Kirat, Hun, Andhra, Pulinda, Pushkas* or *Barewasi, Abhir* or *Ahir, Kank* or *Kathi, Muslim, Khoja, Koli, Tamboli* etc. and people who are of the higher classes by birth, but who have performed vile deeds, will renounce their evil ways, purify themselves and become ardent devotees through their association with the ascetic and *gruhasth* disciples of Purna Purushottam Lord Shree Swaminarayan who will manifest in the future. Therefore, it is needless to say that the higher caste *Brahmins* will also become purified. I bow down to this incarnator of all incarnations (Sarvavtari) Lord Shree Swaminarayan, who will manifest in the future."

Fulfilling the forecasts of these scriptures, Purna Purushottam Lord Shree Swaminarayan manifested to:

- Eradicate irreligion and establish the true religion (*Bhagwat-dharma*).
- Destroy evildoers and protect *sants*.
- Abolish the practice of animal sacrificial ceremonies and instead, to advocate the ideology of non-violence under any circumstances (*ahinsa*).
- Liberate souls from the web of superstition, black-magic, witchcraft, etc.
- Establish loving devotion (*prem-lakshana-bhakti*) unto the Lord.
- Rescue all those who seek salvation from their internal enemies such as lust, anger etc. and to ensure that they attain eternal salvation (*aatyantik-moksh*).

Internal enemies refer to obstacles that reside within people that are encountered as they progress through spirituality and become closer to the Lord. Examples of these are; lust (*kaam*), anger (*krodh*); greed (*lobh*); pride (*maan*); uncontrolled fascination or bewilderment about something or someone (*moh*); arrogance (*mad*); vanity (*matsar*); an intense hope for someone or something (*aashaa*); desires or yearning for things or someone (*trushnaa*); self-pride (*ahankaar*); envy or jealousy (*irshaa*).

Chapter 3

Divine Ordination

Lord Swaminarayan manifested on the earth to:

- Fulfil the devotional desires and wishes of His loving devotees and grant them His divine parental compassion.
- Protect and rejuvenate religious decree (*dharma*) and devotion (*bhakti*) which were being persecuted and degraded by irreligious and evil entities.
- Establish and disseminate His eminence as the incarnator of all incarnations (Sarvavtari), His supreme spiritual knowledge and His true *upasana*.
- Enlighten the previous incarnations and their devotees with His supreme *upasana* and then uplift them to His abode - Akshardham.
- Establish the long-forgotten principles of the *Ekantik-dharma* by destroying evil and thereby protecting the upholders of truth and virtuosity.
- Elucidate the true spiritual knowledge and *upasana* to His devotees, i.e. the souls who seek salvation and then lead them to His divine abode, encouraging other souls to follow the path to salvation.

Purna Purushottam Lord Swaminarayan in His divine
lustrous abode, Akshardham, deliberating with His
Muktas about manifesting upon the earth

The incarnator of all incarnations, Purna Purushottam Lord Shree Swaminarayan resolved to manifest upon the earth.

Is there any particular event that caused Him to manifest? No.
Did anybody pray for Him to manifest? No.

He manifested out of sheer mercy and divine grace.

In order to liberate the souls, who had become inflicted by the illusion of Maya, the cause of all causes, the supreme Lord, Purna Purushottam Lord Shree Swaminarayan decided to manifest upon this earth along with His *Mukta*s.

When deciding to manifest upon this earth, the Lord held a divine congregation with His *Mukta*s in Akshardham.

The *Mukta*s humbly prayed, "Oh Lord, You are the almighty, omnipotent and supreme Lord. Merely through Your will, You are able to remove the miseries of souls. No-one other than You is able to liberate souls and bestow upon them the *Mukta* state. Oh merciful Lord! What need is there for us to accompany You?"

Lord Shree Swaminarayan replied to the *Mukta*s, "What you say is indeed true. However, the souls have become trapped in the illusion of Maya. Who will introduce them to Me? People relate to and have affection for others who are like them – those who are of the same form as them. Therefore, you must accompany Me onto the earth and become like them. They will see you worshipping Me and learn through your teachings. Attract the souls towards you and introduce them to Me. Explain My glory to them and encourage them to become engrossed with devotion unto Me."

With joined hands, the *Mukta*s humbly prayed to the Lord, "Dear Lord! To liberate souls is Your work. Merely by performing the *vartman* ceremony to the souls, You are able to liberate them from their material body and award them the status of *Mukta*."

The Lord smiled as He heard the humble requests of His *Mukta*s and said, "My dear *Mukta*s! If I call a soul to Me and perform the *vartman* ceremony, his body will cease. Others will see this and immediately flee in fear of death. Then, whose salvation will we perform? Dear *Mukta*s, you must come with Me. Let the souls become attracted to you and then, we will do just as you say. However, the process needs to be performed in phases. When the souls have become affiliated with you, we will reveal the reality."

In this manner, the incarnator of all incarnations Lord Shree Swaminarayan resolved to manifest on the earth together with His *Mukta*s.

Karan Satsang
True association with Lord Swaminarayan. See Chapter 1

Acharya
Preceptor

Karma
Sanskrut word meaning deed or action. According to Hindu belief, every action has inevitable consequences which attach themselves to the doer. These deeds result in reward or punishment dependent on their nature. Karma is thus the moral laws of actions and their consequences

Vartman: During the formal and ceremonial initiation of a devotee into the Karan Satsang, Shree Swaminarayan Gadi Sansthan, the Acharya of Shree Swaminarayan Gadi places a few drops of water in the devotee's palm, chants the Lord's *mantra* and then pours the water onto the ground. Only the Acharya of Shree Swaminarayan Gadi can perform true *vartman* because only he has the power to burn away great sins, and free the devotee of all his sins and *karmas* from his present and past lives.

By virtue of this ceremony the soul is free from past sins and the devotee promises to obey the five vows (**panch vartman**):

- Not to consume intoxicating or addictive substances (liquor, drugs etc.) which lead to wrongful temptation.
- Not to kill nor to eat the flesh of any living entity, i.e. pure vegetarianism, non-violence (*ahimsa*).
- Not to commit adultery and other wrongful sexual acts (rape, seduction etc.).
- Not to steal - not only money but also properties and goods.
- Not to perform irreligious, unsociable or immoral deeds or have others perform them.

Renouncers (*tyagis*) have additional vows to abide by:

- *Nirlobh* - being free from greed (to not hoard or keep money or wealth even via another person).
- *Nishkam* - being completely void of lust.
- *Nihswad* - being completely void of all preferences, having no partiality for anything and relinquishing fine articles.
- *Nirman* - being free from all arrogance, pride and anger, and being tolerant of others.
- *Nihsneh* - being free from all affection and attachment to those other than the Lord.

Chapter 4

Divine Manifestation

The Lord's devotees on this Earth are corporeal and have human bodies. When the Lord appears on this Earth for the salvation of souls, He also shows Himself in the same manner. He conceals His greatness and showers affection on His devotees. He takes the form of the devotee's son, companion, friend, or relative. As a result of this relationship, devotees experience a close intimacy with Him and the barrier between the Lord and the devotee does not remain. In this manner, the Lord grants His infinite bliss to the devotee in accordance with the individual's spiritual desires.

Lord Shree Swaminarayan, Vachanamrut Kariyani 5

The divine lustrous darshan of the almighty
Lord Shree Swaminarayan – Shree Sahajanand Swami Maharaj

In the North Indian State of Uttar Pradesh, there is a city called Ayodhya (a holy city that is the birth place of Ramchandraji). Itarpur is a village near Ayodhya. Here, there lived a *Brahmin* called Balsharma, who was of the *Sarvariya Samvedi* caste, with his wife Bhagyavatidevi. In Samvat 1796 Kartik Sud 11, the couple was blessed with a son whom they named Dharmadev.

Chhapaiya is another village near Ayodhya. Here, there lived the *Brahmin* Krishnasharma with his wife Bhavanidevi. In Samvat 1798 Kartik Sud 15, this couple was blessed with a daughter whom they named Bhaktidevi. Krishnasharma arranged for Bhaktidevi to marry Dharmadev, and then kept the couple at his home in Chhapaiya.

Dharmadev and Bhaktidevi lived a devout and religious life, and faithfully worshipped God. All those who came in their contact became inspired to give up their immoral practices and also started to perform devotion unto God. Due to their religious convictions, the couple was harassed by those who followed illicit practices. Nevertheless, Dharmadev and Bhaktidevi remained steadfast. Pleased with their unfaltering devotion, Purna Purushottam Lord Shree Swaminarayan gave *darshan* to the couple and blessed them with a boon; "Dharmadev! I will manifest at your home and protect you from the sinful individuals who are harassing you. I will establish the *Ekantik-dharma* on the earth."

> The birth of the Lord and divine *Muktas* is referred to as 'manifestation' as they are not bound by the cycle of births and deaths or nature. They come on the Earth merely by their will, for granting salvation to the souls.

As Dharmadev had gained the blessings of Lord Shree Swaminarayan, he came to be known as Hariprasad (consecrated by God). His wife Bala had been granted the *darshan* of Lord Swaminarayan because of her devout worship of God and therefore, she came to be known as Bhakti (devotion).

After some time, in Samvat 1837 Chaitra Sud 9 (Monday 2nd April 1781), just after 10pm, the incarnator of all incarnations (Sarvavtari), Purna Purushottam Lord Shree Swaminarayan gave His divine lustrous *darshan* to His mother, Bhakti. He reminded her of His promise and then immediately assumed the form of an enchanting baby.

Manifestation of
Lord Shree Swaminarayan –
Shree Ghanshyam Maharaj

The Lord's divine, lustrous *darshan* is the actual form of Lord Shree Swaminarayan. However, if He gave *darshan* on the earth in this manner, humans would be unable to take His *darshan* and would not become attracted by Him. It is one of His divine episodes, that for the benefit and salvation of all souls, He conceals all this lustre and assumes the form of a baby.

At that time, the melodious sound of drums emanated from the sky. A light, soothing breeze scented with fragrance filled the air and showers of sandalwood paste (*chandan*) and flowers descended upon Chhapaiya. The hearts of *sants* became filled with bliss and enlightenment, whilst the hearts of evil souls became afflicted by pain and they experienced a burning sensation throughout their bodies.

Before Lord Swaminarayan manifested on the earth, His *darshan* could only be attained by His own *Muktas*. The other deities and their *Muktas* were not able to have His *darshan*. However, when He gave *darshan* on the Earth, all were granted His *darshan*. All the deities came for this long awaited *darshan*. The arrival of these divine entities was evident through the sound and the fragrance. As they offered their adoration to the Lord, they showered Him with flowers and sandalwood.

Deities, including Brahma, Vishnu, and Shiv, gather for the darshan of the baby Lord Ghanshyam

Dharmadev and Bhaktimata named the baby Lord 'Ghanshyam'. When the baby Lord Ghanshyam was three and quarter months old, the sage Markandeya Rishi came to their home (Samvat 1837 Ashadh Vad 7, Thursday 12th July 1781). Dharmadev ceremoniously welcomed the *rishi* and offered him an appropriate seat.

Ghan - clouds, shyam - dark in complexion. Therefore Ghanshyam refers to rain filled clouds, which indicates the imminent arrival of rain water - one of the necessities for life, and signifies extreme attractiveness.

Dharmadev knew that the *rishi* was an astrologer. He sat in front of the *rishi* with the baby Lord Ghanshyam in his lap and requested him to formally name his son. Markandeya Rishi gazed at baby Lord Ghanshyam's face. He then took His divine hand to read His palm. The *rishi* proclaimed, "This child was born under the sign of Cancer; therefore, He will be known as 'Hari'. He will have characteristics according to His name, He will therefore alleviate you from all your worries, and of all those who resort to His shelter. He has a dark (*krishna*) complexion, which will attract to Him, all those who are granted His *darshan*. Therefore His name will also be 'Krishna'. Combining the two names, He will also be known as 'Harikrishna'. Your baby son possesses the five virtues: renunciation, spiritual knowledge, austerity, religious decree and yoga. As a result, He will become like Shivji. Therefore, He will become famous by the name 'Nilkanth'."

Letters are associated with each sign of the Hindu zodiac. The letters 'D' and 'H' are assigned to the sign of Cancer and are used for the naming of babies born under this sign.

The *rishi* concluded his forecast by saying, "In His palm, He has the mark of a lotus flower (*padma*). Consequently, He will be the sovereign Lord of multitudes of souls and will possess innumerable characteristics that are capable of bestowing salvation."

Hearing such a forecast about their son's future, Dharmadev and Bhaktimata became overjoyed.

Markandeya Rishi / Muni
Astrologer and sage.
Said to be one of the eight immortals (chiranjivis)

Rishi
Sage, holy person

Hari
From the word hru which means to steal, i.e. the Lord's ability to steal the affection and the hearts of mortals

Krishna
One who attracts all and liberates them from the world

Shivji
One of the trinity of deities (Brahma the creator, Vishnu the sustainer and Shiv the destroyer). Also known as Nilkanth, and as a great ascetic

Padma
From the Samudrik scripture, which states that those who have a lotus (padma) on their palm will be sovereigns

Nilkanth
During the mythological churning of the ocean (samudra manthan) the deity Shivji drank the poison that emerged from it. This turned his throat blue. He was therefore named Nil (blue) kanth (throat). Shivji was renowned for practicing severe austerities. During His forest expedition, the Lord performed severe austerities and therefore assumed the name Nilkanth Varni

Chapter 5

Divine Childhood Episodes

When the Lord appears on the earth in a human form, He possesses the same infinite spiritual powers that He has when He is in Akshardham. Only foolish souls think of Him to be human, just like themselves. They believe that the Lord is born, then becomes a child, reaches adolescence, becomes old and eventually dies. However, these human features do not apply to the Lord. The Murti of the Lord is divine. All His actions are also divine.

Lord Shree Swaminarayan, Vachanamrut Panchala 7

Shree Ghanshyam Maharaj takes His first few steps
and lovingly embraces His father, Dharmadev,
whilst His mother, Bhaktimata, looks on in delight

Akshardham
The divine abode of
Lord Shree Swaminarayan

Murti
Divine image or form of the Lord

Vachanamrut
The words of Lord Shree
Swaminarayan compiled as a
scripture. See Appendix

Chowl-sanskar
A ceremony denoting the first
haircut of Hindu males as
prescribed by Hindu scriptures

Brahmin
Category of the Hindu caste
system whose members are
contemplative, philosophical,
scholastic, impart knowledge
and perform religious rites

Kalidatt
This was in fact the Lord's
maternal uncle

Twelve wives
Dharmadev is the incarnation
of religion (dharma). Dharma has
various characteristics, which
sometimes personify themselves.
The wives mentioned here are the
twelve physical personifications
of the twelve characteristics
of dharma

Just as a magnet draws iron, the baby Lord Shree Ghanshyam attracted everyone's inclination towards Him. Everyone took great pleasure in playing with Lord Ghanshyam. They would carry Him, kiss Him, and cuddle Him.

As time passed, Lord Ghanshyam started to take His first few steps. He was soon running, purifying the ground with each step. When Shree Hari entered His third year, the Chowl-sanskar ceremony was performed (Samvat 1839 Jeth Vad 5, Monday 19th June 1783). As a part of the ceremony, His parents held a feast to which many *Brahmins* had been invited.

Whilst His parents were busy with the hospitalities of serving their guests, Lord Ghanshyam played with His friends. As they played, the children drifted Him away to a park on the outskirts of the town. Kalidatt, an evil demon versed in the ways of black magic, arrived.

Using his black magic, Kalidatt disguised himself as a child and started to play with Lord Shree Ghanshyam and His friends. He then scared the Lord's friends away by showing them his bulging eyes, reptilian tongue, and menacing face. Then seeing the baby Lord Shree Ghanshyam alone, Kalidatt approached Him with a view to kill Him. As he came closer, Lord Ghanshyam looked up at Kalidatt with glaring eyes and unleashed a torrent of fire, striking and burning the evil Kalidatt who retreated in pain. Kalidatt then cast a spell to create a fierce storm. He turned himself into a terrifying and gigantic monster. With all his might, the monster fell onto the tree under which the baby Lord Shree Ghanshyam was sitting. The tree snapped and fell, but it fell in such a way that it formed a protective canopy over the baby Lord Ghanshyam. The evil Kalidatt lost consciousness, thus losing his ability to regain his normal form. The storm he had created took hold of his enormous body and thrashed it against the trees. Kalidatt stumbled and fell to the ground, covered in blood, and died in agony.

By killing the demon Kalidatt in His childhood, and other demons during the forest expedition (see Chapter 7), Lord Swaminarayan fulfilled one of His motives for manifesting on the earth; to destroy evil doers.

Knowing the baby Lord Shree Ghanshyam to be alone, Dharmadev's 12 deity wives manifested and took the opportunity to play with Him. In order to fulfil

Bhaktimata
Another name for Bhaktidevi,
Lord Shree Ghanshyam's mother
when He manifested on this Earth

Darshan
The visualisation of the Lord.
Also the act of looking with
reverence and devotion at the
image or deity in the shrine,
sometimes of seeing a holy person

The demon Kalidatt dies whilst trying
to kill the baby Lord Shree Ghanshyam

their wishes, Lord Shree Ghanshyam assumed 12 forms. By now, Lord Shree Ghanshyam's parents and relatives started to get worried and began to search for Him. Eventually, they arrived at the park. Lord Shree Ghanshyam's aunt, Sundari, spotted Him sitting under the broken tree. She picked Him up and took Him to Bhaktimata.

Lord Swaminarayan assumed 12 forms and fulfilled the wishes of the 12 deity wives of Dharmadev. These deities would not be able to have the *darshan* of the Lord if He was not present on the earth. He fulfilled their wishes and provided them with the opportunity to show their parental compassion to the Lord. This was another motive for the Lord's manifestation.

Deities come for the darshan of
the divine baby Lord Ghanshyam

Vaikunth, Golok, Badrikashram
The celestial abodes of the incarnations Ramchandra (Ram), Krishna and Nar–Narayan, respectively. Akshardham is the abode of the Supreme Lord Swaminarayan

Aarti
Ritual ceremony. See Appendix

Rampratapbhai
Husband of Suvasini. Lord Ghanshyam's elder brother, the younger brother being Ichharambhai

Lord Shree Ghanshyam entertained His friends in many wondrous ways. Sometimes they went bathing in a river, a lake or in a small rapid stream. Whilst bathing, He would make His friends dive under water and would take them to Vaikunth, Golok or Badrikashram for *darshan*. On one occasion, infant Lord Shree Ghanshyam and His childhood friend Veniram went to Lake Narayan where they competed against each other about who could swim across the lake and reach the other side first. The Lord swam swiftly across the lake and went into the village. However, Veniram became tired and started drowning. His friends and some of the villagers who were standing on the banks, began shouting for someone to save him. Unseen by anyone, the omnipresent Lord Ghanshyam picked Veniram from the lake and took him into the village. Everyone was surprised when they saw Lord Shree Ghanshyam coming from the village accompanied with Veniram. They all fell unto the lotus feet of the infant Lord Shree Ghanshyam and bowed to Him in obeisance.

> By the episode with Veniram, Lord Swaminarayan has indicated that one must never compete with the Lord or challenge Him in any manner. Ultimately, He will succeed and His wish will become reality. The power of the Lord is immense. No-one can ever assimilate His true greatness.

Soon after, Dharmadev's family went to live in Ayodhya. Each day, Lord Shree Ghanshyam Maharaj would bathe in the River Saryu and then visit every temple in Ayodhya for *darshan*. He would assume numerous forms and be present in each of the temples during the dusk (*sandhya*) *aarti* ceremony and during the evening religious discourses. Lord Shree Ghanshyam's elder brother Rampratapbhai often witnessed the simultaneous presence of Lord Ghanshyam at each of the temples.

> Lord Shree Swaminarayan assumed many forms and remained present in all the temples during the dusk *aarti* ceremony and during the evening religious discourses. By this, Lord Swaminarayan has highlighted the need to perform devotion to the Lord and the importance of being present at the religious discourses. By assuming many forms, He has revealed His nature of being omnipresent. He is one, but is present everywhere.

On one occasion, Lord Shree Ghanshyam came home after playing. His sister-in-law (*bhabhi*) Suvasini was cooking in the kitchen. She had removed her gold ring and put it aside. Lord Shree Ghanshyam saw the ring. He picked it up and

Shree Ghanshyam Maharaj
playing with His friends

immediately left the house. He went to the confectionery shop and said, "Take this ring and let Me eat as many sweets as I can." The shopkeeper accepted the ring and allowed Lord Shree Ghanshyam to eat the sweets, thinking that such a small child could not possibly eat many sweets. Lord Shree Ghanshyam asked him to close the shop so that no one could see Him eating. The shopkeeper willingly obliged and started serving Lord Shree Ghanshyam. He consumed all the sweets in the shop and left it completely empty.

When Shree Ghanshyam Maharaj returned home, He found everyone searching for the ring. His sister-in-law Suvasini said, "Lord Ghanshyam had come here earlier so ask Him whether He has taken it." Shree Dharmadev questioned Shree Ghanshyam, "Ghanshyam! Have you taken the ring?" Lord Shree Ghanshyam replied, "Yes, I took it." Dharmadev continued, "So, where is it now?" Shree Ghanshyam replied, "I have given it to the confectioner." Everyone decided to go to the confectioner's home.

Shree Ghanshyam Maharaj showed everyone the shopkeeper to whom He had given the ring. They started to scold him, "Why did you coax such a small child? Are you not ashamed of yourself?" The shopkeeper replied, "Actually, it is me that has been cheated. He has eaten my entire stock of confectionery." Hearing this, Lord Shree Ghanshyam immediately protested, "He is lying, look in his shop." The shopkeeper opened his shop. To his surprise, it was completely full of sweets, as if untouched. The amazed shopkeeper immediately returned the ring and bowed in reverence at Lord Shree Ghanshyam's lotus feet.

Chapter 6

Education

न चोरहार्यं न च राजहार्यं, न भ्रातृभाज्यं न च भारकारी ।
व्यये कृते वर्धत एव नित्यं, विद्याधनं सर्वधनप्रधानम् ।।

Na chor-haaryam na cha raaj-haaryam, Na bhraatru-bhaajyam na cha bhaar-kaari, Vyaye krute vardhata ev nityam, Vidyaa-dhanam sarva-dhana-pradhaanam.

Wealth exists in the form of knowledge. This wealth cannot be stolen by a thief, cannot be divided amongst brothers and cannot become burdensome. The more that one uses this wealth (teaches it), the more it multiplies. Therefore, wealth in the form of knowledge, is the greatest of all riches.

Shree Dharmadev places a gold coin, a sword and a holy scripture in front of Shree Ghanshyam Maharaj to find out what He would be most interested in when He grew up. The Lord immediately grabbed the scripture and was totally disinterested in the coin and the sword

53

When He was five years old, the child Lord Ghanshyam commenced His education (Samvat 1842 Chaitra Sud 12, Monday 10th April 1786). He was taught by His father, Dharmadev. The all-knowing Lord easily grasped the knowledge. When He was eight years old, the Yagnopavit Ceremony was performed (Samvat 1845 Fagan Sud 10, Tuesday 5th February 1789). He then started studying the Vedas and the other holy scriptures. Although Dharmadev taught Lord Shree Ghanshyam, there were times when even he became confused. At these times, Lord Shree Ghanshyam Himself would explain the true meanings to His father. Sometimes, Lord Shree Ghanshyam would study subjects and become conversant with them even before His father had taught them. Acknowledging the young Lord's extraordinary divine prowess, Dharmadev bowed down to Him.

> The Yagnopavit Ceremony is an initiation ritual, usually performed around the age of eight, during which a male Hindu *Brahmin* is invested with a sacred thread. After this, he is encouraged to begin the study of the *Vedas*. The thread (*yagnopavit*) is sacrosanct, giving strength and power to perform the *Yagna* ceremony. It hangs around the torso diagonally from the left shoulder to the right thigh. It is also given to ascetic followers of Lord Swaminarayan upon initiation.

Shree Dharmadev teaches the rudiments of the scriptures to Shree Ghanshyam Maharaj

A convention of scholars was held in Kashi to which Dharmadev had been invited. The infant Lord Shree Ghanshyam accompanied Dharmadev to the debate. During the assembly, Lord Shree Ghanshyam spoke in fluent *Sanskrut*

Brahmin
Category of the Hindu caste system whose members are contemplative, philosophical, scholastic, impart knowledge and perform religious rites

Vedas
Ancient Hindu scriptures. Part of the traditional educational process in Hinduism

Kashi
Renowned as a gathering place for learned scholars and regarded as a holy city. It is situated on the banks of the river Ganges (Ganga). It is also known as Varanasi and Banaras

Yagna
Ceremony involving placing items such as flowers, nectars etc into a sacred fire

Sanskrut
Classical language of the Hindu religion. Known as the 'language of the Gods'. It is considered to be the mother of many ancient and modern languages

and eloquently presented a lecture about the *Vishishtadwait* philosophy. He explained that God has a definite form. He affirmed the philosophy founded by Ramanujacharya and then developed this philosophy one step further. He explained, "There are two distinct and identical entities - the Lord and His *Mukta*. When they merge, it appears as if only Lord exists. However, in reality, they are distinct. Lord always remains the master, whilst the *Mukta* remains the devotee."

> During the Kashi convention, Lord Shree Swaminarayan advocated the *Vishishtadwait* philosophy. Even before such great scholars, and at a very young age, Lord Shree Swaminarayan revealed this great prowess in philosophy. He established His true philosophy on the Earth. In this manner, He fulfilled another of His motives for manifesting upon the Earth.

Vishishtadwait
Philosophy of the Swaminarayan faith.
See Appendix

Ramanujacharya
A 11th century philosopher.
See Appendix

Mukta
Liberated soul

Overwhelmed by hearing such an eloquent oration from the child Lord Shree Ghanshyam, the scholars praised Him. They bowed down to Him in respect, and presented Him with garlands of flowers.

Shree Ghanshyam Maharaj explains the Vishishtadwait philosophy during the convention of scholars in Kashi

Chapter 7

Forest Expedition

My nature is such that I like to go to temples for darshan, listen to religious discourses, remain in the company of sants and visit holy places of pilgrimage. When I left My home at an early age, I did not like keeping excess articles with Me. I liked to stay in forests. I had no fear of snakes, lions, elephants or other wild animals. I toured the holy places of pilgrimage and eventually came to Shree Ramanand Swami.

Lord Shree Swaminarayan, Vachanamrut Gadhada Middle Section 55

During My stay in Purushottampuri, I lived only on air as My sustenance for many months. I let My body be dragged away by a river that was three or four miles wide. Whether it was winter, summer or the monsoon season, I stayed without any shelter and only wore a small kopin. I roamed through thick forests that were inhabited by tigers, elephants and wild buffaloes. Even though I travelled in such arduous conditions, My body survived.

Lord Shree Swaminarayan, Vachanamrut Gadhada First Section 29

When He was 11 years old, Lord Shree Ghanshyam enlightened His parents with the knowledge of His true identity. Their physical bodies died and He granted them a divine status. Without the consent of His relatives, He assumed the guise of a *brahmachari* and left home. He embarked on a forest expedition (*van-vicharan*) to bestow salvation upon innumerable souls.

> Bhaktimata was sent to Akshardham in Ayodhya in Samvat 1848 Kartik Sud 10 (Saturday 5th November 1791). Dharmadev was sent to Akshardham in Ayodhya in Samvat 1848 Jeth Sud 4 (Friday 8th June 1792).
>
> Shree Nilkanth Varni left home for His forest expedition at the age of eleven years, three months and one day in Samvat 1849 Ashadh Sud 10 (Friday 29th June 1792).

During His journey He passed through Badrinath, Kedarnath, Muktanath and many other places, where He came across many ascetics practising austerities. To teach them the correct method of performing these acts of self-discipline, He too performed acts of strict austerity. He stood on one foot in the intense cold during constant snowfall. In this manner, He taught the ascetics the manner of true asceticism. Crossing the snow-covered peaks of the Giriraj Himalayan range and the streams and rivers that flow there, He plunged into a four-mile wide river and let its current carry Him away. Eventually, after coming out of the river, He emerged at the foot of Mount Navlakha where He blessed the nine hundred thousand ascetics who lived there and thereby rewarded them for practising their austerities and yoga.

> During the forest expedition, Lord Swaminarayan visited all the pilgrimage sites. In Hinduism, it is said that souls go to pilgrimage sites to rid and cleanse themselves of their sins. All these sins accumulate at the pilgrimage sites. When the merciful Lord visits these sites, He burns away the sins and purifies the pilgrimage sites.
>
> All the ascetics had been performing penances for numerable years to gain the *darshan* of the Lord and attain a spiritual status. Lord Swaminarayan provided them all with the reward of their spiritual endeavours, i.e. granted them His *darshan*. By this *darshan*, they would attain salvation, and their motives for performing their penance would have been fulfilled. This shows that until one is granted the *darshan* of the supreme Lord, true salvation is not attained.

Moving ahead from there, Shree Nilkanth Varni met a sage by the name of Gopal Yogi. In order to accept the *Yogi's* service, Shree Nilkanth Varni used the pretext of wanting to learn yoga. Whenever Gopal Yogi faltered in his yogic

Darshan
The visualisation of the Lord. Also the act of looking with reverence and devotion at the image or the deity in the shrine, sometimes of seeing a holy person

Sants
Ascetics, the closest western equivilent being monks

Vachanamrut
The words of Lord Shree Swaminarayan compiled as a scripture. See Appendix

Kopin
Lower-body undergarment worn by Hindu males

Brahmachari
A Brahmin who is initiated as a renouncer (tyagi) into the Swaminarayan fellowship

Akshardham
The divine abode of Lord Shree Swaminarayan

Yogi
One who has accomplished the virtues of the Yog philosophy

practices, Shree Nilkanth Varni taught him the way to complete them. Eventually, He gave Gopal Yogi the lustrous *darshan* of His divine *sakar Murti*. Acknowledging Shree Nilkanth Varni to be the supreme Lord, Gopal Yogi bowed to Shree Nilkanth Varni's lotus feet with *sashtang-namaskar* and began to serve Him.

Sakar Murti
The Lord exists with a distinct form but not being merely a mass of energy or light

Sashtang-namaskar
The eight–fold bow. A humble bow / prostration in which eight parts of the body are concentrated on the devotion of God, namely; the hands, feet, knees, chest, forehead (all of which touch the ground before His feet), mind, vision and obeisance

Shree Nilkanth Varni learns the rudiments of yoga from Shree Gopal Yogi

During His forest expedition, Shree Ghanshyam Maharaj was known as Nilkanth Varni (as predicted by Markandeya Muni). Lord Ghanshyam left His home, leaving behind all but the necessary possessions. He merely carried: *munj-mekhla* – a grass waistband; *jap-mala* – a rosary; *kamandalu* – a water pot made of gourd; *bhikhsha-patra* – a small bowl made of wood meant for eating food; *Shaligram* – a small round stone worshipped as an idol of Lord Vishnu; *gutko* – a small booklet containing extracts from Hindu scriptures.

Lord Swaminarayan asked to learn yoga, so that He could remain in the service of Gopal Yogi. By this, Lord Swaminarayan has demonstrated the need for offering one's services to elders and great ascetics.

Babulal J. Soni
AMADAVAD-8
1932

Satsang
Fellowship associated with the
Swaminarayan religion

In a nearby village, wild animals had been preying on the farmers' livestock. In desperation, the villagers approached Gopal Yogi and asked him to rid them of this menace. Gopal Yogi told them that he was helpless in this matter and that he could do nothing for them. At that time, Shree Nilkanth Varni was sitting facing Gopal Yogi. He immediately said, "Blow your conch shell. All the wild animals will flee from the regions up to where the sound is heard." Having faith in Shree Nilkanth Varni, Gopal Yogi blew into the conch. The sound generated was such that all the predators fled the region in which the sound was audible, and never again returned. In this manner, Shree Nilkanth Varni resolved the problems of the villagers through Gopal Yogi and subsequently granted him salvation.

A conch shell is usually blown as a signal, or to announce someone's arrival. When Gopal Yogi blew the conch shell, not only did the sound cause all the animals to flee, but also, this sound heralded the imminent arrival of the supreme Lord Swaminarayan to the *Satsang*.

Moving on, Shree Nilkanth Varni arrived at the city of Sirpur where its ruler, King Siddhvallabh, honoured and welcomed Him to the city. On the outskirts of the city, there lived thousands of deceitful ascetics who revered the occult deities and practised black magic. Due to the immense generosity of King Siddhvallabh, they enjoyed a very comfortable life. Shree Nilkanth Varni went to live amongst them. Shree Nilkanth Varni, by His will, created a storm of ferocious winds and lashing rain. Unable to withstand the elements, one by one, the hypocritical, arrogant and deceitful ascetics all retreated into the city to take refuge. Only Shree Nilkanth Varni remained sitting, unperturbed by the harsh conditions. When the storm receded, the King and the city people went to investigate. Everyone proclaimed Shree Nilkanth Varni to be the true ascetic and all the others to be hypocrites. The King surrendered himself to Shree Nilkanth Varni.

Removing the arrogance of these so-called ascetics, Shree Nilkanth Varni moved onwards. Passing through Balvakund and Kapilashram, He arrived at Jagannathpuri, where there lived a large community of demons, disguised as sages. One day, one of the sages ordered Shree Nilkanth Varni to pluck a plant from the ground. Shree Nilkanth Varni refused and said, "The plant is a living entity. If I pluck it, the plant will experience pain. Therefore, I cannot pluck it."

Shikshapatri
Scripture containing the holy commandments of Lord Swaminarayan. See Appendix

The sage became angry by this response and drew out his sword. He threatened Shree Nilkanth Varni, "If You disobey my order, I will kill You." Several other sages heard the dispute. Those who agreed with Shree Nilkanth Varni started to oppose the sage. Differing points of view became apparent amongst the sage community and resulted in a fierce quarrel. First there was just verbal abuse, but soon it escalated into a battle with sticks and weapons, during which ten thousand demons were slain. The unperturbed Shree Nilkanth Varni left the city and went to Manaspur. Here, the King Satradharma honourably welcomed Him to his kingdom.

Lord Swaminarayan has demonstrated His immense compassion for all life. One of His most essential teachings was the ideology of non-violence (*ahinsa*), not killing any animals, even for the performance of rituals or sacrifices. By not even killing a plant unnecessarily, Lord Swaminarayan has shown His absolute adherence to this philosophy of ultimate compassion, as stated in the Shikshapatri Slok 11 and 12.

Some of the surviving demons came from Jagannathpuri and reached Manaspur where they saw Shree Nilkanth Varni. As they considered Shree Nilkanth Varni to be the root cause of the destruction of their community, they plotted to kill Him. During the day, they collected a large amount of stones. At night, they positioned themselves around Shree Nilkanth Varni while He slept alone on a platform. They pelted Him with the stones. However, not a single stone hit Shree Nilkanth Varni. Instead, they formed a fortress-like wall around Him. Seeing this, the demons prepared their weapons to kill Him the next morning. When the King came to know about this, he, along with the villagers, went to investigate at the place where Shree Nilkanth Varni was sleeping. They saw that the stones had piled up on top of each other and formed a wall that was a metre higher than the platform on which Shree Nilkanth Varni slept.

The surprised King bowed down to Shree Nilkanth Varni. He became convinced that Shree Nilkanth Varni was the supreme Lord and became His devotee. The King then used the might of his fierce army to destroy the demons. Shree Nilkanth Varni promised salvation to King Satradharma before continuing His expedition. He travelled to Kanyakumari Rameshwaram and from there He crossed the Konkan range of mountains and the Western regions of India. Eventually, Shree Nilkanth Varni arrived to grace the soil of Gujarat. He sat at the edge of a well in a village called Loj in Saurashtra.

Guptaprayag
Gangotri
Badrinath
Niti
Man Sarovar
Kedarnath
Joshimath
Shreepur
Laxmanpura
Haridwar
Shwetgiri
Pulhashram
Kala Parvat
Brareli
Muktanath
Naimisharanya
Pukhra
Kamakshi
Bansi
Butolnagar
Navlakha Parvat
Lodheshwar
Chhapaiya
Aadivarah
Navdwip
Ayodhya
Shantipur
Balva kund
Vadtal
Dakor
Junagadh
Budhej
Vadodara
Vanthli
Bhavnagar
Bharuch
Mangarol
Loj
Surat
Buranpur
Prabhas
Dharampur
Ganga Sagar
Guptaprayag
Malegam
Kapllashram
Nasik
Puna
Bhuvaneshwar
Sakshigopal
Pandharpur
Jagannathpuri
Kishkindhao
Aadikurma
Pampa Sarovar
Chakratirth
Manaspur
Venktadri
Yadavgirio
Tirumallai
Bhutpuri
Sivkanchi
Shreerangpattan
Malayachal
Vishnukanchi
Shreerang
Janardan
Sundarraj
Rameshwar
Padmanabho
Totadri
Kumarikakshetra

A map of the route taken by Shree Nilkanth Varni during His forest expedition (van–vicharan). Shree Nilkanth Varni left home for His forest expedition at the age of eleven years, three months and one day on Samvat 1849 Ashadh Sud 10 (Friday 29th June 1792), and travelled over 12,000km by foot. He arrived in Loj on Samvat 1856 Shravan Vad 6 (Thursday 21st August 1799). The forest expedition lasted seven years one month and eleven days

Chapter 8

At the Edge of the Well of Loj - Saurashtra

A great sage has arrived at our ashram in Loj. He is a staunch ascetic and possesses great divine qualities. He shows mercy to all. He is more beautiful than the deity of beauty, Kamdev. He uses the name Nilkanth. He remains mostly in meditation. When He talks, He speaks only about the Lord and the divine scriptures. He wears only a deerskin and carries merely a piece of cloth and a tulsi rosary. His heart is like butter and His body is more tender than a flower. Oh Gurudev! He eagerly awaits your darshan.

Shree Muktanand Swami
in his letter to Sadguru Shree Ramanand Swami in Bhuj

Haricharitra Chintamani Part 1 Varta 89

In Samvat 1856 Shravan Vad 6 (Thursday 21st August 1799) Shree Nilkanth Varni came and sat at the edge of the well in Loj - Saurashtra. The village women who came to fetch water from the well became fixated by the *darshan* of Shree Nilkanth Varni and experienced an overwhelming aura of happiness in His presence. News of the arrival of this great ascetic swiftly spread throughout the village.

Shree Sukhanand Swami came to the well to fetch water. He too saw Shree Nilkanth Varni. He requested Shree Nilkanth Varni to accompany him to the *ashram*, "Oh Varniraj! Our guru, Shree Muktanand Swami is in our *ashram*. He is eager for the *darshan* of an ascetic such as You. Please come to the *ashram* to meet him. If it is not Your wish to come there, I will call Shree Muktanand Swami here."

Shree Nilkanth Varni accepted Shree Sukhanand Swami's humble request and went to the *ashram*. Shree Muktanand Swami warmly welcomed Shree Nilkanth Varni and requested Him to stay there. Shree Nilkanth Varni asked Shree Muktanand Swami to describe the forms of the Jeev, Maya, Ishwar, Brahm and Parabrahm. Shree Muktanand Swami replied according to the *sakar* philosophy of his guru Shree Ramanujacharya in which each are described as having a distinct form. Recognising Shree Muktanand Swami to be a true and sincere ascetic engrossed in religious decree, devotion and spiritual knowledge, Shree Nilkanth Varni resided in the *ashram*.

Ashram
Secluded dwellings for ascetics

Tulsi
Sacred basil

Darshan
The visualisation of the Lord. Also the act of looking with reverence and devotion at the image or deity in the shrine, sometimes of seeing a holy person

Muktanand Swami
One of the most senior sants of Ramanand Swami

Sadguru
Status of eminent sant

Haricharitra Chintamani
Scripture written by Sadguru Raghunathcharandasji Swami

Jeev, Maya, Ishwar, Brahm and Parabrahm
The five eternal entities

Sakar philosophy
Philosophy that describes God to exist with a distinct form but not being merely a mass of energy or light

Ramanujacharya
A 11th century philosopher. See Appendix

Shree Sukhanand Swami humbly requests Shree Nilkanth Varni to grace their ashram

Sants
Ascetics, the closest Western equivilent being monks

Satsang
Fellowship associated with the Swaminarayan religion

Sampraday
Holy fellowship

Brahmachari
A Brahmin who is initiated as a renouncer (tyagi) into the Swaminarayan fellowship

Shree Nilkanth Varni noticed a hole in the wall of the *ashram* and the adjoining house. The ascetics exchanged fire with the neighbouring male and female family members. Seeing this, Shree Nilkanth Varni said, "This is not just a hole in the wall, but it is a flaw in the religion. Wherever Nilkanth remains, such a flaw cannot exist. I cannot stay here." Hearing Shree Nilkanth Varni's words, Shree Muktanand Swami immediately had the hole filled.

Before matches were available, people kept a fire burning continuously. Through a hole in the wall the *sants* exchanged burning coals with neighbours, including women, thereby compromising their vow of absolute celibacy.

In Loj, Lord Swaminarayan immediately had the hole in the wall filled and segregated the assemblies of men and women. It is said that the previous incarnations performed such celibacy. However, Lord Swaminarayan ensured that His disciples remained adherent to strict celibacy, to the level observed by the previous great incarnations. Even from the very first day that He arrived in the *Satsang*, Lord Swaminarayan started to make His reforms.

At times of religious discourses, men and women used to sit together. The very next day, Shree Nilkanth Varni segregated the assemblies for men and women and established a unique tradition of absolute celibacy in the *Sampraday*.

Shree Nilkanth Varni became eager to meet Shree Ramanand Swami. Unfortunately, he was residing in Bhuj. So, Shree Muktanand Swami and Shree Nilkanth Varni sent letters to him. As Shree Ramanand Swami opened Shree Nilkanth Varni's letter, a brilliant lustre was emitted from it and emanated throughout the entire vicinity. All the devotees sitting in the assembly were amazed to witness such a spectacle.

All objects become divine if they come into contact with the Lord; even items such as this paper became divine and lustrous as it contained the words of the Lord.

Shree Ramanand Swami said to his followers, "The immensely great *brahmachari* (Shree Nilkanth Varni) has arrived in Loj. All of you should go there for His *darshan*."

Jeevan-mukta
Granter of salvation to souls

Ashtang Yog
Eight-fold yoga

Yogi
One who has accomplished the virtues of the Yog philosophy

Shree Nilkanth Varni writing the letter to Shree Ramanand Swami in Samvat 1856 Fagan Vad 5 (Friday 28th February 1800)

"Swamiji Shree Ramanandji; who is the 'Sun' that has arisen, in the form of a Sadguru, and who is currently presiding at the very holy place, Shree Bhujnagar. Accept the prostrations of your devout devotee, *brahmachari* Nilkanth, also known as Sarjudas; who remains in your service from the town of Loj. Moreover; the purpose of writing this letter is that by the will of God, I have arrived here, having travelled through the four great places of pilgrimage. There, I heard your name and heard that you, the Jeevan-mukta have manifested in the Western region. I then accomplished *Ashtang Yog*, by practising yoga whilst staying with Gopal Yogi in the forest. At that time, the *Yogi* told me that I would meet the *Siddh* (accomplished) in the regions below Girnar (mountain). I then spent many days living only on air. Still, I did not attain the *darshan* of Krishna in person. Now I have stayed here, considering this place to be pious. Kindly enable me to have a contact with Krishna himself. I have heard that you grant such *darshan* to those who long for that state. Having heard this from Swami Muktanandji, and having known him to be void of all deceit, I have stayed here. Swamiji and Bhattji have told me that we will call you here; so I should stay till then. Bhattji Mayaram insists that having read both the letters, you will shower such mercy on us. Just as the Chakor bird remains greatly desirous of the Moon, I wish that you give me *darshan* at the earliest moment; otherwise I will come there, to be in your service. This letter has been written in Samvat 1856 Fagan Vad 5. Show your merciful gaze at the earliest moment after you read this letter. Otherwise, I will not stay here."

A translation of the letter written by Shree Nilkanth Varni

67

A reproduction of the actual letter that Shree Nilkanth Varni wrote to Shree Ramanand Swami

Haricharitra Chintamani
Part 1 Varta 89

At that time, Lalji Suthar came to Bhuj. Shree Ramanand Swami asked, "Why have you come here? Why did you not go to Loj?" Lalji Suthar replied, "You are my God, and you are here. Why should I go to Loj?" Shree Ramanand Swami replied, "The newly arrived Shree Nilkanth Varni is extremely great." Lalji Suthar asked, "How great is He? Is He like Mukunddasji? Ramanand Swami replied, "Mukunddasji is nothing compared to Him." Then again he asked, "Is He like Ramdasbhai?" Shree Ramanand Swami replied, "Compared to Shree Nilkanth Varni, both of these fade into insignificance." Lalji Suthar continued, "Is He as great as you?" Shree Ramanand Swami replied, "In comparison to Him, I am nothing. I am His servant."

The gathered congregation became astounded to hear this conversation and sat contemplating the glory of Shree Nilkanth Varni.

Lalji Suthar
An ardent devotee who later took initiation as a sant and became Shree Nishkulanand Swami

Mukunddasji
Sadguru Shree Muktanand Swami

Ramdasbhai
The first sant initiated by Ramanand Swami. His actual name was Ramdas Swami. Lord Swaminarayan considered him to be His gurubhai, i.e. having the relation of brother, because they both were sants of the same guru, Ramanand Swami. The Lord addressed him as Bhai Swami or Ramdasbhai

Shree Ramanand Swami opens the letter from Shree Nilkanth Varni and a brilliant lustre emanates from it

Chapter 9

The Meeting with Shree Ramanand Swami

It has been 21 years since I first came to Ramanand Swami. During this time, I have met countless devotees who have offered Me endless varieties of clothing, jewellery, food etc. Still, My mind has never been tempted by any of these articles because I have an intense affiliation for renunciation. My only desire is to please the Lord by practising austerities.

Lord Shree Swaminarayan, Vachanamrut Kariyani 10

My nature of renunciation was such that I could not remain in the same place for longer than the time till a cow is milked. I had such an intense sense for asceticism. However, I also had a deep regard for Shree Ramanand Swami. Therefore, when Mayaram Bhatt brought the message of Swami from the city of Bhuj in which it was said, "If You have a desire to remain in the Satsang, You must remain there, even by embracing a pillar." I literally grabbed hold of a pillar and embraced it. He asked Me to remain under the command of Muktanand Swami. Therefore, I stayed in his command for nine months, until I had the darshan of Swami.

Lord Shree Swaminarayan, Vachanamrut Loya 3

Shree Nilkanth Varni and Shree Ramanand Swami
meet for the first time in Piplana

Vachanamrut
The words of Lord Shree Swaminarayan compiled as a scripture. See Appendix

Satsang
Fellowship associated with the Swaminarayan religion

Darshan
The visualisation of the Lord

Padmasan
The lotus pose in which the right foot is placed on the left thigh with the sole uppermost; and the left foot is placed on the right thigh, with the sole upturned. Both hands are placed on the knees with palms upturned

Narshi Mehta
An ardent devotee of Shree Ramanand Swami who lived in the of village Piplana

Samadhi
A trance–like state. The final stage of Yoga

Sants
Ascetics, the closest Western equivalent being monks

Vashishta Rishi
An ascetic sage of the Dwapar–yug era (See Appendix) whom Ramchandraji regarded as his guru

Ramchandraji
One of the 24 incarnations of the Lord

Shree Ramanand Swami travelled from Bhuj to Piplana. Shree Nilkanth Varni and Shree Muktanand Swami left Loj and also arrived in Piplana. Shree Ramanand Swami and Shree Nilkanth Varni met for the first time in Samvat 1856 Jeth Vad 12 (Thursday 18th June 1800). Shree Ramanand Swami lifted up Shree Nilkanth Varni and affectionately embraced Him. Shree Ramanand Swami gazed into Shree Nilkanth Varni's lotus face and tears of love rolled from his eyes.

Eventually, Shree Ramanand Swami took his seat and Shree Nilkanth Varni sat before him in the respectful *padmasan*. The entire congregation also sat down, and watched as Shree Ramanand Swami and Shree Nilkanth Varni stared at each other's lotus faces.

Meanwhile, a merchant from the Sindh region came to the village. As soon as he entered the village, he experienced a divine peace and tranquillity, and his worldly thoughts and volitions all subsided. He thought, "God or a divine prophet must be present in this village." He enquired in the village, "Has God or a prophet come to this village?" One villager said, "Go to Narshi Mehta's home. Many *sants* have come there. One of them may be God or a prophet."

The merchant arrived at the assembly where Shree Ramanand Swami and Shree Nilkanth Varni were seated. As soon as Shree Nilkanth Varni's gaze fell on the merchant, he fell into a trance (*samadhi*) in which he witnessed Shree Nilkanth Varni seated on a majestic throne and Shree Ramanand Swami bowing in obeisance to Him. Upon awakening from the trance the merchant asked, "You Hindus follow a strange practice! The disciple sits on a throne whilst God sits on the floor!"

Shree Ramanand Swami said, "It is a Hindu tradition that when God is in the guise of a devotee, He sits on the floor, just like the sage Vashishta Rishi sat on a prominent seat whilst Ramchandraji sat before him in a lower position."

Shree Ramanand Swami's answer left the merchant speechless. He bowed, first to Shree Nilkanth Varni and then to Shree Ramanand Swami, and then left the assembly.

Prayag-kshetra
Region around the city of Allahbad in Northern India where the holy rivers Ganges and Jamuna meet

Shree Ramanand Swami then proceeded to enquire about Shree Nilkanth Varni's full name, His parents, caste, His origins, family background, etc. Nilkanth Varni answered all his questions in detail and also told him about all the places of pilgrimage He had visited during His forest expedition.

Then Shree Ramanand Swami said, "I gave initiation to Your father, Shree Dharmadev, in Prayag-kshetra. By my command, he preached to all about the religious decree and devotion unto the Lord. Your father was one of my devotees and therefore, You too are mine. However, characteristically, You are far superior than Your father."

Hearing this, Shree Nilkanth Varni gently smiled.

Lord Shree Swaminarayan, even though He is the supreme almighty God, took Shree Ramanand Swami to be His guru. By this, He explained the importance of a guru. Without a guru, one cannot attain knowledge.

To demonstrate the respect that devotees should have for their guru, Shree Nilkanth Varni sat on the floor before His guru, Shree Ramanand Swami.

Chapter 10

Initiation and Coronation

On the auspicious day of Samvat 1857 Kartik Sud 11 (Wednesday 28th October 1800), Shree Ramanand Swami gave initiation (*diksha*) to Shree Nilkanth Varni as a *sant*. Shree Ramanand Swami gave Him two names - Shree Sahajanand Swami and Shree Narayan Muni.

> Shree Nilkanth Varni was initiated as a *sant* at this ceremony, taking on the saffron robes and the vows that go with becoming a *sant*. The initiation here refers to the *Bhagwati diksha* – the initiation of a follower as a renouncer (*tyagi*). *Vaishnavi diksha* is the initiation of an aspirant into the Swaminarayan religion as a householder (*gruhasth*).

Shree Sahajanand Swami travelled extensively with Shree Ramanand Swami and revealed His extraordinary yogic prowess. Shree Ramanand Swami decided to appoint Shree Sahajanand Swami as his successor, as the leader of the *Sampraday* that he had established. Shree Ramanand Swami arranged a grand celebration in which he called all his devotees from all over the land to Jetpur, where he held a vast assembly on Samvat 1858 Kartik Sud 11 (Monday 16th November 1801).

The grand coronation ceremony of
Lord Shree Swaminarayan
– Shree Sahajanand Swami Maharaj

At this extraordinary congregation, Shree Ramanand Swami addressed everyone and said, "I will narrate the way in which our *Sampraday* was established. According to the philosophy of Ramanujacharya, I performed the *sakar upasana* and devotion unto the Lord. Due to this, I had to endure the malice of many individuals who constantly kept harassing me. Still, I did not falter in my devotion. While travelling, I reached Shreerang-kshetra, where Shree Ramanujacharya gave *darshan* to me in a dream. He gave me initiation and commanded me to establish a *Sampraday* that gave prominence to devotion and the religious decree.

"When I awoke from the dream, I discovered the symbols of the initiation, including the *tilak* on my forehead, a *kanthi* around my neck and all the other marks on my body. I then established this *Sampraday*.

"Wherever I have travelled, I have always proclaimed, 'I am merely the drumbeater, awakening and alerting all to the imminent arrival of the God who is truly worthy of worship'. This God is Shree Sahajanand Swami. Finally He has arrived amongst us all."

During the divine ordination in Akshardham, Lord Shree Swaminarayan commanded His *Muktas* to go onto the Earth ahead of Him and announce His imminent arrival. By proclaiming himself to be the drumbeater, Shree Ramanand Swami revealed this was indeed the role he had played.

"You all know and have experienced that Shree Sahajanand Swami has an overwhelming prowess in austerity, religious decree (*dharma*), devotion (*bhakti*), spiritual knowledge (*gnan*), yoga (*yog*), meditation (*dhyan*), and miracles etc. He is greater than anyone in all these respects and furthermore, He has an unsurpassed knowledge about all the scriptures. Therefore, I have decided to entrust the helm of this *Sampraday* to Shree Sahajanand Swami." Everyone applauded in appreciation of their guru, Shree Ramanand Swami's decision.

Shree Ramanand Swami then led Shree Sahajanand Swami to the throne and announced, "Oh Shree Sahajanand Swami! In the eyes of the world, You are my disciple. However, You are the all-powerful, almighty Lord. The six great attributes of power are all inherent within You. I wish to entrust the helm of

this religion to You. Only You have the ability to lead the devotees of this *Sampraday* to remain adherent to the religious decree and only You alone are able to fulfil their devotional desires.

"I am aware that the vows of asceticism and abstinence are dear to You and so You have an aversion to worldly objects. However, it is my command that You must accept everyone's adoration. You must accept all the garments, ornaments, jewellery etc. that are offered to You with love.

"I also realise that you are strict to the vows of a *brahmachari* so You will not agree to ladies offering adoration to You. However, You are pure and immutable like fire. The eight *siddhis* and nine *niddhis*, are ever-present in Your service, and are not able to tempt You. So how can such insignificant worldly objects entice You?

"You are the ocean of mercy and the epitome of grace. So I have complete confidence that You will shower mercy on all and accept all the kinds of services that are offered to You."

Akshardham
The divine abode of Lord Shree Swaminarayan

Muktas
Liberated souls

The six attributes
Along with worldly attributes, the six great attributes of power exist within God. These are knowledge (gnan), divine strength (shakti), immense power (bal), sovereignty (aishwarya), redemptive power (virya), and divine lustre (tej)

Brahmachari
A Brahmin who is initiated as a renouncer (tyagi) into the Swaminarayan fellowship

Yogi
One who has accomplished the virtues of the Yog philosophy

There are eight *siddhis* or accomplishments through which one attains miraculous powers. The true ascetic *yogi* strives to attain:

Anima - the ability to become miniscule; *Mahima* - the ability to grow enormous; *Garima* - the ability to grow heavier than any known element; *Laghima* - the ability to grow lighter than air; *Prapti* - success in achieving desired objects or aims and acquiring supernatural power. When a *yogi* achieves this, he can comprehend all languages, cure disease, read the minds of others and predict the future; *Prakamya* - the ability to attain any desire, the condition of gaining more than one expects; *Ishitva* - the ability to control anything, universal domination either in this or in a future life; *Vashitva* - to master or to control any affair, the ability to tame animals and bring them under control.

The nine *niddhis* represent the immense opulence of the Lord. They represent monetary quantities of the following denominations:

Padma:	10,000,000,000	*Mukund*:	1,000,000,000,000,000
Mahapadma:	100,000,000,000	*Kund*:	10,000,000,000,000,000
Shankh:	1,000,000,000,000	*Nil*:	100,000,000,000,000,000
Makar:	10,000,000,000,000	*Kharv*:	1,000,000,000,000,000,000
Kachhap:	100,000,000,000,000		

Chammar
A silver-handled cluster of sable hair originally used to ward off insects away from the king. It is therefore a symbol of sovereignty

Murti
Divine image or form of the Lord

Aarti
Ritual ceremony.
See Appendix

Shree Sahajanand Swami showed reluctance, but Shree Ramanand Swami affirmed, "This is my command."

Shree Sahajanand Swami said,

आज्ञा गुरूणाम् अविचारणीया ।

Aagnaa Guroonaam Avichaaraniyaa

"The command of a guru should be obeyed, without question."

He continued, "Oh My guru! I accept your command with the utmost of reverence. According to your command, I will lead the followers to abide by the manners of true religion, spiritual knowledge, austerity and devotion. I will ensure that they are immersed into the religious decree."

These words made Shree Ramanand Swami extremely pleased. He lovingly embraced Shree Sahajanand Swami and then seated Him on the throne. He handed over the helm of the *Sampraday* to Shree Sahajanand Swami by impressing a *tilak* of sandalwood paste on His forehead. He then placed a flower garland around His neck. Disciples stood beside Shree Sahajanand Swami holding the ceremonial mace, umbrella and *chammar*. Shree Nilkanth Varni's *Murti* looked truly splendid. Shree Ramanand Swami and all the devotees performed the *aarti* ceremony to Shree Sahajanand Swami. The entire assembly shouted cheers of acclamation.

The delighted Shree Ramanand Swami then addressed the assembly and said, "Oh *sants* and devotees! Today, I have handed over the helm of this religion to Shree Sahajanand Swami. I command you all to remain according to His commands and behave according to His will.

"On many occasions, I have told you that I am merely beating a drum, enlightening all those who seek salvation to the imminent arrival of the supreme Lord. I have awoken you from ignorance and have led you to the supreme Lord, Shree Sahajanand Swami. If you remain under His shelter, you will attain eternal salvation (*aatyantik-moksh*).

Bhaktavatsal
He who is beloved to his disciples

"You must not harbour any arrogance of being older or more senior than Him. Do not think of Him as being young. Shree Sahajanand Swami is superior to you all. The salvation of you all lies with Him. Therefore you all must remain according to His will."

In this way, Shree Ramanand Swami gave his instructions to all. He then addressed Shree Sahajanand Swami and said, "I am extremely pleased with You. Ask me for a boon."

Hearing these words of approval, Shree Sahajanand Swami, seated in the guise of an ascetic, said to Shree Ramanand Swami, "Oh Gurudev! If your disciples are to be inflicted with the pain of a scorpion sting, may the pain of thousands of scorpion stings be inflicted on every pore on My body, but let your disciples be spared from the suffering. Also, if any of your devotees are destined for poverty, may that hardship come to Me, but let your disciples have sufficient food and clothing. Grant Me these two boons."

Hearing these words of the Bhaktavatsal Shree Sahajanand Swami, in which the poignant love for the disciples was evident, Shree Ramanand Swami became extremely pleased and granted the two boons.

The assembled *sants* and devotees became captivated by the immense mercy of Shree Sahajanand Swami, and bowed to Him with sincere reverence.

> Shree Ramanand Swami seated the Lord on the throne and entrusted Him with the leadership of the *Sampraday*. This throne, upon which Lord Swaminarayan presided, is Shree Swaminarayan Gadi.

Chapter 11

Revelation of the Swaminarayan Name

The Lord's prowess is so great that merely by chanting His name, Swaminarayan, at the time of death, even the most sinful soul is freed from all their sins and attains His divine abode.

Lord Shree Swaminarayan, Vachanamrut Gadhada First Section 56

In Samvat 1858 Magshar Sud 13, (Thursday 17th December 1801) Shree Ramanand Swami withdrew his human appearance in the village of Faneni. Prior to his departure, he commanded his disciples, "Do not bury my body, do not cremate it, nor should you submerge it in water. You should merely leave my body in a dense forest." According to his command, the disciples placed Shree Ramanand Swami's body on a palanquin and ceremoniously carried him to a solitary place in a forest, where they left him and returned.

Meanwhile a herdsman, who was minding his goats, came to the vicinity where Shree Ramanand Swami's body had been left. He looked towards Shree Ramanand Swami. All of a sudden, Shree Ramanand Swami opened his eyes and stood up from the *padmasan*. He stretched out his arms and started flapping them like the wings of a bird. Shree Ramanand Swami flew into the sky and eventually disappeared. The herdsman was stunned. The *darshan* of such a divine *sant* was truly magnificent. The herdsman felt a sense of immense bliss in his heart. When he came to the village, he conveyed his experience to Shree Ramanand Swami's disciples. The disciples were all delighted to hear about what the herdsman had witnessed.

> Shree Ramanand Swami disappeared into the sky. This shows that the Lord and His divine personages are not bound by normal human processes of birth and death. They can appear and disappear in any manner they wish.

On the 14th day after Shree Ramanand Swami's departure (Samvat 1858 Magshar Vad 11, 31st December 1801), Shree Sahajanand Swami called a vast assembly of Shree Ramanand Swami's followers. They came from all over the country. He first consoled them in their grief.

अखण्डं स्वस्वरूपस्था महान्तो ये तु पूरुषाः ।
कल्याणार्थं हि जगतां ज्ञेयं तज्जन्म भूतले ॥
आविर्भावतिरोभावौ तेषां स्वातन्त्र्यतः किल ।
भवतो न त्वितरवन्निजकर्मवशात् क्वचित् ॥
तद्देहत्यागमालोक्य मुह्यन्त्यसुभृतोऽसुराः ।
दैवास्तु तत्स्वरूपज्ञास्तेषां लीलां विदन्ति ताम् ॥

Vachanamrut
The words of Lord Shree Swaminarayan compiled as a scripture. See Appendix

Padmasan
The lotus pose in which the right foot is placed on the left thigh with the sole uppermost; and the left foot is placed on the right thigh, with the sole upturned. Both hands are placed on the knees with palms upturned

Darshan
The visualisation of the Lord. Also the act of looking with reverence and devotion at the image or the deity in the shrine, sometimes of seeing a holy person

Sant
Ascetic, the closest Western equivalent being a monk

Karma
Sanskrut word meaning deed or action. According to Hindu belief, every action has inevitable consequences, which attach themselves to the doer. These deeds result in reward or punishment dependent on their nature. Karma is thus the moral law of actions and their consequences

Sampraday
Holy fellowship

Kopin
Undergarment for Hindu ascetics

Dhoti
A lower body garment for Hindu ascetics

Gatadiu
Upper body garment for Hindu ascetics

Tilak
A mark applied on the forehead. The Swaminarayan mark is of a U shape made of yellow sandalwood paste (chandan)

Gruhasth
Those with family associations

Akhandam swaswaroopasthaa mahaanto ye tu purushaahaa,
Kalyaanaartham hi jagataam gneyam tajjanma bhootale;
Aavirbhaava-tirobhaavau tesham swaatantryatah kila,
Bhavato na tvitaravan-nij-karmavashaat kvachit;
Taddeha-tyaagamaalokya muhyantyasubhruto-suraaha,
Daivaastu tatswaroopagnaas-teshaam leelaam vidanti taam;

"The manifestation of great personages, who constantly
remain engrossed in the form of God, is purely for the salvation of souls.
Unlike ordinary beings, they manifest and disappear according
to their will, but not as a result of the influence of their *karma*.
Heretics become pre-occupied at seeing the apparent death of
such great individuals. However, discerning devotees,
who have recognised their true greatness,
believe it to be just another part of their divine episodes."

Addressing the congregation, Shree Sahajanand Swami then said, "Dear *sants*! Amongst the *sants* in our *Sampraday* there are some who wear only a *kopin* whilst others wrap a cloth around their waists. Some wear saffron clothing whilst others wear white. Some wear a cap whilst others tie a cloth around their head. It seems that there is no uniformity amongst us. Therefore, from today, I wish to instigate a common manner of dressing. Oh *sants*! From today, you should all wear a *dhoti* and *gatadiu*. You should wear a turban *(pagh)* on your head. All this clothing should be un-sewn and saffron coloured. It should be the same for you all. Through your appearance, you will be distinguishable from all others wherever you go."

The saffron colour represents the colour of fire. Those who have accepted the path of renunciation (e.g. *sants*) have burnt all worldly affiliations. Their un-sewn clothing symbolises the simplicity of their lives.

"Moreover, oh *sants* and disciples! You all adorn different marks on your foreheads. Some of you impress an upright *tilak*, whilst others make a horizontal line. Some merely have a single vertical line and some have three horizontal lines. Others apply ash on their forehead. Today, I will give you all a unique marking. All *sants* and male *gruhasth* devotees should apply an upright *tilak* using sandalwood paste *(chandan)* on their foreheads. A round

chandlo should be impressed within the *tilak*, using *kanku* or sandalwood paste. Married and unwed women should apply just a round *chandlo* using *kanku*. Widowed ladies must not apply any markings.

"Oh beloved *sants* and devotees! You all are striving hard to attain salvation. Devotion unto God is dear to you all. You are all children of the same father, disciples of the one guru. However, you all chant different *mantras*. Some of you chant 'Ram Ram', some 'Krishna Krishna'. Some of you perform remembrance using 'Datt Datt', whilst others use 'Kapil Kapil'. Some of you recite 'Om namo Bhagawate Vasudevaya' (I bow in reverence to Lord Vasudev). This constitutes different types of *upasana* amongst you. From today, I wish to establish one *upasana*.

"From today you must chant, contemplate, and worship the one and only name that I will shortly reveal. First of all, you must hear about its greatness. Those who chant it, wholeheartedly and with true faith, will be alleviated of all their sins. If Yamduts come to punish a soul on their deathbed, the utterance of this name will banish them away. If a venomous cobra has bitten someone and the poison has pervaded through that individual's entire body, through the chanting of this name, whilst understanding its glory, the effects of the poison will be eradicated. Oh! By merely reciting, uttering or contemplating this name, one will immediately fall into a trance (*samadhi*), during which the divine lustrous *darshan* of the Lord dwelling in Akshardham will be visualised."

After listening to Shree Sahajanand Swami describing the glory of such a powerful name, the fascinated devotees became impatient to hear it. With joyous tears in their eyes, they emotionally prayed, "Oh Shree Sahajanand Swami! Have mercy on us all and reveal Your magnificent, divine name. We are anxious to chant the name, fall into a trance (*samadhi*) and attain the *darshan* of the Lord in Akshardham."

The all-compassionate Shree Sahajanand Swami accepted their prayers and lovingly said, "Oh My beloved devotees! Have patience. No one has been able to understand the glory of My name. Dear devotees! Do not worry. I will definitely tell you this name."

Chandlo
Circular mark applied in the centre of the forehead with sacred red powder (kanku)

Mantras
Chant or incantation used in a rituals, worship and meditation. Words or phrases which possess sacred powers. A sacred phrase or chant given in the initiation ritual

Upasana
Correct understanding of the Lord. See Appendix

Yamduts
Servants of the deity of death

Akshardham
The divine abode of Lord Shree Swaminarayan

Again Shree Sahajanand Swami gently smiled and said, "No one has managed to discover My eternal name. My parents named Me Ghanshyam. Markandeya Rishi called Me Hari, Krishna, Harikrishna and Nilkanth. Shree Ramanand Swami gave Me the names Narayan Muni and Sahajanand Swami. However, no one discovered My true and original name."

Markandeya Rishi
Astrologer and sage. Said to be one of the eight immortals (chiranjivis)

Trividhi taap
Three types of miseries: Adhyatmik miseries arising from one's own deeds; Adhibhautic miseries arising from worldly or material contacts; Adhidaivik miseries arising from natural powers

Internal enemies
Obstacles to the Lord that reside within people. See Chapter 2

Babro
An evil spirit

Lord Shree Swaminarayan had nine names given to Him before He revealed His real, eternal and supreme name **Swaminarayan**, meaning the master of all Lords.

His parents, Dharmadev and Bhaktimata, named Him **Ghanshyam**; Markandeya Muni gave Him the names **Hari, Krishna, Harikrishna** and **Nilkanth**; Sadguru Shree Muktanand Swami, gave the name **Saryudas** (meaning the disciple from the Saryu region - named after the River Saryu in Northern India, which flows through the holy city of Ayodhya); Sadguru Shree Ramanand Swami gave the names **Shree Sahajanand Swami** (He who readily imparts divine bliss to others) and **Narayan Muni**. *Sants* and devotees used **Shreejimaharaj** as an affectionate name of respect and endearment for their beloved Lord.

"By the chanting of My name, all of one's *trividhi taap* will cease. All of one's internal enemies will be abolished. A deep affection for the religion and towards devotion will be evoked. Ultimately, by the remembrance of My name, Akshardham (eternal salvation) will be attained."

Those who were conceited and regarded Shree Sahajanand Swami to be a novice to the religion, still maintained their belief of superiority over Him. They believed that Nilkanath had devised some kind of black magic or had invoked the ghost Babro with which He was brainwashing everyone. These people began to burn with anger but were unable to speak due to the powerful presence of Shree Sahajanand Swami. Instead, they made gestures and signalled to one another, "Do not utter the name. I will not!"

The omniscient Shree Sahajanand Swami was naturally aware of this, but He did not say a word. Those who had faith in Him became spiritually enlightened to His greatness.

Shree Sahajanand Swami said, "There are many names for deities, including Narayan, Surya-narayan, Vairat-narayan, Laxmi-narayan, Nar-narayan, Vasudev-narayan, etc. I am the master (*swami*) of all these deities (*narayans*). Therefore, My name is 'Swaminarayan'. Dear disciples! My name is

'Swaminarayan'. This is My supreme name. You must all recite this name. Those who chant this name will experience divine ecstasy."

As soon as they heard the eternal name, 'Swaminarayan', of the supreme Lord from Shree Sahajanand Swami Maharaj, the assembled masses immediately began to chant, 'Swaminarayan, Swaminarayan'. All those who uttered the name immediately fell into a trance (*Samadhi*). Shree Sahajanand Swami piled the entranced bodies on top of each other, like a stack of logs. Then, as Shree Sahajanand Swami called their names, each person awoke from the trance and emerged from the pile of bodies without disturbing any of the others. They immediately started to pray to Shree Sahajanand Swami Maharaj and performed the eight-fold prostration in reverence (*sashtang-dandvat-pranam*) at His lotus feet.

Sastang-dandvat-pranam
The eightfold bow. A humble bow / prostration in which eight parts of the body are concentrated on the devotion of God, namely: the hands, feet, knees, chest, forehead (all of which touch the ground before His feet), mind, vision and obeisance

Samadhi
The final stage of Yoga

Sinhasan
Ornately decorated shrine where idols of the Lord are installed

In the trance, the devotees witnessed Lord Swaminarayan presiding in a divine *sinhasan*. They saw the deities to whom they had been worshipping, kneeling in prayer before Lord Shree Swaminarayan. The deities said, "We worship Lord Shree Swaminarayan. You too should worship Him and remain devoted to Him. You should offer your services to Him. By this, you will fulfil the true purpose of your human birth (i.e. attain salvation)."

As a result of the experiences during their trance, the devotees became convinced that Lord Shree Swaminarayan was indeed supreme and the incarnator of all the incarnations. With such convictions they started worshipping Him with faith and dedication.

As soon as the devotees chanted the supreme name, Swaminarayan, they immediately fell into a trance

Chapter 12

Glory of the Swaminarayan Name

When vicious desires arise, one should stop meditating and loudly chant Swaminarayan! Swaminarayan! Then, all the awful thoughts will subside and peace will prevail. There is no other way of avoiding such repulsive thoughts, other than this.

Lord Shree Swaminarayan, Vachanamrut Loya 6

There were some who believed that Shree Sahajanand Swami - Lord Shree Swaminarayan had propitiated the evil spirit Babro and that He used black magic. They did not like His phenomenon of inducing trance (*samadhi*).

Many firmly believed that Shree Ramanand Swami was their God. They resented Lord Shree Swaminarayan and were not prepared to accept Him as being the true, supreme Lord.

Shree Vyapkanand Swami and Shree Swaroopanand Swami were two such *sants*. One night they got together and started whispering to each other.

Shree Swaroopanand Swami said, "Vyapkanand! This Nilkanth has started to call Himself Swaminarayan. Not only that, but He has also announced that He is the supreme Lord Himself."

Vyapkanand Swami replied, "Yes Swaroopanand! In addition, He has commanded us to worship Him by the name Swaminarayan."

Swaroopanand Swami continued, "I will never accept that. My God is Shree Ramanand Swami. I will only chant 'Ramanand, Ramanand'."

Vyapkanand Swami said, "I agree. In that case, why don't we go away from here?"

Having decided to leave, the two *sants* fell asleep. During the night, they both had the same dream in which they had the *darshan* of Akshardham. They saw Shree Sahajanand Swami - Lord Shree Swaminarayan, presiding upon a divine Gadi. Shree Ramanand Swami was standing before Him with joined hands. They saw Shree Ramanand Swami praying to Him. In the dream, Shree Ramanand Swami commanded them, "Lord Shree Swaminarayan is my God. I worship Him as my Lord. So you too should do the same."

As soon as the dream was over, both the *sants* awoke and started to discuss what they had just experienced.

Vyapkanand Swami said, "Swaroopanand! That Sahajanand is extremely devious. He hypnotised me."

Vachanamrut
The words of Lord Shree Swaminarayan compiled as a scripture. See Appendix

Samadhi
A trance–like state. The final stage of Yoga

Shree Ramanand Swami
The Lord's guru. See Chapter 9

Sants
Ascetics, the closest Western equivalent being monks

Darshan
The visualisation of the Lord. Also the act of looking with reverence and devotion at the image or the deity in the shrine, sometimes of seeing a holy person

Akshardham
The divine abode of Lord Shree Swaminarayan

Swaroopanand Swami said, "Yes Vyapkanand! I was going to tell you the same thing. He took me to His abode. There was immense lustre all around. At the centre was a magnificent Gadi (Shree Swaminarayan Gadi) on which the conniving Sahajanand was seated. And the one whom we worship, Shree Ramanand Swami, was standing before Him, praying and worshipping Him. It would have been okay if that was all, but He made Ramanand Swami say, 'This Swaminarayan is my God. I worship Him, and you too should worship Him.'"

Hearing this, Vyapkanand Swami proposed, "Swaroopanand! Before He tries any more of His tricks let us get away from here and go where we can worship Ramanand Swami in peace." Swaroopanand Swami concluded, "Yes! Let's do just that, Vyapkanand." In this manner, both the *sants* decided to leave.

The next morning, Vyapkanand Swami and Swaroopanand Swami came to the assembly where Lord Shree Swaminarayan was presiding and sat amongst the congregation. All the *sants* and disciples were attentively listening to the discourses. Just then, a devotee came to perform *pooja* to Lord Shree Swaminarayan. He had brought a bowl of sandalwood paste, a garland and an *aarti* with him. The Lord told the devotee to leave all the offerings beside Him and take a seat in the congregation. The devotee bowed to the Lord and sat down.

The all-knowing Lord Shree Swaminarayan then said, "Vyapkanand Swami, we are both the disciples of the same guru. In this respect, we are brothers. Today, you are going to leave us. Will you not perform *pooja* to Me before you go?"

Vyapkanand Swami was stunned by this remark and became embarrassed. He thought, "How did He know about this?" Then he decided, "Let me perform His *pooja* and then I will be free from Him." He came forward to perform the *pooja*. As soon as he dipped his finger into the bowl of sandalwood paste, Lord Shree Swaminarayan placed both His hands on His chest then stretched them straight out and said, "Swami! *Pooja* is not performed like that. This is the way to perform *pooja*!"

Immediately, the 24 incarnations and *Muktas* emerged from Lord Shree Swaminarayan's *Murti*. On one side of Him was a line of incarnations, on the other was a line of *Muktas*. Shree Ramanand Swami was first in the line of *Muktas*. Shree Vyapkanand Swami became astounded at seeing this spectacle,

Pooja
An act of adoration, also performed as part of one's daily worship

Aarti
Ritual Ceremony. See Appendix

Twenty-four incarnations
Hindu philosophy states that God has incarnated in 24 forms:

Sanak, Varah, Yagnapurush, Hayagreev, Narayan, Kapildev, Dattatreya, Rushabhadev, Pruthraj, Machh, Kachh, Dhanvantri, Mohini, Nrusinh, Vaman, Hanspakshi, Hari, Parshuram, Ram, Vedvyas, Krishna, Buddh, Kartik and Kalki. Lord Swaminarayan is the incarnator of all these incarnations

Muktas
Liberated souls

Murti
Divine image or form of the Lord

Muni
Sage, ascetic (sant)

but he was also pleased to have the *darshan* of Shree Ramanand Swami. As he continued with the *pooja*, Lord Shree Swaminarayan said, "Vyapkanand Muni! Perform the *pooja* to all these incarnations and *Muktas* simultaneously." Hearing this, Vyapkanand Swami became confused and asked, "How is that possible?" Lord Shree Swaminarayan gently smiled and replied, "Utter the name of the one whom you believe to be God and pray to him, that if he is the supreme Lord, then by his prowess, may you assume numerable forms."

> Lord Shree Swaminarayan has revealed His absolute supremacy. He is greater than all the incarnations. All these incarnations and their *Muktas* exist as a result of the power instilled into them by the supreme Lord Shree Swaminarayan. That is why Lord Shree Swaminarayan is able to show them emerging from His *Murti*. Inferior incarnations cannot make a more superior incarnation appear from their *Murti*. No incarnation has revealed the *Murti* of Lord Shree Swaminarayan from his *Murti*.

Vyapkanand Swami proceeded to utter the name of each and every incarnation with this thought. But all was in vain. Finally he thought, "If Shree Ramanand Swami is the supreme Lord then by his prowess may I assume numerable forms." But nothing happened.

Now, Vyapkanand Swami became hesitant. He looked towards Lord Shree Swaminarayan's gently smiling lotus face. Lord Shree Swaminarayan cast His divine gaze on Vyapkanand Swami and transformed his feelings. Vyapkanand Swami questioned, "Are You the supreme Lord?" Lord Shree Swaminarayan replied, "Utter My name and see for yourself."

Meanwhile, Swaroopanand Swami, who was sitting amongst the congregation, decided, "If Vyapkanand Swami now assumes numerable forms, I will become convinced that Shree Swaminarayan is God. I will remain here and worship Him. If Vyapkanand wants to leave, he may go."

Vyapkanand Swami, who was standing before Lord Shree Swaminarayan, had the same thought and immediately said, "If Shree Sahajanand Swami, who is seated before me and who has declared His name to be Swaminarayan, is the supreme Lord, then by His prowess, may I assume multiple forms." As soon as Vyapkanand Swami uttered these words, he instantly assumed multiple forms. In the hands of each form was a bowl of sandalwood paste, a garland of flowers and an *aarti*. As he started to perform *pooja*, each of his other forms

simultaneously performed *pooja* to each of the incarnations and *Muktas*. Lord Shree Swaminarayan then merged all the incarnations and *Muktas* back into Himself. Again Vyapkanand Swami uttered, "If Shree Sahajanand Swami, who is seated before me and who has declared His name to be Swaminarayan, is the supreme Lord, then may my multiple forms all become one." All his numerable forms were merged into one.

Lord Shree Swaminarayan revealed the 24 incarnations and Muktas emerging from His Murti

Lord Shree Swaminarayan then said, "Vyapkanand Swami and Swaroopanand Swami. All the gates are open for you. You may now go wherever you please."

Both *sants* immediately prostrated in reverence at Lord Shree Swaminarayan's lotus feet and begged for forgiveness, "Oh, Lord Shree Swaminarayan! We are ignorant. We were not able to recognise You. Mercifully you gave *darshan* to us in a dream, but we thought You had used a spell on us. Forgive us for our sins. Oh Lord! You are the supreme God. We will chant Your divine name 'Swaminarayan'. Oh Lord! Keep us under Your shelter."

Just as a diamond is required to cut another diamond, the *darshan* of the Lord can only be attained through His grace and one's faith unto the Lord can only be achieved through the Lord Himself.

Lord Swaminarayan, Vachanamrut Gadhada First Section 51

Bhumapurush
One of the personalities in the lineage of deities. His abode being Avyakrit-dham

Yampuri
The closest Western equivalent is Hell

Lord Shree Swaminarayan replied, "Oh Vyapkanand Swami and Swaroopanand Swami! I will allow you to remain with Me, if you do one thing for Me." Both *sants* said, "Oh Lord! Our Master! Give us Your command. We will immediately do as You ask." Lord Shree Swaminarayan said, "During My forest expedition, Bhumapurush came to Me and prayed to Me. I promised him that I would take him to Akshardham. So Vyapkanand Swami! Go to the abode of Bhumapurush and tell him that the supreme Lord Shree Swaminarayan is now presiding as the sovereign king. Inform him that I have sent you there in accordance with the promise I had given to him, that I would send him to Akshardham. When they chant the name 'Swaminarayan', he and all his subjects will attain Akshardham."

"Oh Swaroopanand Swami! When a sovereign king takes office, he grants his pardon to all and releases all prisoners from captivity. Similarly, I have now taken My Gadi. So I want to relieve all the suffering souls in Yampuri and award them the abode of Bhumapurush. Go to Yampuri and recite My name 'Swaminarayan' three times. All the souls will be dispatched to the abode of Bhumapurush."

Bhumapurush came to Lord Swaminarayan during the forest expedition. It is only when the merciful Lord is on this Earth that these incarnations are able to have the *darshan* of the supreme Lord.

Hearing Lord Shree Swaminarayan's commands, both the *sants* asked, "How can we reach there?" Lord Shree Swaminarayan replied, "Why have you both become confused? Think about My power. Look at Me."

As soon as the gaze of Lord Shree Swaminarayan and the two *sants* met, they fell into a trance. With divine bodies, they embarked on their journeys, during which they had to encounter numerous obstacles. Each hindrance was overcome by the power of chanting the 'Swaminarayan' name. Vyapkanand Swami reached Bhumapurush's abode and conveyed Lord Shree Swaminarayan's message. He made everyone chant 'Swaminarayan'. By the power of the 'Swaminarayan' name, Bhumapurush and his servants attained Akshardham.

Shree Swaroopanand Swami arrived in Yampuri. He clapped loudly and exclaimed the name 'Swaminarayan' three times. All the souls were

immediately liberated from the bond of Narak and were relieved of their suffering. They gathered around Shree Swaroopanand Swami despite vain attempts by the Yam to stop them. Shree Swaroopanand Swami pointed upwards and said, "Look!" When they looked up, they saw divine aircraft descending from the sky. The souls sat in the aircraft, which took them to the abode of Bhumapurush. Dharmaraja then asked, "What will I do here alone?" Swami replied, "You reigned here as the king. Now, take the place of Bhumapurush and reign in his abode as Bhumapurush." Dharmaraja went to the abode and became Bhumapurush.

> Dharmaraja became Bhumapurush by the command of Lord Swaminarayan. This shows that Lord Swaminarayan ultimately controls the entire hierarchy of incarnations.

The glory of the 'Swaminarayan' name is boundless. Lord Shree Swaminarayan Himself has described its greatness;

જે સ્વામિનારાયણ નામ લેશે, તેનાં બધાં પાતક બાળી દેશે
છે નામ મારાં શ્રુતિમાં અનેક, સર્વોપરી આજ ગણાય એક

Je Swaminarayan naam leshe, tenaa badhaa paatak baadee deshe,
Chhe naam maaraa shrutimaa aneka, sarvopari aaj ganaay eka.

Whoever utters the name Swaminarayan will have their sins burned away.
The Lord is referred to by many names in various scriptures,
but this is the supreme name of the Lord.

Reciting the name Swaminarayan just once, is equivalent to reciting the names of deities or incarnations a thousand times.
The fruits attained by the mere utterance of this name are indescribable.

This six-syllable *mantra* is so powerful that it fulfils the ultimate aims of human life.
It brings bliss and destroys all sorrows, ultimately it bestows Akshardham.

This name is a hundred thousand times more powerful than the *Gayatri mantra*.
This magnitude can only be comprehended by Mahesh.
Wherever *Muktas* reside, it is only this *mantra* that is recited.

Narak
Yampuri, the closest Western equivalent is Hell

Yam
Attendants of Yampuri

Dharmaraja
The King of Yampuri

Mantra
Chant or incarntation using rituals, worship or meditation. The words or phrases possess sacred powers

Ultimate aims of human life
Dharma – religion
Arth – wealth
Kaam – virtuosity
Moksh – salvation

Gayatri Mantra
A famous Hindu verse

Mahesh
Anadi–mukta, the highest status of a liberated soul

If this *mantra* is heard at the last moments of one's life,
even a sinful person attains salvation.
This *mantra* dispels evil spirits and enlightens true wisdom.
Yam will be repelled away from whoever chants this *mantra*.

The name Swaminarayan, whether uttered in reverence or with evil
sentiment, grants eternal salvation.
This six-syllable *mantra* is the epitome of all six principle Hindu scriptures,
it enables a soul to transgress the ocean of life and death.

Throughout the entire year and every day,
this *mantra* should be recited whilst performing every deed.
Whether your body is in a purified state or in an impure state,
this name should be remembered daily with love.

Just as water washes away bodily dirt,
this *mantra* cleanses one internally (i.e. the soul).
Those who have committed numerous great sins, and abused *Brahmins*,
cows or *sants*, are ashamed even to speak the name Swaminarayan.

The name Swaminarayan is the most potent destroyer of sin.
Even within extremely sinful persons, none of their sins
remain un-burned if they chant the name Swaminarayan.

Brahmins
Category of the Hindu caste system whose members are contemplative, philosophical, scholastic, impart knowledge and perform religious rites

Rishi
Sage, holy person

Shat means six and *shastra* means scripture. The six principal Hindu philosophies are: Sankhya (written by Kapil Rishi) - Describes the nature of the universe; Yog (written by Patanjali Rishi) - Describes the interaction of the soul with the Lord; Nyay (written by Gautam Rishi) - Describes methodology and logic; Vaisheshik (written by Kanad Rishi) - Describes physics; Mimansa (Purva Mimansa) (written by Jaymini Rishi) - Stipulates the rules of the religious decree; Vedant (Uttar Mimansa) (written by Badarayan Rishi also known as Vyas Muni) - Describes the rituals of Hinduism

Cows are considered to be sacred by Hindus.
God's first four creations are said to be the Vedas (scriptures), fire, the cow and Brahmins. The cow is considered so pious that even its urine and dung are regarded as being the most purifying of articles. The other three items derived from the cow, which are considered equally purifying are its milk, curd and clarified butter (*ghee*). These five products of the cow are called *panch-gavyam* and are used together for self-purification in religious ceremonies. Cow-dung is applied to the floor in order to purify the ground.

Chapter 13

The Faith of Shree Muktanand Swami in the Lord

Shree Muktanand Swami was renowned as the mother of the Satsang. In order to explain the supremacy of Lord Shree Swaminarayan to all, he used himself as an example. He showed that he had human sentiments for the Lord. Eventually, by the divine mercy of the Lord, Shree Muktanand Swami came to understand His greatness and revealed His supremacy to everyone.

There are few individuals in the Satsang who will never become tempted or corrupted by worldly objects. Shree Muktanand Swami is one such eminent sant.

Lord Shree Swaminarayan, Vachanamrut Gadhada Last Section 33

Purna Purushottam Lord Shree Swaminarayan continued with His chapter of instigating trance (*samadhi*). Numerable souls became His devotees through these episodes.

However, there were some who did not like this phenomenon of inducing trance and the manner in which the Lord made devotees chant His name 'Swaminarayan'. Shree Muktanand Swami prayed to Shree Ramanand Swami, "Oh my Lord Shree Ramanand Swami! Instil some understanding into Shree Sahajanand Swami."

Once, Shree Muktanand Swami was in the village of Kalvani. Early one morning, Shree Muktanand Swami was performing his daily ablutions near a pit. All of a sudden, he saw a lustrous figure approaching him from an Easterly direction. Amidst the lustre was a figure that was travelling one yard off the ground. As the figure approached, he realised who it was and exclaimed, "Oh! It is my guru, my Lord, Ramanand Swami."

Shree Muktanand Swami bowed and prostrated in reverence before his guru's feet and tears rolled down his cheeks. He said, "Oh my Lord! After your departure, Sahajanand has ruined everything. He is now being worshipped as God."

Shree Ramanand Swami replied, "Muktanand! You have forgotten my words! I used to say that I am merely the drumbeater, awakening all who seek salvation to the imminent arrival of the supreme Lord. That supreme God is Shree Sahajanand Swami – Lord Shree Swaminarayan. He has finally arrived. He is the paramount Lord to whom I offer my worship. You too should worship Him."

After saying this, Shree Ramanand Swami placed his hand on Shree Muktanand Swami's head and relieved him from his grief. By the grace of his guru, Shree Muktanand Swami developed a deep faith in Lord Shree Swaminarayan and started to consider Him to be the supreme Lord.

Shree Muktanand Swami then gathered flowers and made a garland. With his own hands, he prepared a bowl of sandalwood paste and immersed wicks in *ghee*, to perform the *aarti* ceremony. Carrying all these articles, Shree Muktanand Swami came to the congregation.

Satsang
Fellowship associated with the Swaminarayan religion

Sant
Ascetic. the closest Western equivalent being a monk

Vachanamrut
The words of Lord Shree Swaminarayan compiled as a scripture. See Appendix

Purna Purushottam
Almighty supreme Lord of Lords

Samadhi
A trance-like state. The final stage of Yoga

Ramanand Swami
The Lord's guru. See Chapter 9

Ghee
Clarified butter

Aarti
Ritual Ceremony. See Appendix

Pooja
An act of adoration, also performed as part of one's daily worship

Kirtan
Devotional song praising the Lord

Nar
Human

Brahmin
Category of the Hindu caste system whose members are contemplative, philosophical, scholastic, impart knowledge and perform religious rites

When Lord Shree Swaminarayan, in the guise of Shree Nilkanth Varni, arrived in Loj, He met Shree Muktanand Swami and resided with him. (In this capacity, Shree Nilkanth Varni lived with Muktanand Swami for ten months and six days). Therefore, He referred to Shree Muktanand Swami as His guru. When Shree Muktanand Swami approached the Lord in readiness to perform *pooja*, He said, "Oh Muktanand Swami! You are considered My guru. What are you doing?" Shree Muktanand Swami replied, "I have realised today who the guru is and who the disciple is. Shower mercy on me and allow me to perform my adoration to You. Pardon me for all my misunderstandings."

Shree Muktanand Swami adorned Lord Swaminarayan's forehead with the sandalwood paste and garlanded Him. He lit the wicks and started to perform the *aarti*. At that moment, some of the elderly *sants* questioned him, "Muktanand Swami! What are you doing?"

Shree Muktanand Swami retorted, "The wicks are burning away. Let me first perform the *aarti* and then I will answer you all."

Shree Muktanand Swami then performed the *aarti* ceremony, whilst singing a *kirtan*.

જય સદ્‌ગુરુ સ્વામી, પ્રભુ જય સદ્‌ગુરુ સ્વામી
સહજાનંદ દયાળુ (૨) બળવંત બહુનામી.....જય ૦ ટેક

Jay Sadguru Swami, Prabhu Jay Sadguru Swami
Sahajanand dayaalu (2) balavant bahunaami

Hail to Sadguru Swami, Oh dear Lord! My hail to You.
Oh merciful Sahajanand! You are the all-powerful Lord.
Your names are also infinite.

With joined hands, I bow to Your lotus feet. By merely placing my
head at Your lotus feet, You have ended all my miseries.

Oh Lord Narayan! You are the brother of *Nar* and manifested
in the guise of a *Brahmin*.

Through Your manifestation, You have emancipated innumerable wretched and degenerated men and women.

Oh eternal Lord! Each day, You perform new and enchanting divine episodes.

The 68 great sites of pilgrimage lie at Your lotus feet. The *darshan* of Your lotus feet is greater than sites of the merit attained by visiting the holy pilgrimage sites, Kashi, Gaya etc., millions of times.

Oh manifest Lord Purushottam! Those who perform Your *darshan*, will be freed from the bond of *kaal* and *karma*. They, together with their families, will attain liberation.

Oh treasury of mercy! During this very age, You have showered Your divine grace over all. Muktanand firmly acclaims, You have made it easy for all to attain salvation (*aatyantik-moksh*).

From the time Shree Muktanand Swami first sang this *aarti*, it has been sung in the entire Swaminarayan *Sampraday*.

When the *aarti* concluded, Shree Muktanand Swami described the *darshan* that Shree Ramanand Swami had given him. Then addressing the entire assembly, he said, "If you seek salvation, you must worship Lord Shree Swaminarayan. He is indeed the almighty Lord."

Darshan
The visualisation of the Lord. Also the act of looking with reverence and devotion at the image or the deity in the shrine, sometimes of seeing a holy person

Lord Purushottam
Supreme Lord Swaminarayan

Kaal
The power of the Lord that provides souls with the rewards of their deeds

Karma
Sanskrut word meaning deed or action. According to Hindu belief, every action has inevitable consequences, which attach themselves to the doer. These deeds result in reward or punishment dependent on their nature. Karma is thus the moral law of actions and their consequences

Sampraday
Holy fellowship

Chapter 14

The Flourishing of the Satsang

શૂરા જીતે શસ્ત્ર વડે સદાય, વિધ્ધા વડે વિપ્ર જીતે સભાય
સેના વડે રાજ્ય જીતે દિગંત, સદ્ધર્મથી વિશ્વ જીતે સુસંત

*Sooraa jeete shastra vade sadaay, vidyaa vade vipra jeete sabhaaya
Senaa vade raajya jeete digant, saddharmathi vishwa jeete susanta*

*In this world, brave soldiers win battles using weapons, scholars win
assemblies (debates) with their knowledge, and rulers gain sovereignty
over other kingdoms using their armies. Similarly, sants conquer the
entire world through their religiosity.*

Lord Shree Swaminarayan primarily travelled on His mare, Manki,
whom He had brought with Him from Akshardham

Purna Purushottam Lord Shree Swaminarayan began to tour the land of Gujarat and Kutch. He bestowed the bliss of trance (*samadhi*) effortlessly to all, regardless of whether they were worthy or not. In the trance, the individuals were given *darshan* by the incarnation whom they worshipped. That incarnation was seen praying to Lord Shree Swaminarayan. In the trance, the incarnations would tell their disciples, "I worship Lord Shree Swaminarayan. You too should worship His name, Swaminarayan. He is the supreme Lord."

Lord Shree Swaminarayan revealed His supremacy to many devotees such as Abhay Khachar, by showing the 24 incarnations emerging from His divine *Murti* and then merging them back into Himself.

Consequently, people of all statures in life, from kings to peasants, became ardent followers of Lord Shree Swaminarayan and began to worship Him by chanting His name, 'Swaminarayan'.

Lord Shree Swaminarayan began a unique tradition of performing the *vartman* ceremony. All salvation seekers who came to His shelter underwent this *vartman* ceremony. Whilst performing the *vartman* ceremony, the Lord says, "All the good or evil deeds and actions of all your past lives are placed at the lotus feet of Shree Swaminarayan. You now reside in His *Murti*."

By performing the *vartman* ceremony, the Lord motivated innumerable people to give up their addictions to drugs, alcohol, smoking, gambling etc. and made them His loyal disciples. Lord Shree Swaminarayan convinced evil bandits such as Joban Vadtala to give up their unlawful activities and made them His ardent devotees.

On one occasion, a new *Kathi* follower who had undergone the *vartman* ceremony, came across his previous guru. The guru called him and asked, "Oh Somla! What did you see in Swaminarayan that caused you to become His devotee?"

The *Kathi* replied, "Lord Shree Swaminarayan performs *vartman* and surrenders all the sins, merits and *karma* of all our previous lives at His lotus feet. Through this process, He purifies us all."

Satsang
Fellowship associated with the Swaminarayan religion

Akshardham
The divine abode of Lord Shree Swaminarayan

Purna Purushottam
Almighty supreme Lord of Lords

Samadhi
A trance–like state. The final stage of Yoga

Darshan
The visualisation of the Lord. Also the act of looking with reverence and devotion at the image or the deity in the shrine, sometimes of seeing a holy person

Murti
Divine image or form of the Lord

Vartman
An oath taken, when an aspirant joins the faith to abide by the five sacred vows. See Chapter 3

Kathi
Member of Kathi caste

Karma
Sanskrut word meaning deed or action. According to Hindu belief, every action has inevitable consequences, which attach themselves to the doer. These deeds result in reward or punishment dependent on their nature. Karma is thus the moral law of actions and their consequences

The guru questioned, "Exactly what is *vartman*? And tell me! How does Swaminarayan surrender the sins at His feet?" The *Kathi* devotee replied, "He places some water in our palm and then, holding our hand He says, 'All your sins and *karmas* are now at My feet.' Saying this, He allows the water to fall to the ground." The guru retorted, "Ah! What is the big deal in Swaminarayan doing that! Even I can do that."

> During the 49 years, 2 months and 1 day that the Lord gave *darshan* on the earth, He made more than 1.2 million disciples and gave initiation into the ascetic fraternity to over 2500 individuals.
>
> It is not mentioned anywhere in any scriptures that an incarnation has burnt away the *karmas* of their disciples. It is said that they, on occasions, have managed to delay the consequences of their actions, but they have not managed to eradicate them. This demonstrates the supremacy of Lord Shree Swaminarayan over all the previous incarnations.

Just then, they saw another *Kathi* passing. He was an extremely sinful character. The devout *Kathi* stopped him and said to the guru, "Surrender the sins of this man at your feet."

The guru then asked, "Oh Vasta! Bring some water." Water was bought and the guru started to perform *vartman*. He placed the water in the palm of the sinful *Kathi* and held his hand. Then he said, "Let the sins and *karmas* of your innumerable lives fall at my feet!" As soon as the guru uttered these words, his body was repeatedly thrown into the air, just like a bouncing ball. Eventually, he fell to the ground and started foaming at his mouth. He experienced great pain and eventually became unconscious. The *Kathi* devotee brought him to Lord Shree Swaminarayan and explained what had happened. The merciful Lord showered mercy on him and surrendered all his sins at His feet. The guru immediately regained consciousness and humbly fell at Lord Shree Swaminarayan's lotus feet. He begged for forgiveness and became a devotee. The other sinful *Kathi* also became a devotee.

In this way, many people of varying doctrines and creeds became followers of Lord Shree Swaminarayan and started worshipping Him by chanting His name, 'Shree Swaminarayan'. Lord Shree Swaminarayan abolished various evil practices that were prevalent in the society, including *doodh piti*, *sati* and *fatana*

Doodh piti
Drowning of a new born female baby in milk

Sati
Burning of a widow in her husband's funeral pyre

Fatana
The singing of obscene, immoral songs during wedding ceremonies

He prohibited the use of addictive substances such as alcohol and drugs, and banned theft, adultery and the consumption of meat.

He freed innumerable individuals from their blind beliefs of ghosts, spirits, spells, curses, charms, superstitions etc. and led them to live devout, religious lives. Recognising the great prowess of Lord Shree Swaminarayan, many souls who aspired for salvation renounced the material world, became *sants* and started preaching about the religion. Lord Shree Swaminarayan had five hundred principal preaching *sants* called *paramhans*, who with the strength and grace of Lord Shree Swaminarayan, spread the faith far and wide. The faith blossomed in all directions. Such prowess cannot be achieved by anyone else, other than the supreme Lord.

> **Paramhans:** Lord Swaminarayan initiated 500 major preaching *sants* as *paramhans* in one night at Kalvani. By the command of the Lord, these *sants* did not keep any external signs of affiliation to the Swaminarayan Faith, such as *shikha, sutra, tilak-chandlo* etc. In this manner, they were able to travel from village to village without being harassed by spiteful ascetics of other faiths who actively sought out Swaminarayan *sants* and tortured them. These *sants* were the *Muktas* who had accompanied the Lord from the divine abode.

Sants
Ascetics, the closest Western equivalent being monks

Shikha
A circular cluster of hair on the crown of the scalp signifying asceticsm

Sutra
Sacrosanct thread

Tilak- chandlo
A mark applied on the forehead, The Swaminarayan mark is of a U–shape made of yellow sandalwood paste (chandan) at the centre of which is a circular mark applied in the centre of the forehead with sacred red powder (kanku)

Muktas
Liberated souls

સહેજે કરાવે જનને સમાધિ, રહે નહિ અલ્પ કશી ઉપાધિ
જુએ જઈને જન શ્રીજી ધામ, એ તો ખરું ઈશ્વરનું જ કામ ....

Saheje karaave jan ne samaadhi, rahe nahi alp kashi upaadhi
Jooe jaee ne jan Shreeji dhaam, e to kharu Ishwar nu ja kaam

He leads one to trance with the utmost of ease
During which all experience great peace
They witness the divinity of the Lord in His abode
This is the prowess of the Lord alone.

People are attracted by affluence and riches
Many kingdoms are conquered by armies and weapons
But to conquer all without such resources
This is the prowess of the Lord alone.

He, whose name is worshiped by millions,
Upon whom meditate multitudes, with pure and sincere hearts
Wealth, women and home are renounced by His command
This is the prowess of the Lord alone.

Koli
Member of the Koli class

Firm and staunch followers of differing creeds
Who cannot be won over by any means
They become disciples and bow down to Him
This is the prowess of the Lord alone.

Believers of many deities exist
They see their cherished deities praying to Him
They then start to chant His name
This is the prowess of the Lord alone.

Violent thieves, bandits and crooks
All become pious and adhere to the faith
He, in whose hands lies the reins of all
This is the prowess of the Lord alone.

Tasks that humans can complete
These can be performed by all
But the tasks that no-one else can do
This is the prowess of the Lord alone.

Gradually and steadily, the religion is spread
Gradually and steadily, great scriptures are created
He who does all, in the shortest of times
This is the prowess of the Lord alone.

Deeds which can be learnt and then performed
These are the deeds that humans can perform
Attracting millions of souls to Him
Such an ability, exists with the Lord alone.

The Swaminarayan religion soon spread all over Gujarat, Saurashtra and
Kutch. Lord Shree Swaminarayan's disciples were living pious and moralistic
lives. This attracted the attention of Vadodara's King Sayajirao II who used to
say, "If one wishes to rid the *Kathis*, *Kolis* and all the other people that live in
a village from their addictions and illicit practices, a Swaminarayan temple
should be built there." Sayajirao often gave donations for building temples.
In this manner, the flag of the Shree Swaminarayan religion was made to
fly far and wide.

Chapter 15

Philosophy

Lord Shree Swaminarayan imparts His supreme divine philosophy to the eminent sants who collated these teachings into the Vachanamrut scripture

Purna Purushottam Lord Shree Swaminarayan preached His supreme knowledge that:

The Lord is not *sagun*, nor is He *nirgun*. His true, original form is beyond both these attributes and is divine and lustrous. The *sagun* and *nirgun* attributes of the Lord exist as a result of His extraordinary divine prowess.

Vachanamrut Kariyani 8

It is impossible to visualise the soul or Brahm without having *sakar upasana* unto the Lord.

Vachanamrut Gadhada Last Section 36

The supreme Lord Shree Swaminarayan dispelled the belief that, "Salvation can be attained through worshipping the Lord's *pratima* only after an extensive period of time." He said, "My *pratima* is Me. The divine *Murti* that exists in Akshardham is the same as this human form of the *Murti* that gives *darshan* to you all, and is the very same divine, salvation-granting *pratima Murti*. There is no difference between these forms. Not even an iota of a difference exists between them."

Vachanamrut Gadhada First Section 9, 48 and 68

Through merely realising that Lord Shree Swaminarayan is the doer and controller of all, salvation is attained. All other spiritual means are performed in order to please Him.

Vachanamrut Kariyani 10

There are many means to please Lord Shree Swaminarayan. Amongst these, to have true loving devotion unto the Lord is the best means of all. One should develop this true loving chaste devotion unto the Lord, together with an understanding of the religious decree, spiritual knowledge and asceticism. By developing such devotion, the devotees should think of their own form to be *Purushottam-roop*.

Vachanamrut Vadtal 3

Sants
An ascetic, the closest Western equivalent being monks

Vachanamrut
The words of Lord Shree Swaminarayan compiled as a scripture. See Appendix

Purna Purushottam
Almighty supreme Lord of Lords

Sagun
Possesses attributes related to illusion (Maya)

Nirgun
Not possessing any attributes of illusion (Maya)

Brahm
The Lord

Sakar upasana
The philosophy that describes the Lord to exist with a distinct form but not being merely a mass of energy or light. See Appendix

Pratima
Divine form of the Lord as an idol, painting etc.

Murti
Divine image or form of the Lord

Akshardham
The divine abode of Lord Shree Swaminarayan

Darshan
The visualisation of the Lord

Purushottam-roop
God-like

Lord Shree Swaminarayan has said, "My philosophy is the *Vishishtadwait* philosophy." He has elucidated its meaning.

विशिष्टं च विशिष्टं च विशिष्टे ।
विशिष्टयोः अद्वैतम् इति विशिष्टाद्वैतम् ।।

Vishishtam cha Vishishtam cha Vishishte
Vishishtayoho adwaitam iti Vishishtadwaitam

"The Lord and His *Muktas* have distinct forms. By the grace of God, the distinct form of the *Mukta* becomes merged into the *Murti* of God, and there appears just one entity, the Lord."

Vachanamrut Sarangpur Section 11
and Shikshapatri Slok 1

Such supreme spiritual knowledge is explained in the scripture, Vachanamrut with its commentary, the Rahasyarth Pradeepika Tika.

Vishishtadwait
Philosophy of the Swaminarayan faith. See Appendix

Muktas
Liberated Souls

Shikshapatri
Scripture containing the holy commandments of Lord Swaminarayan. See Appendix

Rahasyarth Pradeepika Tika
Accompanying commentary to the Vachanamrut. See Appendix

By His own will, Lord Shree Swaminarayan manifests Himself in different forms. The *Sankalp* and the *Sankalpi*, are exactly the same. They grant salvation to numerable souls.

By accepting adorations and offerings of food *(thal)*, and conversing with devotees through His *pratima*, Lord Shree Swaminarayan has demonstrated that no difference exists between His *pratima* and His divine form.

Vachanamrut Gadhada First Section 48

At the last moments of the devotees' life, Lord Shree Swaminarayan gives His divine *darshan* to their relatives and others. He converts the devotee's soul to become *sakar* like Himself and merges the soul into His *Murti*. In this manner, He enlightens souls to experience the reality of the *Vishishtadwait* philosophy.

Lord Shree Swaminarayan's faithful loving devotees were so engrossed in His devotion that they became unified with His *Murti* to such an extent that Avalbai and other disciples proclaimed, "I am Sahajanand Swami – the omniscient God of all."

The almighty power and supremacy of the name 'Swaminarayan' is such that at the time of their death, many witness amazing miracles. Chariots, horse-drawn carriages and aircraft would be seen taking the soul to His abode, and then being merged into His *Murti*.

Vachanamrut Gadhada First Section 1

Sankalp
Thought – the thoughts of the Lord that take physical form are called Sankalp–swaroop, i.e. the Lord gives darshan through the personification of His thoughts

Sankalpi
One who thinks. i.e the originator of the sankalp – the Lord Himself

If someone has recognised the true essence of the form of God, there remains nothing more for that individual to know. God is extremely competent, extremely lustrous and infinitely great. He conceals His supremacy and lustre within Himself, and assumes the form of a human for the salvation of souls. He assumes a form that can be visualised by humans, in order that they can serve and offer worship etc. to that form. If a tiny thorn pricks the leg of an ant, the thorn cannot be removed using a lance or a knife. A minute needle would be required. Similarly, God conceals His greatness within Himself and assumes an incredibly minute form.

Vachanamrut, Gadhada First Section 63

Chapter 16

The Sants of the Swaminarayan Sampraday

Those who offer food to the great, eminent sants with love and affection attain the spiritual rewards of performing millions of religious ceremonies and ultimately, they are granted salvation. People who touch the feet of such sants become free from the sins of their innumerable past lives. Those who donate clothing to such sants attain eternal salvation (aatyantik-moksh). The rivers and lakes into which these sants dip their feet become places of pilgrimage. Any tree under which they sit or eat the fruits of, gains spiritual merit. If anyone performs darshan of these sants with sincere love, and bows down to them in reverence, their sins become destroyed.

Lord Shree Swaminarayan, Vachanamrut Jetalpur 4

Just like Lord Shree Swaminarayan, His *sants* possess amazing, miraculous and divine prowess. Each greater than the other. Shree Vyapkanand Swami arrived in Botad and stayed on the top floor of Daha Khachar's royal court. All of a sudden, he heard cries of grief. Daha Khachar's mare had just died. The *Kathis*, to whom a mare is more beloved than a son, were grieving their loss. Concerned about all the commotion, Shree Vyapakanand Swami went down and asked, "I have come here and you are all lamenting. Why?" One of the *Kathis* explained, "Swami! The King's mare has died. That is why we are weeping." Shree Vyapkanand Swami approached the dead mare and resting his chin on the tip of his staff he said, "This mare has legs, a face, a tail and eyes. Everything is intact and yet you say she is dead. What is dead in her?"

Hearing these remarks, the bystanders thought, 'Does Swami not even understand such simple things!' One *Kathi* said, "Swami! She has lost her breath?" Shree Vyapkanand Swami said, "Oh! Is that so?" Saying this, Shree Vyapkanand Swami encircled his hand in the air behind him. He made a fist, as if he was grabbing something and then brought his hand forward.

He then placed his hand near the mare's mouth and opened his fist. As soon as he snapped his fingers, the mare immediately became alive again and stood up. Everyone was amazed to witness the miracle.

It is said:

એક વ્યાપકાનંદ મુનિ, આચરજકારી છે
તે પર મહેર મોટી પ્રભુની, આચરજકારી છે
એક મુઇ જીવાડી ઘોડી, આચરજકારી છે

Ek Vyapkanand Muni, aacharaj-kaaree chhe
Te par maher motee prabhu-nee, aacharaj-karee chhe
Ek muee jeevaadee ghodee, aacharaj-kaaree chhe

The Muni Vyapkanand, is admirable.
Upon him remains the grace of God, therefore he is admirable.
He resurrected the dead mare. He is immensely admirable.

Sants
Ascetics, the closest Western equivalent being monks

Sampraday
Holy fellowship

Darshan
The visualisation of the Lord. Also the act of looking with reverence and devotion at the image or the deity in the shrine, sometimes of seeing a holy person

Vachanamrut
The words of Lord Shree Swaminarayan compiled as a scripture. See Appendix

Kathi
Member of the Kathi community

Muni
Sage, sant

Murti
Divine image or form of the Lord

> There may be many people who show miracles and perform magic tricks. However, this does not make them God. One should remain vigilant about being enticed by such illusions.

After few days, Shree Vyapakanand Swami came to Gadhada for Lord Shree Swaminarayan's *darshan*. As he approached Him, Lord Shree Swaminarayan said, "Vyapakanand Swami, you have become God! The nature of worldly humans is such that they have deep affection for their relatives. As soon as someone dies, they will bring them to you to bring them back to life. Will you restore life to everyone again?"

Shree Vyapakanand Swami replied, "Oh Lord! There are many lost souls wandering around in this universe. If I take one of these souls and place it in the body of another, surely that does not make me God. He who frees souls from the illusory world and transforms them into a divine form, and keeps them in His *Murti*, only He is God. Such a God are You, but no other!"

Hearing these words, Lord Shree Swaminarayan became extremely pleased.

સ્વામિનારાયણ ભગવાન બીજો કોઇ નહિ
એના સર્વોપરીપણામાં બીજી જોડ નહિ

Swaminarayan Bhagwan beejo koee nahi
Enaa Sarvopari-panaa-maa beejee jod nahi

Lord Swaminarayan is God, there exists no other
In His supremacy, there exists no equal.

Purna Purushottam
Lord Shree Swaminarayan

Chapter 17

Shreeji-sankalp-murti Shree Gopalanand Swami

Devotees who have an immense love for God wish only for the darshan of God and to listen to the discourses about God. Obviously, they want to constantly live with God, wherever He presides. However, if they have true love for God, they remain more committed to abiding by the will of God rather than their own preferences. This is the characteristic of those who possess the highest category of humbleness. Gopalanand Swami is a sant of that eminent stature.

Lord Shree Swaminarayan, Vachanamrut Gadhada Middle Section 62

Shreeji-sankalp-murti
The physical embodiment of the thoughts of Lord Shree Swaminarayan i.e. those who give darshan upon this earth by the will of the Lord; they are synonymous to the Lord Himself

Sant
Ascetic, the closest Western equivalent being a monk

Vachanamrut
The words of Lord Shree Swaminarayan compiled as a scripture. See Appendix

Muktas
Liberated souls

Akshardham
The divine abode of Lord Shree Swaminarayan

Murti
Divine image or form of the Lord

Sadguru
Status of eminent ascetics (sants)

Darshan
The visualisation of the Lord

Bhaktachintamani
Biographical scripture of Lord Shree Swaminarayan written by Shree Nishkulanand Swami. It consists of 8527 verses organised in 164 chapters and portrays the life and episodes of Lord Shree Swaminarayan in chronological order

Lord Shree Swaminarayan and His divine *Muktas* deliberated in Akshardham about manifesting on the earth. These *Muktas* always remain in the *Murti* of the Lord. They are merged in the *Murti*; they neither leave nor return to the *Murti*. The Lord Himself manifested on the Earth to grant salvation to the souls.

Vachanamrut Sarangpur 11

Amongst all the *sants* of Lord Swaminarayan, Sadguru Shree Gopalanand Swami was supreme. He had an immensely powerful, miraculous prowess.

Sadguru Shree Nishkulanand Swami has said:
"The firm ascetic who had an immense love for the Lord, manifested with Him, assuming the name Khushal."

Bhaktachintamani, Prakaran 142

Sadguru Shree Gopalanand Swami's name before he took initiation as a *sant*, was Khushal Bhatt. He manifested (Samvat 1837 Maha Sud 8, Monday 1781) in the village of Todla near the town of Idar. This is approximately 15 miles away from the town of Shamlaji. Even in his childhood, he showed many miraculous and amazing feats.

There was an alley behind Khushal Bhatt's home where he used to play. The deity Shamlaji, from the Shamlaji Temple would personify himself and come to play with Khushal Bhatt. Shamlaji would remove his anklet, jingle it and show it to Khushal Bhatt. He would take off his upper garment and adorn Khusal Bhatt with it. In this way, they both would make each other laugh. Each day, Shamlaji would come to play with Khushal Bhatt.

One day, when Shamlaji was playing with Khushal Bhatt in Todla, the Shamlaji temple priest hurriedly went to the temple to awaken the deity. He rang the ceremonial bell. However, Shamlaji was not at the temple, he was in Todla playing with Khushal Bhatt. Shamlaji heard the bell. He immediately left Todla and flew back to the temple, where he took his usual place. However, in his haste, he forgot his golden anklet and upper garment in Todla. When the temple administrators came for *darshan*, they saw that the golden anklet was missing from Shamlaji's foot and accused the priest of stealing it. There was nothing that the innocent priest could do. He humbly prayed to Shamlaji with joined hands. Even if Shamlaji retrieved the anklet and placed it on his

foot, the priest would still not be cleared from the accusation of theft. Everyone would think that the priest became scared and replaced the anklet. Therefore, Shamlaji gave *darshan* to one of the administrators and told him that he had gone to play with Khushal Bhatt in Todla, and had forgotten the anklet and upper garment there. Shamlaji told the administrator to go to Todla and retrieve them. The administrator brought them back, and the priest was acquitted. Khushal Bhatt was so powerful that even the deity Shamlaji came to play with him.

Once, the region was afflicted with a severe famine and everyone migrated to the town of Idar. Khushal Bhatt and his friends used to go to play in the neighbouring forest. With his divine powers, he would produce sweet roots from the soil and give them to his friends to eat. He would amuse them all and teach them methods of worship and meditation. On one occasion, he made his friends sit in meditation and then led them into a trance (*samadhi*), in which he took them for a bathe in the River Saryu in Ayodhya. He then led them to the temples of Ayodhya for *darshan*. In one of these temples they saw a divinely lustrous child. This child was none other than Shree Ghanshyam Maharaj. They saw Khushal Bhatt and Shree Ghanshyam Maharaj speaking to each other, but could not understand what was being said. They were then returned to Idar and then brought back from the trance. They were absolutely amazed at what they had just experienced.

Khushal Bhatt was a teacher in the village of Todla. Together with his other teachings, he would describe the greatness and glory of the Lord.

Once, a house in the village caught fire. A four year old child was sleeping inside the house. His parents and the other family members were away from the house at that time. Who would rescue the child? Whilst sitting in his classroom, Khushal Bhatt extended his arm and lifted the child from the burning house. He brought the child back and seated him beside his chair in the classroom, where he began to play with the other children. The child's home was completely destroyed. His parents began to weep and mourn for their child who they thought had perished in the fire. The child's mother was grief-stricken. Sensing the anguish of the child's mother, Khushal Bhatt said to the child, "Go home! Your mother is crying after you." The child immediately hurried home and told everyone what had happened to him. Everyone was

amazed to hear how Khushal Bhatt saved him. They all came to Khushal Bhatt and bowed in reverence to him.

Brahmin
Category of the Hindu caste system whose members are contemplative, philosophical, scholastic, impart knowledge and perform religious rites

Pradakshina
Method of honour or form of worship which involves circumambulating in a clockwise direction around the object of worship

Khushal Bhatt resurrects the dead boy and cow

Early one morning, a *Brahmin's* son was taking his cow to drink water from the river. All of a sudden, a tiger came out of the forest and attacked them. Both were killed. The growling tiger stood there. Commotion and uproar arose throughout the village. Hearing the news of his son, the dead boy's father became distraught. He decided that life was no longer worth living without his one and only child. Lamenting in grief he decided to confront the tiger. People tried to restrain him from doing so, but he did not listen. At that time, merciful Khushal Bhatt appeared on the scene and stopped him. The *Brahmin* fell down at Khushal Bhatt's feet and wept. Having consoled the *Brahmin*, Khushal Bhatt approached the tiger and slapped it on its face. The tiger immediately fell to the ground in a dizzy haze and was led into a trance, during which it was reminded of its previous births. In the trance, the tiger received the divine *darshan* of Khushal Bhatt. When it awoke, it proceeded to honour Khushal Bhatt by performing *pradakshina* to him. The tiger then sat down on its knees in front of Khushal Bhatt. Khushal Bhatt commanded, "From today onwards, give up violence and savageness. Whenever you are hungry, you should come to the village and show the villagers your belly. Knowing you are hungry, they will all give you food." Accepting His commands, the tiger bowed in obeisance and retreated into the forest.

Khushal Bhatt then sprinkled some water over the dead boy and the cow. Both became alive again. Everyone was amazed to witness this miracle. They all fell at Khushal Bhatt's feet in reverence. They started praising him and performed adoration to him.

Thereafter, whenever the tiger became hungry, it would come into the village and show everyone its belly. Everyone gave food to the tiger. The children soon became so acquainted and friendly with the tiger that they started to play with it. Several children would sit on the tiger's back and ride around the village. Everyone enjoyed stroking and playing with it. Such was the majesty and glory of Khushal Bhatt – Sadguru Shree Gopalanand Swami.

Purna Purushottam Lord Shree Swaminarayan was presiding in Jetalpur. Khushal Bhatt went there for His *darshan*. This was to be the first time that they had met. As soon as their gazes met, tears of love rolled down from their eyes. Lord Shree Swaminarayan called Khushal Bhatt to Him and affectionately embraced him.

Just then, Damodarbhai (an ardent devotee) came with a message from Gangama. The food was ready, so she was requesting the Lord to go and dine. Lord Shree Swaminarayan asked, "Shall I come alone or with the entire assembly?" Damodarbhai replied, "The food has been prepared only for You, but do as You wish." Lord Shree Swaminarayan went to dine, accompanied by all the disciples. Lord Shree Swaminarayan and Khushal Bhatt led the entourage of devotees who were all chanting and singing. On their way, they came across a well from which they heard sounds of wailing and weeping. Everyone stopped. Lord Shree Swaminarayan said to Khushal Bhatt, "Go to the well and see what is making the commotion." Khushal Bhatt went to look in the well and then said, "There is a weeping hoard of spirits and ghosts in the well." Lord Swaminarayan said, "Grant them salvation." Immediately, Khushal Bhatt went to the well and removed the scarf from his shoulder. He waved it over the well and said, "Go to Akshardham!" Instantly, a thick cloud of smoke emerged from the well and divine light emanated from Shreejimaharaj and Khushal Bhatt. The spirits were freed from all their sins and were given a divine form. At that moment, divine aircrafts descended from the sky. All the spirits sat on them and were carried to Akshardham.

Purna Purushottam
Almighty supreme Lord of Lords

Gangama
An ardent disciple of Lord Shree Swaminarayan, who accompanied Him wherever He travelled. She carried a burning stove on her head, so that she could immediately prepare food for the Lord, as soon as He asked for it

Through this episode, Lord Shree Swaminarayan revealed to all that Khushal Bhatt (Sadguru Shree Gopalanand Swami) is just as competent as He at dispatching all souls, even unworthy souls, to Akshardham.

The entourage was delighted to witness this phenomenon and loudly sang and chanted as they walked. Eventually, they arrived at Gangama's home. Shreejimaharaj sat everyone to dine. All the devotees started chanting the Lord's name.

Gangama approached Lord Shree Swaminarayan and humbly prayed, "Oh Lord! I have made the meal only for You, but You have arrived with the entire assembly." Lord Shree Swaminarayan replied, "Don't worry. This Khushal Bhatt has amazing powers. He will serve everyone with what you have. There will not be a shortage of food. Just bring the food."

Gangama brought the food. Khushal Bhatt removed half the contents and began to serve the assembled devotees. He served everyone in the assembly but still, the food did not lessen. Then, Lord Shree Swaminarayan and Khushal Bhatt sat down to dine. Gangama approached them to serve the food. However, she saw two divine, lustrous figures. She could not recognise which was Lord Shree Swaminarayan and which was Khushal Bhatt. Lord Shree Swaminarayan gave this *darshan* to show the divine majestic prowess of Khushal Bhatt. After a short while, Lord Shree Swaminarayan withdrew the lustrous *darshan* and Gangama was able to serve them both. From this episode, Lord Shree Swaminarayan showed to all that Khushal Bhatt had manifested with Him from Akshardham and therefore, he is a Shreeji-sankalp-murti.

In Samvat 1864 Kartik Vad 8 (Sunday 22nd November 1807), Lord Shree Swaminarayan initiated Khushal Bhatt as a *sant* and named him 'Shree Gopalanand Swami'.

Shortly after Sadguru Shree Gopalanand Swami's initiation, Parvatbhai came for Lord Shree Swaminarayan's *darshan* and humbly prayed, "Oh Lord! Have mercy on us and send a group of eminent *sants* to stay in Agatrai for six months." Shreejimaharaj appointed Shreeji-sankalp-murti Sadguru Shree Gopalanand Swami head of the group, and assigned thirty great Sadgurus,

including Santdasji, Vyapkanand Swami, Swaroopanand Swami, Krupanand Swami, Ramdasbhai, Aatmanand Swami, etc. to accompany him. Hearing this, Ramdasbhai said, "Oh Maharaj! It may be better to appoint a *sant*, other than Gopalanand Swami, as the head of the group as he has only recently been initiated as a *sant*." Lord Shree Swaminarayan replied, "He forever dwells within My *Murti*. He is the greatest *sant* of all. Parvatbhai has asked Me to send him as the head. That is why I have appointed him your leader. So you all must obey and respect him. Do not let any arrogance arise within you and think that you are more senior or more experienced than he is. And Santdasji! You too must remain with Gopalanand Swami for six months, but do not go elsewhere." The group of *sants* went to Agatrai and stayed at Parvatbhai's home for six months. There, Sadguru Shree Gopalanand Swami and then Parvatbhai in turn, described the glory and greatness of Shreejimaharaj. Parvatbhai was also immensely powerful.

It is said:

એક હરિજન પર્વતભાઇ, આચરજકારી છે
સદા રહે મૂર્તિમાંહી, આચરજકારી છે

Ek harijan Parvatbhai, aacharaj-kaaree chhe
Sadaa rahe Murti-maahee, aacharaj-kaaree chhe

The devotee Parvatbhai, is admirable
He always remains in the *Murti*, so is greatly admirable

Throughout the six-month period Sadguru Shree Gopalanand Swami remained there, he did not allow Kaal to enter the village. Instead, he took all the souls who died to Akshardham.

He suppressed the influence of Kaal and dispatched all the souls to Akshardham, regardless of whether they were worthy or not - such was the great prowess of Sadguru Shree Gopalanand Swami.

Parvatbhai
An ardent devotee who had accompanied the Lord from Akshardham. He lived in the village of Agatrai

Santdasji
An eminent sant who had a reputation for wandering around according to his own will

Ramdasbhai
The first sant initiated by Ramanand Swami. His actual name was Ramdas Swami. Lord Swaminarayan considered him to be His gurubhai, i.e. having the relation of a brother, because they both were sants of the same guru, Ramanand Swami. The Lord addressed him as Bhai Swami or Ramdasbhai

Kaal
The power of the Lord that provides souls with the rewards of their deeds

Chapter 18

Amazing Divine Prowess

Those who have accomplished a firm detachment from worldly objects, a resolute faith in God, observe absolute strictness in their observance of celibacy and the ideology of non-violence, and have a true understanding about the nature of their soul, are freed from the cycle of birth and death. The grace of God is only attained by those who possess these qualities. They acquire the same characteristics as God. At times, they remain merged within the Murti and sometimes, they separate themselves from Him and remain in His humble service. Just as God is autonomous, these Muktas too are independent.

Lord Shree Swaminarayan, Vachanamrut Sarangpur 11

One day, Lord Shree Swaminarayan was presiding before a vast congregation, giving His divine *darshan* to all. He was adorned with a gold crown (*mugat*) and golden garments. At that time, the immensely merciful Lord Shree Swaminarayan asked Shreeji-sankalp-murti Sadguru Shree Gopalanand Swami, Sadguru Shree Brahmanand Swami, Sadguru Shree Nityanand Swami and Sadguru Shree Muktanand Swami, "Reveal the amazing divine prowess that you all possess."

The entire assembly became eager to hear about the divine characteristics of each of the *sadgurus* and attentively awaited their responses.

Sadguru Shree Muktanand Swami

Murti
Divine image or form of the Lord

Muktas
Liberated souls

Vachanamrut
The words of Lord Shree Swaminarayan compiled as a scripture. See Appendix

Darshan
The visualisation of the Lord. Also the act of looking with reverence and devotion at the image or the deity in the shrine. sometimes of seeing a holy person

Shreeji-sankalp-murti
The physical embodiment of the thoughts of Lord Shree Swaminarayan i.e. those who give darshan upon this earth by the will of the Lord; they are synonymous to the Lord Himself

Sadguru
Status of eminent ascetics (sants)

Firstly, Sadguru Shree Muktanand Swami humbly said, "Oh Maharaj! However sceptical and stonehearted a person may be, if they listen to my preaching, their conscience becomes pure and they will be diverted to the moral path of God. By your grace, such amazing prowess exists in me."

Lord Shree Swaminarayan said, "Yes! You do possess such qualities." The entire assembly bowed in respect to Sadguru Shree Muktanand Swami.

Muni
Sage, ascetic (sant)

Sadguru Shree Brahmanand Swami

Then, Sadguru Shree Brahmanand Swami humbly said, "Oh Maharaj! Whenever I compose poems about devotion unto You, religious decree and spiritual knowledge, I do not have to think about the words. The words spontaneously come to me. There is never a mistake regarding the rules of poetry in any of the poems. There is no-one who can compete with my poetic genius. Such an amazing prowess exists in me, by Your divine grace."

Lord Shree Swaminarayan said, "Brahm Muni! What you say is the truth." The assembly bowed in respect to Sadguru Shree Brahmanand Swami.

Sadguru Shree Nityanand Swami

Then, Sadguru Shree Nityanand Swami humbly said, "Oh Maharaj! This Bharatkhand is divided into four main spiritual regions. If any scholar from any of these places debates with me about the interpretation of the scriptures, they will never be able to defeat me. By Your grace, I possess such amazing scholastic prowess."

Bharatkhand
The Land of India. The four regions refer to North, South, East and West India. In each region there is a holy centre of scholastic excellence. Jagannathpuri is in the East, Dwarika is in the West, Badrikedar is in the North and Rameshwar is in the South

Lord Shree Swaminarayan said, "Yes Swami! You are indeed the greatest of all the scholars." *Sants* and devotees in the entire assembly bowed in respect to Sadguru Shree Nityanand Swami.

The assembly now turned its attention to Sadguru Shree Gopalanand Swami, as he humbly prepared to speak with joined hands. They became eager to know which great characteristic this amazing and miraculous *sant* was going to describe.

Sadguru Shree Gopalanand Swami

Sadguru Shree Gopalanand Swami said, "Oh Maharaj! In this world, it is said that nothing is possible without the will of God. By your grace, I am able to do anything that I wish. Such amazing prowess exists in me by Your grace."

Lord Shree Swaminarayan gently smiled. He stood up, lovingly embraced Sadguru Shree Gopalanand Swami and said, "Swami! I am indeed aware of all your greatness."

Everyone understood and realised that although Lord Shree Swaminarayan and Sadguru Shree Gopalanand Swami appear as two different entities, actually, they are one.

શ્રીજી પ્રભુ ને ગોપાળમુનિમાં, કાંઈ જુદાઈ નથી
એક છે છતાંય દેખાય બે, આપણને એ ખબર નથી
જાણ્યું આજે સ્વયં શ્રીજી, સ્વામી દ્વારે કાર્યો કરે
પતિત જનના ઉદ્ધાર માટે, સંત બની જગમાંહી ફરે

Shreeji Prabhu-ne Gopalmuni maa kaee joodaaee nathee
Ek chhe chhataay dekhaay be, aapannee e khabar nathee
Jaanyu aaje swayam Shreeji, Swami dwaare kaaryo kare
Patit jana naa udhaar maate, sant banee jag-maahee fare

Between Lord Shreeji and Gopal *Muni*
Exists no difference at all
They are one, yet appear as two
this is not understood by all.
Today we have come to realise
Shreeji Himself works through this Swami
Who appears upon the Earth in the guise of a *sant*
For the upliftment of the degenerated souls

The assembled devotees sat, engrossed by the divine *darshan* of Lord Shree Swaminarayan and Sadguru Shree Gopalanand Swami lovingly embracing each other. Their bliss and heartfelt love expressed itself through tears of joy. The *darshan* of both the divine *Murtis* appeared as one. Words of exclamation emanated from the devotees, 'Hail to the Lord! Hail to the Swami!'

Thereafter, Lord Shree Swaminarayan presided on His Gadi and sat Sadguru Shree Gopalanand Swami beside Him. Then, addressing the entire assembly, He said, "My dear *sants* and devotees, you all know and have experienced that Shree Gopalanand Swami is the greatest of all and is an immensely powerful *sant*. Out of these four *sadgurus*, he possesses the most superior and marvellous attributes.

Darshan
The visualisation of the Lord. Also the act of looking with reverence and devotion at the image or the deity in the shrine, sometimes of seeing a holy person

Sankalp-swaroop
The physical embodiment of the thoughts of Lord Shree Swaminarayan i.e. those who give darshan upon this earth by the will of the Lord; they are synonymous to the Lord Himself

Sampraday
Holy Fellowship

Satsang
Fellowship associated with the Swaminarayan religion

Upasana
Correct understanding of the Lord
See Appendix

"Shree Gopalanand Swami is My Sankalp-swaroop. Therefore, I command you all to live according to his will. In our *Sampraday*, he is the greatest of all. Therefore, I am handing the responsibility of this *Satsang* to him. If you remain under his authority, and remain vigilant that his every command is My decree, there is no doubt that you will attain My abode and experience the bliss of My *Murti*."

In the presence of the entire assembly, Lord Shree Swaminarayan then turned to Sadguru Shree Gopalanand Swami and said, "Swami! Ensure that all remain adherent to the religious decree. If someone needs reprimanding, you must do so. You are just as able and miraculous as I. You are My Sankalp-swaroop. You and I are one. Your aims are the same as Mine. This *Sampraday* which is Mine, is also naturally yours. Therefore you must look after this *Satsang* and spread My supreme *upasana*."

Sadguru Shree Gopalanand Swami bowed in reverence to Lord Shree Swaminarayan and respectfully accepted His command.

Chapter 19

Secret Ordination

Once, a congregation of eminent *sants* was held in the presence of Purna Purushottam Lord Shree Swaminarayan. Shreeji-sankalp-murti Sadguru Shree Gopalanand Swami, Sadguru Shree Brahmanand Swami, Sadguru Shree Nityanand Swami and Sadguru Shree Muktanand Swami were gazing, without blinking their eyes, at the Lord's lotus face.

Lord Shree Swaminarayan gently smiled and said, "Dear *sants*! Temples have been built. Scriptures have been written. The *Satsang* has been spread everywhere. Now, the *Sampraday* has become firmly established."

Sadguru Shree Gopalanand Swami said, "Yes Maharaj. Everything has happened according to Your will."

Sadguru Shree Brahmanand Swami said, "Oh Maharaj! There are still many souls who cannot understand Your supreme *upasana*."

Sadguru Shree Muktanand Swami added, "Oh merciful Maharaj! Shower Your grace so that all can understand Your true glory and attain Akshardham."

Sadguru Shree Nityanand Swami continued, "Merciful Lord! Everything lies in Your will. Shower mercy so that all, even those who are new to the faith and seek salvation, can easily understand Your glory and attain Akshardham."

The benevolent Lord Shree Swaminarayan said, "Dear *sants*! It is indeed My intention to do as you say. Through Sadguru Shree Gopalanand Swami, My supreme *upasana* and the Karan Satsang will be spread everywhere. The origin of the Karan Satsang lies with Shree Gopalanand Swami. He is the guardian of the religion. Through Shree Gopalanand Swami's spiritual lineage, the era of attaining eternal salvation (*aatyantik-moksh*) will always remain in the form of an ever-blossoming spring season. In the future, a great new entity will arise in Shree Gopalanand Swami's heritage, through which all souls in the *Sampraday* will be able to easily and clearly understand My supreme *upasana* and attain Akshardham."

Hearing such a wonderfully divine and amazing oracle, all the *sadgurus* bowed in respect to Lord Shree Swaminarayan.

Soon after, Purna Purushottam Lord Shree Swaminarayan adopted two sons – the sons of each of His two brothers.

> Shree Ayodhyaprasadji Maharaj is the son of the Lord's elder brother Rampratapbhai and Shree Raghuvirji Maharaj is the son of His younger brother Ichchharambhai. They are the Acharyas of the two worldly thrones (*vyavaharik gadis*) established by Lord Shree Swaminarayan for administrative purposes.
>
> Lord Shree Swaminarayan adopted Shree Ayodhyaprasadji Maharaj and Shree Raghuvirji Maharaj and appointed them as the Acharyas of Shree Narnarayan Gadi and Shree Laxminarayan Gadi, respectively. These were the thrones established for temporal reasons. They were **not** established to bestow absolute salvation; only Shree Swaminarayan Gadi can bestow salvation.

Sants
Ascetics, the closest Western equivalent being monks

Purna Purushottam
Almighty supreme Lord of Lords

Shreeji-sankalp-murti
The physical embodiment of the thoughts of Lord Shree Swaminarayan i.e. those who give darshan upon this earth by the will of the Lord; they are synonymous to the Lord Himself

Sadguru
Status of eminent ascetics (sants)

Satsang
Fellowship associated with the Swaminarayan religion

Sampraday
Holy fellowship

Upasana
Correct understanding of the Lord. See Appendix

Akshardham
The divine abode of Lord Shree Swaminarayan

Karan Satsang
True association with Lord Shree Swaminarayan. See Chapter 1

Gadi
Throne

Acharya
Preceptor

Chapter 20

Karan Satsang

Shree Ghanshyam Maharaj said, "Dear Suvasinibhabhi. When I will preside on this earth as the sovereign King, I will not forget you." In order to fulfil this wish to His elder sister-in-law, Suvasinibhabhi, Lord Shree Swaminarayan established two thrones for temporal purposes and established the sons of His elder and younger brothers as their Acharyas.

Ghanshyam Leelamrut Purvardh Tarang 49

Satsangi Bhushan Ansh 1 Adhyay 30

Whilst Purna Purushottam Lord Shree Swaminarayan was presiding in the Akshar-ordi, Sadguru Shree Gopalanand Swami came for *darshan* and sat down.

Purna Purushottam Lord Shree Swaminarayan gazed at him. Swami was gently smiling. The Lord asked, "Swami! Why are you smiling?"

Swami replied, "Your divine actions are truly incomprehensible. According to the stipulations in the scriptures, only one heir can be adopted. However, You have adopted two."

The Lord said, "Swami! I am not bound by the scriptures." Swami said, "Oh Maharaj! You are supreme. But dear Lord! Do tell. Whom do You love the most?" The Lord replied, "To Me, they are both equal. But Swami! Why do you ask such a question?" Swami answered, "Oh Maharaj! You have one Gadi and two adopted sons. To whom will You give the Gadi?"

The Lord replied, "Swami! My salvation granting Gadi will not be given to either. That is the Gadi for *tyagis*. It is the Gadi of the Karan Satsang. A *gruhasth* cannot preside on that Gadi. At present, I will not reveal its existence, but I will entrust that Gadi to you. Protect this Gadi of the Karan Satsang. I will arrange for the livelihood of My two adopted sons as I think appropriate and thereby fulfil the boon that I gave to Suvasinibai that when I preside as the supreme sovereign, I will not forget her."

Swami said, "Oh Maharaj! As You will."

The Lord continued, "Swami! At the moment, there is much disorder in the *upasana*. However, just wait and see what transpires when the souls understand My supreme *upasana*. The fourth in your heritage will disclose the essence of the Karan Satsang. It is then that all people will understand My true will. The souls will understand My supreme *upasana* and attain our abode.

Swami said, "Oh Maharaj! You are difficult to understand. Who can know Your secret wishes?"

Saying this, Sadguru Shree Gopalanand Swami placed his head at Lord Shree Swaminarayan's lotus feet and then they lovingly embraced.

Karan Satsang
True association with Lord Shree Swaminarayan. See Chapter 1

Suvasinibhabhi
Shree Ghanshyam Maharaj's sister-in-law; the wife of Rampratapbhai

Ghanshyam Leelamrut
The Lord's divine episodes written by Bhoomanand Swami

Satsangi Bhushan
Scripture written by Vasudevanand Varni describing The Lord's divine episodes

Purna Purushottam
Almighty supreme Lord of Lords

Sadguru
Status of eminent ascetics (sants)

Akshar-ordi
Name of Lord Swaminarayan's residential chambers in Gadhada

Darshan
The visualisation of the Lord

Tyagi
someone who has renounced worldly objects – an ascetic (sant)

Gruhasth
Those with family associations

Upasana
Correct understanding of the Lord. See Appendix

Chapter 21

The Lord's Successor

The Lord commanded, "Listen attentively Gopalanand! You are the controller of both lands (deshs). Look after the devotees of both lands well." The entire congregation listened and took a vow to obey his (Gopalanand Swami's) command.

Acharya Shree Viharilalji Maharaj, Harileelamrut Kavya Kalash 10 Vishram 3

Lord Shree Swaminarayan places the hands of both Shree Ayodhyaprasadji Maharaj and Shree Raghuvirji Maharaj into the hands of Shree Gopalanand Swami. In this manner, the Lord Himself entrusted the sovereignty of the entire Satsang to Shree Gopalanand Swami

131

A huge congregation of *sants*, devotees, Acharyas and *parshads* had assembled in the presence of Lord Shree Swaminarayan. Addressing them all, He said, "Oh My beloved devotees! I command you all to obey Sadguru Shree Gopalanand Swami. If you remain obedient to him, you will attain My Akshardham."

સાધુ વર્ણી પાળા સુણી લેજો રે
ગોપાળ મુનિની આજ્ઞામાં રહેજો રે ....

Sadhu varni paalaa sunee lejo re
Gopal Muni-ni aagnaa-maa rahejo re

Sants, varnis and *palas*; all listen,
Stay under Gopal Muni's authority.

Sadguru Shree Nishkulanand Swami
Bhaktachintamani Prakaran 160 Verse 49

अस्याऽऽज्ञायां वर्तितव्यं भवद्भिर्मामकैर्जनैः ।
वर्तिष्यतेऽन्यथा योऽसौ न मदीय इति ध्रुवम् ।।

Asyaagnaayaam vartitavyam bhavadbhir-maamakair-janaihi
Vartishyate-anyathaa yosau na madeeya iti dhruvam

All My disciples must follow the commands of this Gopal Muni.
Anyone who does not implicitly obey him is not My devotee.
Of this, you must be sure.

Shree Shatanand Muni
Satsangi Jeevan Prakaran 5 Adhyay 55

At that time, Lord Shree Swaminarayan was at the centre of the assembly, presiding on a magnificent Gadi. The two Acharyas were seated on either side of Him, on their own separate seats. Lord Shree Swaminarayan called Sadguru Shree Gopalanand Swami to Him and seated him with Him, on His own Gadi. He placed His hand on Sadguru Shree Gopalanand Swami's shoulder and then addressed the entire assembly, "This Swami, is now in My place. He

Acharya
Preceptor

Harileelamrut Kavya
A biography of Lord Swaminarayan written by Shree Viharilalji Maharaj in poetic form

Shree Ayodhyaprasadji Maharaj / Shree Raghuvirji Maharaj
See Chapter 19

Satsang
Fellowship associated with the Swaminarayan religion

Sants
Ascetics, the closest Western equivalent being monks

Parshad / Palas / Bhagat
The first stage of initiation into ascetic life. These ascetics wear white clothing

Sadguru
Status of eminent ascetics (sants)

Akshardham
The divine abode of Lord Shree Swaminarayan

Varni
Brahmchari, Brahmin who is initiated as a renouncer (tyagi) in the Swaminarayan fellowship

Muni
Sage, ascetic (sant)

shall act on My behalf. He and I are one. Be sure about this fact, he and I are one and the same. From today, My salvation-granting Gadi of the Karan Satsang is being entrusted to him. The Gadi that I enthrone is the Gadi for ascetics. *Gruhasths* can never enthrone this Gadi."

Saying this, Lord Shree Swaminarayan removed some sandalwood paste from His own forehead and impressed it on Sadguru Shree Gopalanand Swami's forehead. He presented Sadguru Shree Gopalanand Swami with a divine garland of flowers taken from His own neck.

Lord Shree Swaminarayan then took the hands of both Acharyas, placed them in the hands of Sadguru Shree Gopalanand Swami and said, "This Swami is the paramount leader of you both and everyone else. You all must respect his every wish and act according to his command."

It is said;

જેને શ્રી ભક્તિપુત્રે નિજજન બહુના ઉપરી આપ કીધા
બંને આચાર્ય કેરા ઉપરી કરી વળી હાથમાં હાથ દીધા

Jene Shree Bhakti-putre, nijajan bahunaa, uparee aap kidhaa
banne Acharya keraa, uparee karee vadee, haath-maa haath deedhaa

He who is the son of Bhakti (i.e. Lord Shree Swaminarayan)
To all His disciples said, he (Sadguru Shree Gopalanand Swami) is above all
He proclaimed him to be above both Acharyas
And placed their hands in his.

Shree Viharilalji Maharaj
Harileelamrut Kavya Kalash 1 Vishram 1

Lord Shree Swaminarayan then turned to Sadguru Shree Gopalanand Swami and said, "Swami! I have entrusted the salvation-granting Gadi of the Karan Satsang to you. You are the leader and are superior to all. Nourish the *Sampraday* by touring the regions and bestowing your bliss to all. Ensure that everyone abides by the religious decree, and preach about the spiritual knowledge and asceticism to all. Take care of the whole *Satsang*."

Bhaktachintamani
Biographical scripture of Lord Shree Swaminarayan written by Shree Nishkulanand Swami. It consists of 8527 verses organised in 164 chapters and portrays the life and episodes of Lord Shree Swaminarayan in chronological order.

Satsangi Jeevan
Biographical scripture of Lord Shree Swaminarayan written in Sanskrut by Shree Shatanand Swami. It is divided into 5 parts and contains a total of 13,000 verses, with an emphasis on one's religious duties

Gruhasth
Those with family associations

Karan Satsang
True association with Lord Shree Swaminarayan. See Chapter 1

Sampraday
Holy fellowship

Chapter 22

Ordination to Withdraw His Human Darshan

After entrusting His Gadi, i.e. the throne of the Karan Satsang and the throne of ascetics, to Sadguru Shree Gopalanand Swami, Purna Purushottam Lord Shree Swaminarayan decided to withdraw His human *darshan*.

He called Shreeji-sankalp-murti Sadguru Shree Gopalanand Swami, Sadguru Shree Muktanand Swami, Sadguru Shree Nityanand Swami, Sadguru Shree Shukanand Swami and other Sadgurus to Him in the Akshar-ordi. He first welcomed them all and asked about their welfare. He then said, "Dear *sants*! The *Ekantik-dharma* has been established. All other doors have been closed and the gateway to Akshardham has been opened."

It is said:

પૃથ્વીમાં અવતાર ધર્યો છે, જીવોને કરવા ભવ પાર
અક્ષરધામનું દ્વાર ઉઘાડી, બંધ કીધાં બીજાં સૌ દ્વાર
એ..... દિન દિન પ્રત્યે સત્સંગ કેરી વૃદ્ધિને કરનારા રે ....

Pruthvee-maa avtaar dhaaryo chhe, jeevo-ne karvaa bhav paar
Akshardham-nu dwaar ughadee, bandh keedhaa beejaa sau dvaar
e....din din pratye satsang keree vrudhi-ne karnaaraa re

By incarnating on the Earth for the salvation of souls
All other doors have been closed and the gateway to Akshardham has been opened

> Until Lord Swaminarayan's manifestation on the earth, virtuous souls were sent to the abodes of other incarnations and deities, but none were able to attain Akshardham. When Lord Swaminarayan manifested, He stopped all souls from entering all these other abodes. The only divine abode that can now be attained is that of Lord Swaminarayan, the supreme Akshardham.
>
> *Jeevanpran Swamibapa ni Vato Part 1, Varta 62*

Shreejimaharaj continued, "Gopal Muni! Ensure that everyone abides by the religious decree. Propagate My supreme *upasana* to all. Now, I am going to withdraw My......." The Lord stopped. His divine eyes met those of Sadguru Shree Gopalanand Swami. Tears were rolling down from Sadguru Shree Gopalanand Swami's eyes, preventing Him from speaking further.

Sadguru Shree Gopalanand Swami tearfully said, "Oh Maharaj! Your actions are indeed incomprehensible. Every deed You perform is purifying and emancipating. My dear Lord! In Akshardham, when we were deliberating about coming onto the earth, You decided to shower Your *darshan* on the earth for 125 years. However, it has not even been 50 years since You placed Your divine feet on the earth. What is the reason for Your early departure?"

Purna Purushottam Lord Shree Swaminarayan replied, "Swami! What you say is true. We did indeed decide that. However, My glory is too great for the souls to easily comprehend. And therefore, when you describe My true glory, they create many difficulties for you. In the future, I will fulfil My intention to give *darshan* in a human form for 125 years."

Sadguru Shree Gopalanand Swami said, "Oh Maharaj! Souls are trapped by the ignorance of the illusory world. Oh 'Ocean of Mercy'! Have compassion on them all. Let them have Your *darshan*. Let them have the opportunity to take the dust of Your lotus feet and place it on their heads. If they feel the wind that has touched You, by Your grace they will ultimately become worthy and attain the abode. However, if Your *darshan*........." uttering this, Sadguru Shree Gopalanand Swami became emotional and tears started to flow from his eyes.

Lord Shree Swaminarayan placed His divine hands on Sadguru Shree Gopalanand Swami's head and lovingly wiped away his tears with His own scarf. He then said, "Swami! We both are the almighty. For now, I will

Darshan
The visualisation of the Lord

Karan Satsang
True association with Lord Swaminarayan. See Chapter 1

Purna Purushottam
Almighty, Supreme Lord of Lords

Shreeji-sankalp-murti
The physical embodiment of the thoughts of Lord Swaminarayan, i.e. those who give darshan upon this earth by the will of the Lord; they are synonymous with the Lord Himself

Akshar-ordi
The name of Lord Swaminarayan's residential chambers in Gadhada, Gujarat – India

Sants
Ascetics, the closest Western equivalent being monks

Ekantik-dharma
Unsurpassed religion

Akshardham
The divine abode of Lord Shree Swaminarayan

Jeevanpran Swamibapa ni Vato
Discourses of Shree Muktajeevan Swamibapa

Muni
Sage, ascetic (sant)

Upasana
Correct understanding of the Lord. See Appendix

withdraw My human *darshan*, but when the time comes, I will manifest again and you will accompany Me. Then, the supreme *upasana* and the status of *Anadi-mukta* that we wish to promote will be easily disseminated to all."

Sadguru Shree Gopalanand Swami was well aware of Lord Shree Swaminarayan's innermost intentions. However, in order that all the others could understand them, he pleaded, "Oh Maharaj! As time passes, different interpretations of the *upasana* will arise and therefore, there will be numerable forms of the *upasana* in one *Sampraday*. This will confuse the souls and it will become difficult for them to ascertain the truth. Therefore, it will be better if You continue to give Your *darshan*."

> Sadguru Shree Gopalanand Swami predicted that as soon as the Lord's human *darshan* disappeared, several factions of the Swaminarayan *Sampraday* would arise because of their differing interpretations about the status of Lord Shree Swaminarayan.

Lord Shree Swaminarayan replied, "Swami! Incarnations from the different abodes and their *Muktas* have come here. Eventually, they will understand My supreme *upasana*. When we give *darshan* here again, they will have become mature and will readily accept our principles. They will then understand our supreme *upasana* and become aware of the status of *Anadi-mukta*. This understanding will be spread all over the world. By My will, through the fourth in your lineage, a unique divine entity will be revealed, which will bring an end to all the confusion. Everyone will be able to enjoy the magnificent bliss of My ever-present (*pragat*) *Murti*."

> The unique, divine entity that the Lord referred to is Shree Swaminarayan Gadi.
>
> In this manner, Lord Shree Swaminarayan Himself announced that Shree Swaminarayan Gadi will attain a physical embodiment in the future.

Anadi-Mukta
Highest state of the liberated soul.
See Chapter 1

Sadguru
Status of eminent ascetics (sants)

Sampraday
Holy fellowship

Muktas
Liberated souls

The assembled Sadgurus were immensely delighted to hear Lord Shree Swaminarayan and Sadguru Shree Gopalanand Swami giving this forecast. They became extremely pleased to know that in the future, the Swaminarayan *Sampraday* will flourish in a remarkable manner. The time will come when the stream of sweet nectar will start to flow and then all mortals who seek salvation, will be able to partake in drinking this divine nectar, and thereby attain Akshardham. At the same time, they were sad because the almighty sovereign, Lord Shree Swaminarayan had decided to withdraw His human *darshan*.

Sensing their sorrow, Lord Shree Swaminarayan pleased them all with His delightful words and affectionately embraced them all.

Shreejimaharaj's personal attendants, Bhaguji Parshad and Mulji Brahmchari lovingly serve the Lord

Chapter 23

Disappearance of the Lord's Human Darshan

The Lord is never born, although He may show that He is going through the process of human birth. He never ages and never dies. Such a powerful Lord manifested at the home of Murti (Bhakti) and Dharmadev. He shows His body and actions to be just like those of all others. Those who understand His deeds to be divine, and understand that He never ages and is immortal, are released from the cycle of birth and death.

Lord Shree Swaminarayan, Vachanamrut Ahmedabad 4

Purna Purushottam Lord Shree Swaminarayan manifested on the Earth out of sheer mercy, to relieve the souls from the miseries of worldly illusions and fulfil the desires of His beloved disciples. He established the *Ekantik-dharma* and commenced the unprecedented practice of bestowing eternal salvation (*aatyantik-moksh*). He gave *darshan* in a human form for forty-nine years, two months and one day, and in Samvat 1886 Jeth Sud 10 (Tuesday 1st June 1830), He decided to renounce His human form.

He arose early that morning and bathed with warm water. He then dressed Himself in white clothing and proceeded with His normal daily routine. He had the floor purified by smearing it with holy cow dung and then matting of the sacred grass (*Darbha*) was placed over it. The Lord then presided on the purified floor in the *padmasan*. He said, "Jay Swaminarayan" to all the *sants* and disciples present and then closed His lotus eyes.

A few moments later, a divine lustre emanated from Lord Shree Swaminarayan's *Murti* and spread everywhere. The rays of lustre pervaded the entire sky. By the will of the Lord, divine lustrous *Muktas* appeared, surrounding Him with divine offerings of adoration. The sky was filled with divine aircrafts. All these *Muktas* performed adoration to the almighty Lord. They adorned His forehead with sandalwood paste (*chandan*), garlanded Him with flowers and performed *aarti*.

Whilst performing the *aarti*, the sound of drum rolls was heard and a shower of fragrant sandalwood fell from the sky, onto the Lord. Speckles of sandalwood were visible everywhere and the atmosphere became intensely fragrant. After performing their adoration to the Lord, the *Muktas* started praying in praise to Him.

Within a moment, an extremely intense lustre radiated from the Lord's *Murti*. The lustre was so powerful, that the combined light of millions of suns would be insignificant in comparison. The *Muktas* merged into the *Murti* and the almighty Lord withdrew His human *darshan*. The *sants* and disciples realised that Lord Shree Swaminarayan had ceased to give *darshan* in a human form, through His own will.

Darshan
The visualisation of the Lord. Also the act of looking with reverence and devotion at the image or deity in the shrine, sometimes of seeing a holy person

Vachanamrut
The words of Lord Shree Swaminarayan compiled as a scripture. See Appendix

Purna Purushottam
Almighty, Supreme Lord of Lords

Ekantik-dharma
Unsurpassed religion.

Padmasan
The posture in which the right foot is placed on the left thigh with the sole uppermost and the left foot is placed on the right thigh with the sole upturned. Both hands are placed on the knees with palms upturned

Sants
Ascetics, the closest Western equivalent being monks

Murti
Divine image or idol of the Lord

Muktas
Liberated souls

Aarti
Ritual ceremony. See Appendix

Sadguru
Status of eminent ascetics (sants)

Dada Khachar
An ardent devotee of Lord Shree Swaminarayan who lived in Gadhada. The Lord stayed principally at the home of Dada Khachar. He is regarded as a loyal and loving disciple

The *sants* and disciples bowed down to the Lord, who was still seated in the *padmasan*. Tears of love and grief rolled down from everyone's eyes. A piercing bolt of grief inflicted all the loving disciples. Many disciples fainted and many lost their sanity. Remorse spread everywhere. Every atom in the atmosphere was tearful. Who could make everyone understand? Who would console them?

To comfort everyone, Sadguru Shree Gopalanand spoke, "*Sants* and devotees!" As soon as they heard these words, everyone looked up and gazed in the direction from where the voice had come. This voice seemed so much like that of their dear Lord Shree Swaminarayan. As they looked at Sadguru Shree Gopalanand Swami, they received the *darshan* of Lord Shree Swaminarayan within him. They understood that Sadguru Shree Gopalanand Swami was indeed, in the place of Shreeji.

Consoling them and relieving their grief, Sadguru Shree Gopalanand Swami uttered, "Lord Swaminarayan is supreme. He is never born nor does He die. He is forever present and will always be with us. We must accept His will and observe whatever He wishes us to see."

These words comforted everyone's hearts. However, Dada Khachar was inconsolable due to his intense love for the Lord. He realised that he would no longer have the Lord's *darshan* and felt, "The Lord is my life. Now that He has gone, there is nothing in this world for me to live for." He ran towards to the cremation pyre to die. Two *sants* stopped him and took him to Sadguru Shree Gopalanand Swami.

Dada Khachar burst into tears as he fell at Sadguru Shree Gopalanand Swami's lotus feet and cried, "Swami! My God has gone. Lord Swaminarayan has passed away. How can I survive without Him?"

The merciful Sadguru Shree Gopalanand Swami said, "Dada! The Lord has not gone. He is always present here. If you want proof of this, go to the place where He used to sit."

Dada Khachar was surprised to hear these words. However, he knew that Sadguru Shree Gopalanand Swami was in the place of Shreeji and had faith in

Muni
Sage, ascetic (sant)

Shree Harileelamrut Kavya
A biography of Lord Swaminarayan written by Acharya Shree Viharilalji Maharaj (3rd successor of Shree Laxminarayan Gadi)

his words. Immediately, he went to where Lord Shree Swaminarayan used to sit. There, he received the *darshan* of Shree Sahajanand Swami - Lord Shree Swaminarayan. He was gently smiling and was adorned with a three-tasselled golden turban, robed in brocaded garments and was wearing a garland of roses around His neck. As if a new lease of life had entered Dada Khachar, he ran and fell at the lotus feet of Lord Shree Swaminarayan. The Lord lifted him up and said, "For so many years I lived with you. Still, you think of Me as human!

The inconsolable Dada Khachar runs into the Lord's cremation pyre, but two sants stop him and take him to Sadguru Shree Gopalanand Swami

Do you think I have gone? I am always present. Whatever Sadguru Shree Gopalanand Swami says, is what I am saying. To fulfil his words, I have given you this *darshan*." Saying this, Lord Shree Swaminarayan gave him the rose garland that He was wearing and said, "Preserve this." He then withdrew His *darshan*. Dada Khachar immediately went to Sadguru Shree Gopalanand Swami with the garland, prostrated in reverence at his lotus feet, and said, "Swami! You are indeed correct. The Lord has not gone. He is always present and will always give *darshan*." Sadguru Shree Gopal Muni became pleased with him and placed his hand on Dada Khachar's head.

Shree Harileelamrut Kavya, Kalash 10 Vishram 5

Lord Shree Swaminarayan convinces Dada Khachar that He is ever-present and gives darshan through Sadguru Shree Gopalanand Swami. He then presents Dada Khachar with a garland of roses

The rose garland that Lord Shree Swaminarayan gave to Dada Khachar did not wither but remained fresh and fragrant for a very long time.

Meanwhile, a large group of devotees was on its way to Gadhada for Lord Shree Swaminarayan's *darshan*. They had not yet heard that Lord Shree Swaminarayan had withdrawn His human *darshan*. They loudly and joyously chanted the Lord's name and sang devotional songs as they walked. Their hearts were overflowing with the loving desire to reach Gadhada, where they would be granted the *darshan* of the Lord, listen to His discourses, offer adoration to Him and enjoy His immense bliss.

Succumbing to the devotion and unflinching love of His devotees, the merciful Lord Shree Swaminarayan appeared before them. He assumed numerous forms along different routes. He was riding on His mare, Manki, and was accompanied by many others who were also on horseback. The disciples became extremely pleased to see Him on His mare, and sang and praised His glory. They adorned Him with garlands, performed *aarti* to Him and ecstatically shouted hails of acclamation. Lord Shree Swaminarayan said to them, "Go to Gadhada. I am visiting a nearby village and will then come there." He then disappeared.

Karan Satsang
True association with
Lord Swaminarayan.
See Chapter 1

On the way to Gadhada, some devotees heard the news that Lord Shree Swaminarayan had withdrawn His human *darshan*. They broke down in tears. Some lost their senses and many became insane with grief.

Jetha Bhakta was on his way to Gadhada for the *darshan* of Lord Shree Swaminarayan. During the journey, he heard that the Lord had withdrawn His human *darshan*, and immediately became delusional.

When the group reached Gadhada, Jetha Bhakta was brought to Sadguru Shree Gopalanand Swami who asked, "Jetha! Why have you become delusional?" Jetha Bhakta recognised those words. They sounded just like the words of Lord Shree Swaminarayan. He realised that the Lord was truly there and immediately came to his senses. He fell at Sadguru Shree Gopalanand Swami's lotus feet and cried, "Oh Swami! You have showered immense mercy on me. Lord Swaminarayan gives *darshan* through you."

In this manner, Sadguru Shree Gopalanand Swami comforted and consoled everyone in their grief and removed their sorrow. Everyone experienced that Sadguru Shree Gopalanand Swami was indeed in the place of Lord Shree Swaminarayan.

Thus, the grief and distress of all the devotees was removed through the Gadi of the Karan Satsang - the Gadi of ascetics. Everyone experienced that the words of Sadguru Shree Gopalanand Swami were indeed those of the Lord Himself.

143

Chapter 24

Shree Gopalanand Swami - The Heir of Shreeji

Above all the abodes is a place where all of God's (Lord Shree Swaminarayan's) servants reside. Above all these servants presides this satsangi (Sadguru Shree Gopalanand Swami). I vow in the name of God and His devotees that this is the absolute truth.

Lord Swaminarayan, Vachanamrut Gadhada Last Section 21

Lord Shree Swaminarayan had said, "Sadguru Shree Gopalanand Swami is the supreme head of the entire *Sampraday* and superior to all. I Myself will work through him and will remain present and perceptible in the *Satsang* forever." It was apparent to all, that these blessed words of Lord Shree Swaminarayan were the absolute truth.

Bhaga Doshi lived in Botad. A Jain ascetic constantly harassed Bhaga Doshi. He used to say, "God cannot exist in Kali-yug. You have been deceived into believing such hypocrisy." Once, Sadguru Shree Gopalanand Swami came to Botad. Bhaga Doshi went to welcome him from the outskirts of the village and explained his predicament. Sadguru Shree Gopalanand Swami consoled him. Just as Sadguru Shree Gopalanand Swami entered the village boundary, he met that Jain ascetic Nemivijayji.

The ascetic asked Sadguru Shree Gopalanand Swami, "Who are you?" Swami replied, "I am the God; the controller of the entire universe." Again, Nemivijayji asked, "Then who is Shree Swaminarayan?" Swamishree replied, "He is my God." With his merciful gaze, Swami looked towards Nemivijayji. He immediately fell into a trance (*samadhi*) and dropped to the floor.

In the trance, he saw Lord Shree Swaminarayan and Sadguru Shree Gopalanand Swami presiding on a divine Gadi surrounded by an aura of great lustre. He also had the *darshan* of the twenty-four Jain prophets (*tirthankars*), who were standing before the Lord, humbly worshipping and praying to Him. From there, Nemivijayji was taken to Yampuri where he experienced overwhelming pain and suffering. As a result of the pain, his body started to be thrown around on the floor. His disciple *munis* began to pray to Sadguru Shree Gopalanand Swami, "It is our mistake, forgive us."

Sadguru Shree Gopalanand Swami awakened Nemivijayji from the trance. He immediately bowed in obeisance and said, "Oh Swami! What you say is indeed the truth. You are God, and your God is Lord Shree Swaminarayan. I had witnessed this in the trance. Forgive me for my errors." Merciful Swamishree showed compassion towards him and forgave him.

Shree Swaminarayan Bhagvat, Skanda 3 Adhyay 3

Satsangi
Devotee, member of the satsang

Sadguru
Status of eminent ascetics (sants)

Vachanamrut
The words of Lord Shree Swaminarayan compiled as a scripture. See Appendix

Sampraday
Holy Fellowship

Satsang
Fellowship, associated with the Swaminarayan religion

Jain
A religious sect

Kali-yug
Era of immorality and sin. See Appendix

Darshan
The visualisation of the Lord. Also the act of looking with reverence and devotion at the image or deity in the shrine. sometimes of seeing a holy person

Yampuri
The closest Western equivalent being Hell

Munis
Sages, ascetics (sants)

Shree Swaminarayan Bhagvat
Scripture written by Narayanji Jaduram Pandya

The ability to entrance souls just as Lord Shree Swaminarayan did, and in that trance to give them the *darshan* of Lord Shree Swaminarayan sitting on a divine throne, can only exist in him who gives *darshan* on behalf of Lord Shree Swaminarayan. Only they can accomplish such great feats.

According to the command of Purna Purushottam Lord Shree Swaminarayan, everyone, ascetics and *gruhasths* alike, remained obedient to Sadguru Shree Gopalanand Swami's wishes.

Shree Gopalanand Swami – Sovereign of the Entire Sampraday

After Purna Purushottam Lord Shree Swaminarayan withdrew His human *darshan*, the first two temples to have completed construction were those in the town Muli, and another in the village of Dholera. The *Murti* installation ceremony was to be performed in both temples. Shree Raghuvirji Maharaj went to Gadhada and requested Sadguru Shree Gopalanand Swami to install the *Murtis* in the temple at Dholera.

By the command of Lord Shree Swaminarayan, Shree Brahmanand Swami was overseeing the construction of the temple at Muli. Sadguru Shree Brahmanand Swami and Shree Ayodhyaprasadji Maharaj met to decide about the arrangements for the *Murti* installation ceremony. Shree Ayodhyaprasadji Maharaj asked, "Brahm Muni! How shall we perform the *Murti* installation ceremony?"

Sadguru Shree Brahmanand Swami replied, "The *Murti* installation ceremony must be performed by Sadguru Shree Gopalanand Swami, because he is in the place of Shreeji. Only if he installs the *Murti*, it can be certain that the *Murtis* have been installed by Lord Shree Swaminarayan Himself."

Hearing Brahm Muni's words, Shree Ayodhyaprasadji Maharaj asked, "Whom shall we send to invite Sadguru Shree Gopalanand Swami?"

Sadguru Shree Brahmanand Swami replied, "I myself will go to Gadhada to invite Sadguru Shree Gopalanand Swami here."

Then Sadguru Shree Brahmanand Swami went to Gadhada to invite Sadguru Shree Gopalanand Swami. Immediately, he went for *darshan*. Sadguru Shree Gopalanand Swami greeted Sadguru Shree Brahmanand Swami and said, "Welcome Shree Brahm Muni! At your old age, why have you travelled such a long distance and come here?"

Shree Brahm Muni replied, "Swami! You are in the place of Shreejimaharaj. Your *darshan* is equivalent to the *darshan* of Shreejimaharaj. I have come to take you with me."

Sadguru Shree Gopalanand Swami asked, "Brahm Muni! Where do you intend to take me? You can see that I am not physically well."

Shree Brahm Muni replied, "Swami, you are an independent (*swatantra*) personage. If you wish, you can dismiss such an illness. But, Swami! The temple at Muli is ready and the *Murti* installation ceremony is to be performed. The auspicious day has been decided; so come and perform the *Murti* installation ceremony."

Sadguru Shree Gopalanand Swami said, "Brahm Muni! I have to perform the *Murti* installation ceremony in the temple at Dholera on the day after the day you speak of. I have already agreed with Shree Raghuvirji Maharaj to go to Dholera and perform the installation ceremony in the temple there."

Brahm Muni replied, "Swami! You can still keep your word. First come to Muli and perform the *Murti* installation ceremony. I will make all the necessary arrangements for you to reach Dholera the day after. However, if it is not your wish to come there now, we will postpone the date of the installation ceremony, but it must be performed only by you. Only then would we have obeyed the commands of Shreejimaharaj, because today, Lord Shree Swaminarayan acts through you. We will abide by whatever you say."

Hearing Sadguru Shree Brahmanand Swami's humble requests, Sadguru Shree Gopalanand Swami accompanied him to Muli. Shree Ayodhyaprasadji Maharaj greeted Sadguru Shree Gopalanand Swami by garlanding him. As soon as he saw the temple at Muli, Sadguru Shree Gopalanand Swami exclaimed, "Brahm Muni! You have built a temple that touches the sky!" These

147

Brahm Sanhita
Scripture written by
Mavdanji Gadhvi

words reminded Sadguru Shree Brahmanand Swami of the words that were spoken by Lord Shree Swaminarayan. When Sadguru Shree Brahmanand Swami commenced the construction work for the temple of Muli, Lord Shree Swaminarayan came to lay the foundation stone. Seeing the vast area acquired for the temple, the Lord said, "Brahm Muni! Are you going to build a temple that touches the sky?"

These words, and the words of Sadguru Shree Gopalanand Swami sounded so alike that Sadguru Shree Brahmanand Swami began to stare at Sadguru Shree Gopalanand Swami's lotus face in amazement. He saw the gently smiling divine face of Lord Shree Swaminarayan in the face of Sadguru Shree Gopalanand Swami. Sadguru Shree Brahmanand Swami immediately fell at Sadguru Shree Gopalanand Swami's lotus feet in reverence.

Sadguru Shree Gopalanand Swami exclaimed, "Brahm Muni! What are you doing?" and lifted him off the floor. He lovingly embraced Sadguru Shree Brahmanand Swami and garlanded him.

Then they both walked around the temple. All around they could see the droves of ardent followers who had come to celebrate the ceremony. As soon as they saw Sadguru Shree Gopalanand Swami, they cheered loudly with great delight. Sadguru Shree Gopalanand Swami blessed them all with his benevolent, salvation-granting divine gaze.

Sadguru Shree Gopalanand Swami asked, "Brahm Muni! The Lord will arrive here tomorrow, so hundreds of thousands of followers have gathered here. Have you made sufficient arrangements for their meal?" Sadguru Shree Brahmanand Swami replied, "Now that you are here, why should I worry?"

Shree Brahm Muni took Sadguru Shree Gopalanand Swami to the kitchen and showed him the heaps of confectionery. Sadguru Shree Gopalanand Swami said, "There is plenty of food here. It will be sufficient, regardless of the number of people that will come and eat." Everything proceeded according to his words.

Brahm Sanhita, Prakaran 5 Adhyay 8

The following day, with great pomp and ceremony, the *Murti* installation was performed by the sacred hands of Sadguru Shree Gopalanand Swami. After performing *aarti*, he took *prasad* from the *thal*. And then according to the arrangements made by Sadguru Shree Brahmanand Swami, Sadguru Shree Gopalanand Swami departed for Dholera, seated on a carriage drawn by two bullocks.

Aksharanand Swami ni Vato, Chapters 716, 717
Sadguru Shree Brahmanand Swami Jeevan-darshan, Laher 57

The next day, in Dholera, with the same great pomp and ceremony, Sadguru Shree Gopalanand Swami performed the *Murti* installation.

At both temples, everyone experienced that it was Lord Shree Swaminarayan Himself who was performing the *Murti* installation ceremonies.

Shree Harileelamrut Kavya, Kalash 10 Vishram 14 - 15

One should worship and perform the adoration of the *Murtis* that have been installed by, or given for worshipping by, the Acharya of the Karan Satsang - through whom Lord Shree Swaminarayan Himself acts.

According to the command of Lord Shree Swaminarayan, eminent *sants* and *gruhasth* disciples associated with Sadguru Shree Gopalanand Swami. Sadguru Shree Gunatitanand Swami used to say, "Oh Swami! Through you, one can experience the ecstasy of Shreejimaharaj."

Hari-charitra Chintamani, Part 3 Varta 68

Aarti
Ritual Ceremony. See Appendix

Prasad
Consecrated offerings, blessed by the Lord

Thal
Food platter

Aksharanand Swami ni Vato
The discourses of Shree Aksharanand Swami

Shree Brahmanand Swami Jeevan-darshan
A biography of Sadguru Shree Brahmanand Swami

Shree Harileelamrut Kavya
A biography of Lord Swaminarayan written by Acharya Shree Viharilalji Maharaj (3rd successor of Shree Laxminarayan Gadi)

Acharya
Preceptor

Sadguru Shree Gunatitanand Swami
An eminent Nand-padvi ascetic (sant)

Hari-charitra Chintamani
Scripture written by Sadguru Raghunathcharandasji Swami

Sadguru Shree Gopalanand Swami explains the supremacy of the Lord to Sadguru Shree Gunatitanand Swami

**Shree Shukanand Swami /
Shree Chaitanyanand Swami /
Shree Sarvanivasanand Swami**
Eminent Nand–padvi
ascetics (sants)

Brahm-nishth Santo
Holy scripture written by Shree
Dharmavalabhdasji Swami

Sadguru Shree Gopalanand Swami
explains the true meanings of the
scriptures to Shree Shukanand
Swami, who was famed as the
Lord's scribe

Sadguru Shree Gunatitanand Swami, Sadguru Shree Shukanand Swami and many others often expressed in assemblies; "We remained very close to Shreejimaharaj and we heard, wrote and compiled the Vachanamruts (nectar in the form of divine discourses of by Lord Shree Swaminarayan). Still, we could not fully understand them at that time. That understanding has now been fully gained through our close association with Sadguru Shree Gopalanand Swami. Now, we are able to experience the Vachanamrut's fresh, rejuvenated ecstasy, immense peace and happiness therein.

Hari-charitra Chintamani, Part 3 Vartas 60, 61, 68

Shamaliya Chaitanyanand Swami often used to say, "If I had not been able to attain the close association of Sadguru Shree Gopalanand Swami, I would have died without ever having understood the true philosophy of the *Satsang*."

Aksharanand Swami ni Vato, Chapter 738
Hari-charitra Chintamani, Part 3 Varta 63
Brahm-nisth Santo, Prakaran 8

Shree Sarvanivasanand Swami renounced his leadership (*mahantai*) of the Ahmedabad Temple so that he could reside with and have the association of Sadguru Shree Gopalanand Swami for the rest of his life.

Aksharanand Swami ni Vato, Chapter 739

In his unique, divine style, Sadguru Shree Gopalanand Swami explicitly and unreservedly explained about having a firm determination and understanding regarding the true *upasana* of Lord Shree Swaminarayan, the strength of the faith unto Lord's *Murti*, chaste devotion (*pativrata-bhakti*) unto Him, and a true understanding regarding the status of *Anadi-mukta*. This true understanding can only be gained from his spiritual lineage of the Karan Satsang. Therefore, whosoever becomes a disciple of the Gadi of the Karan Satsang and remains associated with its Acharya, will gain a true understanding of this great philosophy, and with such an understanding, will attain the same status as the eminent Nand-padvi *sants*, i.e. they will achieve eternal salvation (*aatyantik-moksh*).

Sadguru Shree Gopalanand Swami was residing in Vadtal and was sometimes showing signs of illness. By his orders, his beloved disciple, Sadguru Shree Nirgundasji Swami was residing in Ahmedabad, preaching the supreme *upasana*. Hearing the news of Sadguru Shree Gopalanand Swami's illness, he came to Vadtal and remained in Swami's service.

A large assembly of senior *sants* and ardent devotees was seated in the presence of Sadguru Shree Gopalanand Swami. Sadguru Shree Nirgundasji Swami was seated beside him.

Upasana
Correct understanding of the Lord. See Appendix

Anadi-mukta
Highest state of a liberated soul. See Chapter 1

Karan Satsang
True association with Lord Swaminarayan. See Chapter 1

Sants
Ascetics, the closest Western equivalent being monks

Sadguru Shree Gopalanand Swami entrusts the helm of the Satsang to Sadguru Shree Nirgundasji Swami

Mukta
Liberated soul

Sadguru Shree Gopalanand Swami took hold of Sadguru Shree Nirgundasji Swami's hand and announced, "Swami! Lord Shree Swaminarayan assigned the leadership of this Karan Satsang to me. From today, I hand over this responsibility to you. From now, you must continue to propagate and preach the supreme *upasana* and glory of Lord Shree Swaminarayan. You must look after the *Satsang*. You are as able as I. You are an independent divine *Mukta*, who constantly resides in the *Murti* of Lord Shree Swaminarayan. From today, you are in my place. The key to eternal salvation, which Lord Shree Swaminarayan had given to me, I am now giving to you." After saying these words, Sadguru Shree Gopalanand Swami took off the garland of flowers from his own neck and garlanded Sadguru Shree Nirgundasji Swami. Showing that he was immensely pleased with him, he affectionately placed his hands on Sadguru Shree Nirgundasji Swami's head.

Brahm-nisth Santo Prakaran 15

Sadguru Shree Nirgundasji Swami humbly prayed, "Oh dear Guru! You are in the place of Lord Shree Swaminarayan and ultimately the supreme head of the *Satsang*. You are my almighty Guru and I am your humble servant. You give *darshan* by the will of Shreejimaharaj. You are ever-present and omnipresent. Therefore, I will obey your command. I pray to Lord Shree Swaminarayan and to you, that you remain with me in everything that I do and be pleased with me forever."

Sadguru Shree Gopalanand Swami became extremely pleased on hearing these humble words of Sadguru Shree Nirgundasji Swami. Then, addressing the entire assembly, he said, "Dear *sants* and devotees! From today, this Sadguru Shree Nirgundasji Swami is in my place. Obey his commands and accept that what he says is the ultimate truth with utmost faith. By obeying this, the paramount bliss of Lord Shree Swaminarayan and me is attained. Lord Shree Swaminarayan entrusted the key to eternal salvation to me. From today, I am handing over this key to Sadguru Shree Nirgundasji Swami. Whoever resorts to his shelter and remains obedient to him, will attain eternal salvation."

All the *sants* and devotees respectfully accepted Sadguru Shree Gopalanand Swami's command. Shortly after, in Samvat 1908 Vaishakh Vad 5, Sadguru Shree Gopalanand Swami withdrew his human *darshan* by his own will (at an age of 71 years, 3 months and 12 days).

Chapter 25

Sadguru Shree Nirgundasji Swami

The supremacy and nature of the Lord cannot be truly understood by oneself or even by studying the scriptures. Even though these facts are contained within the scriptures, it is only when a Satpurush appears on the earth and explains it, that one can understand them.

Lord Shree Swaminarayan, Vachanamrut Gadhada Middle Section 13

Sadguru Nirgundasji Swami will preserve the Satsang. Shreejimaharaj has sent Him from the abode Akshardham for that very reason. This Nirgun Swami was given the helm of the Satsang in Samvat 1907 Kartik Sud 15, in Vadtal.

From the scripture, Sadguru Swamishree Balmukunddasji Swami

According to the commands of Sadguru Shree Gopalanand Swami, Sadguru Shree Nirgundasji Swami preached the supreme *upasana* and glory of Lord Shree Swaminarayan. Everyone experienced great delight when they heard these discourses.

Bhaguji Parshad, the personal attendant of Lord Shree Swaminarayan, used to say, "When listening to the discourses of Sadguru Shree Nirgundasji Swami, I experience the same divine peace and tranquillity that was sensed when listening to the words of Shreejimaharaj and Sadguru Shree Gopalanand Swami. The respect that the eminent *Nand-padvi sants* commanded is present in Sadguru Shree Nirgundasji Swami. Just as Sadguru Shree Gopalanand Swami was in the place of Shreeji, Sadguru Shree Nirgundasji Swami is in the place of Sadguru Shree Gopalanand Swami."

Sadguru Shree Nirgundasji Swami ni Vato, Supplementary Chapter 50

The Lord Reprimands Ayodhyaprasadji Maharaj

Sadguru Shree Nirgundasji Swami preached about the supremacy of Lord Shree Swaminarayan. However, there were some *sants* and devotees who could not understand these teachings and started creating problems. Some of them held discussions with Shree Ayodhyaprasadji Maharaj and conspired to evict Sadguru Shree Nirgundasji Swami from Ahmedabad Temple.

Purna Purushottam Lord Shree Swaminarayan had placed Shree Ayodhyaprasadji Maharaj's hand, in the hands of Sadguru Shree Gopalanand Swami and had told him, "He is your superior. He is in My place." Such was the greatness of Sadguru Shree Gopalanand Swami, and now in his place was Sadguru Shree Nirgundasji Swami. How can anyone tell him to leave the Ahmedabad Temple?

Purna Purushottam Lord Shree Swaminarayan showered mercy on Shree Ayodhyaprasadji Maharaj and awakened him one night to give him His divine *darshan*. He immediately woke up and started prostrating in reverence to Lord Shree Swaminarayan. The Lord said, "Stop prostrating. Why have you told Sadguru Shree Nirgundasji Swami to leave? I have sent him (from

Glossary (sidebar)

Sadguru
Status of eminent ascetics (sants)

Satpurush
Saintly person

Vachanamrut
The words of Lord Shree Swaminarayan compiled as a scripture. See Appendix

Satsang
Fellowship associated with the Swaminarayan religion

Akshardham
The divine abode of Lord Shree Swaminarayan

Sadguru Swamishree Balmukunddasji Swami
Scripture written by Sadguru Swami Madhavprasaddasji

Upasana
Correct understanding of the Lord. See Appendix

Parshad
The first stage of initiation into ascetic life; ascetics who wear white clothing

Nand-padvi Sants
Ascetics (sants) initiated by the Lord Himself

Sants
Ascetics, the closest Western equivalent being monks

Shree Nirgundasji Swami ni Vato
Discourses of Sadguru Shree Nirgundasji Swami

Shree Ayodhyaprasadji Maharaj
See Chapter 19

Purna Purushottam
Almighty, supreme Lord of Lords

Darshan
The visualisation of the Lord

Muktas
Liberated souls

Murti
Divine image or form of the Lord

Akshardham) for the eternal salvation (*aatyantik moksh*) of innumerable souls and to explicate and propagate My glory and supreme *upasana*. He is an independent (*swatantra*) *Mukta* who resides constantly within My *Murti*, though he gives *darshan* here (on the Earth) by My will. Such is his greatness. Therefore, do not allow him to leave. He is like a precious jewel. If he goes, your honour will also go. I had commanded you to obey the wishes of Sadguru Shree Gopalanand Swami, but you disobeyed him too. You were wrong to do this. This Swami is in the place of Sadguru Shree Gopalanand Swami. If you let him go, who will explain My supreme *upasana*? Therefore, I command you to have utmost faith in his words and do not let anyone insult him. If you will obey My command, I will become pleased. That Swami is an independent *Mukta* who resides in My *Murti*. If he withdraws his *darshan*, My *upasana* will not be spread. Therefore, you must not let him leave." After giving this command, Shreejimaharaj withdrew His *darshan*.

The next day, Shree Ayodhyaprasadji Maharaj went to Sadguru Shree Nirgundasji Swami and humbly begged him to stay. Sadguru Shree Nirgundasji Swami accepted his plea and remained.

However, the *sants* and disciples who did not agree with Swamishree's preachings started to argue with Shree Ayodhyaprasadji Maharaj. So Shree Ayodhyaprasadji Maharaj told them all about the *darshan* that Lord Shree Swaminarayan had given him the night before. He clearly stated to all,

Lord Shree Swaminarayan gives darshan to Ayodhyaprasadji Maharaj and reprimands him for not obeying the wishes of Sadguru Shree Nirgundasji Swami

157

Mansi-Pooja
Mental worship of the Lord

"Sadguru Shree Nirgundasji Swami will indeed remain here. Therefore, if you want to please Lord Shree Swaminarayan and attain eternal salvation, you must abide by Sadguru Shree Nirgundasji Swami's wishes. You must believe, wholeheartedly, that what he preaches is the absolute truth. No-one must ever insult him. He is in place of Sadguru Shree Gopalanand Swami and therefore, he is in place of Lord Shree Swaminarayan."

Just then, the *sants* sat down to dine. They called Shree Ayodhyaprasadji Maharaj to come and serve them. Shree Ayodhyaprasadji Maharaj said, "I will only come to serve you if you all take a solemn oath to accept Sadguru Shree Nirgundasji Swami's words as the truth, do not insult him, and do not allow others to insult him." All the *sants* took this oath. Only then did Shree Ayodhyaprasadji Maharaj serve them. Such was the greatness of this eminent and independent personage - Sadguru Shree Nirgundasji Swami.

Whilst living in Ahmedabad, Sadguru Shree Nirgundasji Swami preached about Lord Shree Swaminarayan's glory and supreme *upasana*. He preached with unsurpassed eloquence. Even though he was a learned scholar, he spoke in a simplistic and delightful manner. His words immediately struck the hearts of the listeners and all continued to further themselves in their path to salvation.

Ever-increasing crowds of devotees came throughout the day and night to associate with him and listen to his discourses. At times, Sadguru Shree Nirgundasji Swami would deliver sermons to them. At other times he would give *darshan* whilst chanting with a rosary, meditating or performing *mansi-pooja*. They even sat whilst he slept; as well as at times when he showed signs of illness.

The Lord Reminds Parmanand Swami of Shree Nirgundasji Swami's Identity

On one occasion, Sadguru Shree Nirgundasji Swami took on an illness in the form of a severe cough. Multitudes of disciples came for Swamishree's *darshan* and remained sitting, even when he was not able to deliver discourses due to his illness. At night, Swamishree would show his human characteristics and, showing the frailty in him, he would allow the cough to develop and annoy him. As a result, he stayed awake all night.

It is said:

પ્રાકૃત દિવ્ય ચરિત્ર મનોહર, મુમુક્ષુને છે સદાય સુખકર
દિવ્ય દિવ્ય કહી ગાવે......તમને અનંત પ્રણામ

Prakrut divya charitra manohar, mumukshu-ne chhe sadaay sukhakar
Divya divya kahee gaave tamane anant pranaam

The human and divine activities of the Lord and His *Muktas*
are all divine and fascinating to those who seek salvation.
All their episodes are forever divine.

Shree Harignanamrut Kavya

Shree Harignanamrut Kavya
A compilation of devotional songs written by Shree Muktajeevan Swamibapa

Sadhuram
Affectionate term for a ascetic (sant)

Shree Parmanand Swami used to sleep alongside where Sadguru Shree Nirgundasji Swami rested. During the day the droves of devotees and during the night, Swamishree's cough meant that Shree Parmanand Swami was unable to sleep or get any rest. Consequently, he perceived human characteristics in Sadguru Shree Nirgundasji Swami. He started whispering to those who where close to him, "How did I get to sleep alongside Sadguru Shree Nirgundasji Swami? I cannot get even sufficient rest!"

Shree Parmanand Swami had a truly compassionate nature and was very pious. He had gained the favour of Lord Shree Swaminarayan. Consequently, that night, Lord Shree Swaminarayan granted him His divine lustrous *darshan* and said, "Sadhuram! If you do not like to have your bed beside him, how will you like residing within My *Murti*?" Shreejimaharaj then revealed from within Himself, the divine lustrous form of Sadguru Shree Nirgundasji Swami, which was identical to His own form. Shree Parmanand Swami started prostrating in reverence to them and began to pray to both for forgiveness. Shreejimaharaj said, "Sadhuram! Not here to Me. Go in the morning to where Swamishree daily presides and ask for his pardon." He then merged Sadguru Shree Nirgundasji Swami back into His *Murti* and withdrew His *darshan*.

In the morning, Sadguru Shree Nirgundasji Swami was presiding in the assembly. *Sants* and disciples prostrated in reverence to him and sat amongst the congregation. Shree Parmanand Swami arrived and began to prostrate in reverence to Sadguru Shree Nirgundasji Swami. One of the other *sants* whispered to Swamishree, "Shree Parmanand Swami is prostrating to you." Swamishree exclaimed, "Parmanand Swami! Stop! You are known as a *Nand-padvi sant* and

Das
Servant to the Lord

Bavas
Impolite term for ascetics (sants)

I am merely of a *das* status. You need not prostrate to me." Shree Parmanand Swami replied, "Swami! You are the *Nand* of all *Nands*. You are an independent *Mukta* who resides in the *Murti* of Lord Shree Swaminarayan. You are in the place of Sadguru Shree Gopalanand Swami and therefore, you are in the place of Lord Shree Swaminarayan. You alone are able to pardon my faults."

After praying in this way, Shree Parmanand Swami told the congregation about how he had come to regard Sadguru Shree Nirgundasji Swami as a mere mortal and about the *darshan* that Lord Shree Swaminarayan had given him during the night. He described the divinely lustrous *darshan* of Sadguru Shree Nirgundasji Swami emerging from the Lord's *Murti*. Seeing nobleness in him, Swamishree became pleased with him and forgave him.

After hearing this story from Shree Parmanand Swami, many eminent *sants* and disciples started to appreciate the glory of Swamishree. Such was the extraordinary prowess of Sadguru Shree Nirgundasji Swami.

The Wicked Dolatsang is Transformed into a Devotee

The prowess possessed by Sadguru Shree Nirgundasji Swami was extraordinary. By the village of Lavad runs the River Mesvo. Once, Sadguru Shree Nirgundasji Swami and his devout *sants* were bathing in the river. They had not quite finished bathing when all of a sudden they heard a loud commotion, "You *bavas*! Why are you bathing in this river and spoiling my village? You have no right to be here!" On the North bank of the river was a fearsome looking man, who stood hurling abuse at them in an extremely aggressive manner.

This man was Dolatsang, the dreadful chief of the village of Lavad and the neighbouring territories of Mevas and Bhil. News had reached him of the arrival of Lord Shree Swaminarayan's *sants* at the river and so he had rushed there with his accomplices. He shouted again, "Are you coming out of the river now or not?" He then turned to his accomplices and said, "These *bavas* will not obey my words. So Vajesang, Tapubha, hurl stones at them and force them away from here."

By Dolatsang's command, a torrent of stones were thrown towards the *sants*. The *sants* began to chant the 'Swaminarayan' name and retreated from the river.

Lord Shree Swaminarayan has commanded His *sants*:

गालिदानं ताडनं च कृतं कुमतिभिर्जनैः ।
क्षन्तव्यमेव सर्वेषां चिन्तनीयं हितं च तैः ॥

Gaalidaanam taadanam cha krutam kumatibhir janaihi
Kshantavyamev sarveshaam chintaniyam hitam cha taihi

"If anyone demonstrates cruelty towards you,
either verbal or physical, you must endure this malice,
but must never retaliate.
You should forgive these cruel people and pray for their welfare.
Not even a bad thought should enter your mind."

Shikshapatri, Slok 201

According to this command of the Shikshapatri from Lord Shree Swaminarayan, Sadguru Shree Nirgundasji Swami willed to grant salvation to Dolatsang.

Some time passed. The occasion came for Takhubha, Dolatsang's one and only son to be married. The village of Lavad was filled with joy and celebration. The melodious sound of *sharnais* echoed throughout the village. The young landlords of the Mevas territory had tied turbans on their heads and dressed in lavish clothing and perfumed themselves. They enjoyed themselves by dancing in the festivities, whilst becoming intoxicated on alcohol, opium and other drugs. The *pithi* ceremony had been performed to Takhubha. The bridegroom's procession proceeded through the entire village. The celebrations continued late into the night. The wedding party was going to depart early next morning for the main marriage ceremony and everyone was exhausted and they soon fell fast asleep.

Just before daybreak, Takhubha woke up from his bed to urinate. He went to the backyard of the house. As he was returning after urinating under a large tamarind tree, he stepped on something that felt smooth and soft and screamed in fright, "Help! I am dead."

Shikshapatri
Scripture containing the holy commandments of Lord Shree Swaminarayan
See Appendix

Sharnais
Traditional Indian instrument played at weddings

Pithi ceremony
Traditional Indian ritual conducted at weddings

The landlords of the Mevas who were asleep were awakened by the horrible screams and rushed to the back of the house where they saw a deadly black cobra bite Takhubha and then quickly retreat into the hollow portion of the tamarind tree. Takhubha's body became pale and rigid, just like glass and fell onto the ground. Instead of the celebratory melodies, the atmosphere was filled with the sad songs of mourning. The distressed Dolatsang began to cry and exclaimed, "Save my son! I will grant you anything you ask for!" Various conjurers and practitioners of black magic tried to save his son, but their efforts were in vain. All their spells failed to save Takhubha's life.

All of a sudden, amidst the darkness of despair, came a ray of hope. From the direction of the riverbank, the sound of chanting, 'Swaminarayan, Swaminarayan' could be heard. Sadguru Shree Nirgundasji Swami had returned to the river with his *sants* after much travelling, during which they propagated religion to society. They were bathing in the river and melodiously chanting the name 'Swaminarayan'.

It is said that an owl remains unaware that the Sun has risen, whereas humans are able to see the lustre of the Sun, and realise that dawn is upon them.

The immense prowess of Sadguru Shree Nirgundasji Swami had not yet dawned on the owl-like, ignorant Dolatsang, but some of the villagers did know about his greatness. They recognised the melodious chanting to be that of Swamishree's *sants*. One such villager said to Dolatsang, "Sir! Can you hear that chanting? The head of that group is extremely powerful. Some time ago, they were bathing in the river and you had ordered others to throw stones at them to frighten them away. You have committed a crime against them. As a consequence, this grief has been inflicted on you. However, he is immensely merciful. Go under his shelter and beg for his forgiveness. If he showers his grace on you, you will be relieved of your distress."

These words gave Dolatsang some hope, just like the relief experienced by a drowning man when he is rescued. Dolatsang enthusiastically rushed to the river. The *sants* were surprised to see Dolatsang hurriedly coming towards them. But all were astonished when Dolatsang bowed down at Sadguru Shree Nirgundasji Swami's lotus feet. With tears flowing from his eyes, he begged for forgiveness and repeatedly slapped his own face. He cried out, "Oh Swami! I have committed a great offence against you. As a result, I have to endure this pain. Forgive me for my faults. Have mercy on me. Save my son. Now, I only have your mercy to rely on."

The multitude of sins began to be washed away by the tears of his remorse. Tears rolled down the face of this great embodiment of sin, like the streams that run down from the mountains of the Himalayas. The tears fell down at Sadguru Shree Nirgundasji Swami's lotus feet.

The evil Dolatsang begs for forgiveness from Sadguru Shree Nirgundasji Swami

शरणागतपापपर्वतं गणयित्वा न तदीयसद्गुणम् ।
अणुमप्यतुलं हि मन्यते सहजानन्दगुरुं भजे सदा ।।

Sharanaagata-paapa-parvatam ganayitva na tadeeya-sadgunam
Anumapyatulam hi manyate Sahajanand gurum bhaje sadaa

I worship always, my guru Sahajanand; who disregards the multitudes
of sins of those who resort to Him, and considers even the smallest of
good deeds to be immensely great.

Sadguru Shree Nirgundasji Swami, through whom Lord Shree Swaminarayan Himself acts, forgave this mountain of sins, Dolatsang, and took him into his divine shelter. Merciful Sadguru Shree Nirgundasji Swami showered his divine

Mantra
Chant or incantation used in rituals, worship or meditation. Words or phrases which posses sacred powers

Lord Krishna
One of the 24 incarnations of the Lord

Bapji
An affectionate term for an ascetic (sant)

grace on Dolatsang and together with his *sants*, visited his home to relieve him of his distress. Takhubha lay pale, weak and unconscious. Swamishree asked his *sants* to sit down and said, "Dear *sants*! Let us all chant the name Shree Swaminarayan to please the Lord Shree Swaminarayan."

They commenced the chanting of the supreme *mantra* 'Swaminarayan'. The melody of the *sants*' sweet voices reverberated everywhere. It was as if the mountains were swaying and oceans were roaring with the rhythm of the chanting.

Sadguru Shree Nirgundasji Swami was meditating and was completely engrossed in the *Murti* of Shreejimaharaj. The chanting of the supreme *mantra* Shree Swaminarayan continued. There was an amazing potency in this supreme *mantra*. The crowd attentively watched on, engrossed and fascinated. The *sants* being engrossed in the *Murti* of Lord Shree Swaminarayan were melodiously chanting the *mantra*. Swamishree was gently smiling. It was then the miracle occurred.

The black cobra hissed and slithered out from the hollow portion of the dense tamarind tree. The people started to scatter in fear. The cobra stared at Swamishree with its hood up. Swamishree was gently swaying with the rhythm of the chanting. The snake too started to sway with that rhythm, just like when, with the melody of the flute (played by Lord Krishna), the whole cosmos started swaying. Sadguru Shree Nirgundasji Swami opened his eyes and gazed upon the snake. As soon as the vision of both of them met, the cobra jumped up and hurtled towards Takhubha's leg. The cobra sucked out all the poison from where it had previously bitten him. Immediately, Takhubha's pale body regained its original colour. Having completed its task, the cobra circumambulated Sadguru Shree Nirgundasji Swami three times, bowed down to him in reverence and disappeared into the hollow portion of the tamarind tree.

Takhubha stretched out and then stood up. The crowd exclaimed with cheer. Dolatsang ran up to his son and embraced him. Due to their overwhelming joy they both wept profusely and fell before Swamishree's lotus feet. Once again, Dolatsang started to pray, "Bapji! I am undeserving. Forgive me for all my faults. Pardon me! Bapji! Pardon me." Swamishree lifted Dolatsang from his feet. Due to his repentance, Dolatsang's sinful heart started to melt like

heated wax. Swamishree said, "Dolatsang! Take an oath that from today you will never harass *sants* or pilgrims and you will never commit evil on a woman." Dolatsang replied, "Swami! You have revived my entire human life. I take the vow from today that I will never harass anyone."

Having blessed Dolatsang, Swamishree and the *sants* proceeded to leave. Dolatsang halted them and cried, "Swami! I cannot let you leave today. You have given my son a new life, and it is his wedding today. If you leave without dining today, my entire life would become unworthy. It would be shameful for me to allow you to leave." Swamishree replied, "Dolatsang! We cannot accept your food." Hearing these words, the imploring Dolatsang asked, "Why Bapji!? Why can you not eat my food? What is the reason for this?" Swamishree replied, "Dolatsang! Do not take offence. You are a life-long consumer of alcohol and opium. Your house is stacked with barrels of wine, pots of opium and sacks of drugs. We cannot eat there."

Hearing Swamishree's words, Dolatsang immediately took a stick and smashed the barrels of wine and pots of opium and tobacco. He ordered the villagers, "Go, bring water from the River Mesvo to wash and clean my home. Bring cow dung and smear it to purify the house. Light auspicious incense sticks to purify the entire atmosphere. I wish my saviour, my guru, to enter my home and lovingly offer food to him. So hurry!"

Again, Dolatsang fell at Sadguru Shree Nirgundasji Swami's lotus feet and requested him to stay. According to Swamishree's command, Dolatsang and the others went to the river for a purifying bathe. When they returned, Swamishree performed *vartman* to Dolatsang, Takhubha and other relatives. He tied *kanthis* around their necks and made them his disciples. Merciful Sadguru Shree Nirgundasji Swami accepted Dolatsang's food and then continued in his tour to preach about the faith.

Sadguru Shree Nirgundasji Swami was in the place of Sadguru Shree Gopalanand Swami and Sadguru Shree Gopalanand Swami was in the place of Lord Shree Swaminarayan. He was the truly powerful, immensely miraculous Shreeji-sankalp-murti.

Vartman
An oath taken when an aspirant joins the faith, to abide by the five sacred vows, see Chapter 3

Kanthi
A double stranded necklace of wooden beads (usually basil) worn by Swaminarayan disciples. See Appendix

Shreeji-sankalp-murti
The physical embodiment of the thoughts of Lord Swaminarayan. i.e. those who give darshan upon this earth by the will of the Lord; they are synonymous with the Lord Himself

Chapter 26

Shreeji-sankalp-murti Abji Bapashree

Just as Lord Shree Swaminarayan announced His own name 'Swaminarayan', He also gave His own name when He manifested in the form of Bapashree, 'Abji'. The meaning of this name is, 'He who will manifest shortly'.

Just as the deities and celestial entities came for the darshan of the Lord when He manifested in Chhapaiya in Samvat 1837, these deities also came for the darshan of Bapashree when he appeared on the earth and showered him with auspicious items of adoration. This demonstrates that the two forms are the same.

Shreeji-sankalp-murti
The physical embodiment of the thoughts of Lord Swaminarayan, i.e. those who give darshan upon this earth by the will of the Lord; they are synonymous with the Lord Himself

Darshan
The visualisation of the Lord. Also the act of looking with reverence and devotion at the image or deity in the shrine, sometimes of seeing a holy person

Sadguru
Status of eminent ascetics (sants)

Upasana
Correct understanding of the Lord. See Appendix

Purna Purushottam
Almighty, supreme Lord of Lords

Kamdev
The deity of love and passion

Sadguru Shree Gopalanand Swami and Sadguru Shree Nirgundasji Swami preached and propagated the supreme glory and *upasana* of Lord Shree Swaminarayan. However, there were still many who could not understand these teachings.

In the presence of Sadguru Shree Gopalanand Swami and other eminent Sadgurus, Purna Purushottam Lord Shree Swaminarayan had said, "For now, I will withdraw My human *darshan*, but when the time comes, I will manifest again." Lord Shree Swaminarayan decided to fulfil this promise.

Near the village of Vrushpur in the Kutch district, there is a lake called Lake Krishna, which had been blessed by Shreejimaharaj. The pious, devout and chaste disciple, Devuba used to bathe in Lake Krishna every day. Becoming pleased with her faithful, loving devotion, Purna Purushottam Lord Shree Swaminarayan granted Devuba His divine, lustrous *darshan* at the bank of the lake. The beauty of the Lord's gently smiling lotus face and loving eyes was so enchanting, that the beauty of millions of Kamdevs would be insignificant.

Lord Shree Swaminarayan gives darshan to Devuba at Lake Krishna

Devuba became overwhelmed by the beautiful, lustrous *darshan* of Shree Ghanshyam Maharaj and stared at the Lord. She became lost in the Lord's beauty.

Being pleased with her, the merciful Lord said, "Lady! I am pleased with you. Ask for a boon."

Devuba's attention was completely engrossed in the Lord's beautiful lotus face. To her, nothing except the Lord's divine lotus face existed. She had become fascinated by the enchanting *darshan* of the Lord's *Murti* and was experiencing tremendous pleasure and tranquillity. Therefore, she said, "I want a son like You."

Lord Shree Swaminarayan gently smiled and said, "Lady! There is no-one else who is the same as Me. However, My *Anadi-muktas* reside within My *Murti* and have the same form as Me. They constantly remain within My *Murti* and enjoy My divine bliss, they never come or go. However, as you have asked upon my request, I will fulfil your wish. My Sankalp swaroop will manifest at your home and gratify your wish. He will manifest 'Ab' (shortly), therefore you must name him Abji." After saying these words, Shreejimaharaj withdrew His *darshan*.

Murti
Divine image or form of the Lord

Anadi-mukta
Highest state of the liberated soul. See Chapter 1

Sankalp-swaroop
The physical embodiment of the thoughts of Lord Swaminarayan, i.e. those who give darshan upon this earth by the will of the Lord; they are synonymous with the Lord Himself

As Devuba returns home divine Muktas flank her path and proclaim 'The Shreeji–sankalp–murti will manifest at your home'

The delighted Devuba departed from Lake Krishna to go home. On the way, she received the *darshan* of divine *Muktas* who were lining both sides of her path. They repeatedly proclaimed, "Lady! The Shreeji-sankalp-murti will manifest at your home. The Shreeji-sankalp-murti will manifest at your home." This *darshan* continued until she reached home.

As soon as she arrived home, Devuba told her husband Panchabhai about the divine *darshan*. Panchabhai also became overwhelmed and started praying to Lord Shree Swaminarayan.

In Samvat 1901 Kartik Sud 11 (Monday 20th November 1849), the Shreeji-sankalp-murti, Prasiddh Swasiddh Shree Abji Bapashree manifested in the village of Vrushpur.

Purna Purushottam Lord Shree Swaminarayan first granted Devuba His divine lustrous *darshan*. She became engrossed by the divine *darshan* of Lord Shree Swaminarayan. After a short while, Lord Shree Swaminarayan withdrew His *darshan* and immediately, she had the divine *darshan* of Jeevanpran Bapashree lying next to her. Baby Bapashree's forehead was adorned with sandalwood paste and he was garlanded with rose flowers. He lay there, lovingly gazing at his mother.

Muktas
Liberated souls

Prasiddh
Well–known

Swasiddh
Self–accomplished

Jeevanpran
Life and soul

Lord Shree Swaminarayan gives His divine darshan to Devuba and then immediately assumes the form of the baby Abji Bapashree

As soon as Bapashree manifested, *Muktas*, incarnations and deities came invisibly, to perform adoration to him. Shreeji-sankalp-swaroop Bapashree was a miraculous, powerful, entrancing and independent divine *Murti*.

Immediately after manifesting, he commenced his episodes of assuming a trance (*samadhi*) state. He would close his eyes and through his own will, enter into a trance. To fulfil his mother's maternal desires, he would awaken from the trance and suckle her. He would remain in a trance for four days, eight days, sometimes for fifteen days and, on occasions, for several months. There were occasions when the trance lasted six months. He would lie motionless in his cradle with his eyes closed. Still, baby Bapashree's *Murti* remained healthy and strong. Those who came for his *darshan* were always attracted to him and experienced divine happiness. To them, it would seem that Bapashree had only recently fallen asleep. What amazing episodes!

Gradually, Bapashree began to crawl and then walk. So adorable was this baby that everyone who saw him would carry him, cuddle him and play with him. When they carried him, he would seem light to some and heavy to others.

Jeevanpran Bapashree assumed as many forms as he had friends and simultaneously pleased them all

Akshardham
The divine abode of
Lord Shree Swaminarayan

Soon, Bapashree started to play with his friends. They would play chase and catch (*pakad dav*). The friends would run to catch Bapashree. However, Bapashree would assume as many forms as there were friends, and run in different directions. Each friend would think that Bapashree was in front of them and they would easily be able to catch him. However, just as they get close and stretch to grab him, Bapashree would vanish. Eventually, the friends would look around and see Bapashree laughing, and standing at the centre of the group having assumed a single form.

Bapashree used to go to Lake Krishna to bathe with friends. They would dive from a rock into the water and compete to see who could remain under the water for the longest time. With the exclamation, 'Glory to Shree Ghanshyam Maharaj', they would dive into Lake Krishna. The friends would emerge from the water after one, two or three minutes. However, Bapashree would not come up at all. The friends would become worried and dive into the water to look for him. They would search the entire lake but would not be able to find Bapashree. Eventually, when the friends start to cry, Bapashree would come out from the water. The friends would become delighted to see Bapashree again and would ask, "You were not in the lake. Where had you gone?" Bapashree would reply, "I went to Akshardham for the *darshan* of Lord Shree Swaminarayan." Through such experiences, the friends came to understand the glory of Bapashree and realised that although he looked like them, he was actually a divine, independent *Murti*.

Whenever teams were formed for playing games, the friends would quarrel amongst themselves to have Bapashree in their team, because invariably, the team in which Bapashree was playing for always won. Bapashree pleased everyone by alternating between all the teams.

On one occasion, Panchapita became ill. He had a severe fever for four or five days and had not eaten anything. Devuba asked, "Do you want to eat anything?" Panchapita replied, "If there are dates, I want to eat some." Devuba became upset. It was not the season for dates. Moreover, their financial situation was such that she could not afford to buy dates to give to her husband to eat. Tears started to flow from her eyes.

The merciful Bapashree could not bear to see the sorrow of his mother and said, "Mother! Do not worry. I will immediately go and get some dates." Saying this he went out of the house and soon returned carrying some divine dates. His mother was astonished and asked, "How did you get these dates without any money?" Bapashree replied, "As I left the house, I met Shree Ghanshyam Maharaj. He gave me these dates to bring here. They are divine dates. Give them to my father to eat and you too eat some of this *prasad*."

Prasad
Consecrated offerings:
food or other articles that
have been blessed by the Lord

Kirtans
Devotional songs praising the Lord

એ... રસ્તામાં ચાલતાં ઘનશ્યામ મળિયા, ખજૂર હાથમાં લઈને
આપણું દુઃખડું દૂર કર્યું છે, ખજૂર મુજને દઈને, (હરિએ)
ખજૂર મુજને દઈને...........બાળપણે પરચા આપે બાપાશ્રી

Shree Harignanamrut Kavya

"Whilst walking down the road I met Shree Ghanshyam Maharaj carrying dates in His hands"

This event, immediately reminded Devuba of the boon that Lord Shree Swaminarayan gave to her – 'He is the Shreeji-sankalp-swaroop'. With the dawning of such a realisation, she bowed in respect to Jeevanpran Bapashree. She then fed the divine dates to her husband and ate some *prasad* herself.

Even in his childhood, Jeevanpran Bapashree had memorised 1100 *kirtans*, each of four cantos. He would melodiously sing these *kirtans* one by one in the temples and even when he fetched water from the well in the field. He would recite them when walking and whilst performing all other activities and thereby, he attracted everyone's attention to him. He would always be present at the religious discourses, where he would explain the supreme *upasana* of Lord Shree Swaminarayan.

Chapter 27

Shreeji-sankalp-swaroop Bapashree and Sadguru Shree Nirgundasji Swami

To both tyagis and gruhasths he is their life and soul (Jeevanpran). Such were the words of my guru's guru (Sadguru Shree Nirgundasji Swami).

Shree Harignanamrut Kavya

Who would be able to recognise that Jeevanpran Bapashree gives *darshan* by the will of Purna Purushottam Lord Shree Swaminarayan? Who would be able to understand his glory?

Only those independent (*swatantra*) divine *Muktas* who have come from Akshardham and give *darshan* by the will of Shreeji whilst remaining in His *Murti*, are able to recognise him and appreciate his glory.

Sadguru Shree Gopalanand Swami had handed over the responsibility of the Karan Satsang to Sadguru Shree Nirgundasji Swami and ordered him to propagate the supreme *upasana* and glory to the entire *Sampraday*, and had entrusted him with the key to absolute salvation (*aatyantik-moksh*). Only such a personage knows perfectly who Jeevanpran Bapashree was and why he had manifested.

Sadguru Shree Nirgundasji Swami often went to Kutch and stayed with Jeevanpran Bapashree. Sadguru Shree Nirgundasji Swami and Jeevanpran Bapashree would both deliver divine discourses in the assembly and grant divine bliss to all.

In Samvat 1942, Jeevanpran Bapashree travelled to Muli on a pilgrimage with a group of 600 devotees. From Muli, the group went to Gadhada, Dholera and then they reached Dholka. At that time, Shreejimaharaj gave *darshan* to the last of the *Nand-padvi sants*, Sadguru Shree Dhruvanand Swami, who was in Jetalpur, in order to take him to His divine abode - Akshardham. From Dholka, Shreeji-sankalp-swaroop Jeevanpran Bapashree prayed to Lord Shree Swaminarayan, "Oh Maharaj! In two days, this group will arrive in Jetalpur. If You keep Sadguru Shree Dhruvanand Swami alive for two days, the group would be able to have his *darshan* and it would be a memorable occasion for them all." So Lord Shree Swaminarayan kept Sadguru Shree Dhruvanand Swami on the earth.

At the same time, the disciple Jasa, who was in Jetalpur, had the divine *darshan* of Shreejimaharaj with an overgrown beard, riding on the mare Manki. The disciple Jasa asked, "Oh Maharaj! Why are You giving *darshan* in such an exhausted state? Your mare also looks tired and You are unshaven. Why is this?" Shreejimaharaj replied, "Bapashree, who is My form, is touring with a group of pilgrims from Kutch. The group is large. Therefore, from the time

Shreeji-sankalp-swaroop
The physical embodiment of the thoughts of Lord Swaminarayan, i.e. those who give darshan upon this earth by the will of the Lord; they are synonymous with the Lord Himself

Sadguru
Status of eminent ascetics (sants)

Tyagis
Individuals who have renounced worldly objects – ascetics (sants)

Gruhasths
Those with family associations

Shree Harignanamrut Kavya
A compilation of devotional songs written by Shree Muktajeevan Swamibapa

Darshan
The visualisation of the Lord. Also the act of looking with reverence and devotion at the image or deity in the shrine, sometimes of seeing a holy person

Purna Purushottam
Almighty, supreme Lord of Lords

Muktas
Liberated souls

Akshardham
The divine abode of Lord Shree Swaminarayan

Murti
Divine image or form of the Lord

Karan Satsang
True association with Lord Swaminarayan. See Chapter 1

that they left, I have been travelling with them. As the group is large, pilgrims are walking according to their own pace. I am staying with them so that no-one is looted or loses their way. I have been accompanying them, and that is why I look like this." Having said these words, Shreejimaharaj disappeared.

Two days later the group arrived in Jetalpur and everyone was able to have the *darshan* of Sadguru Shree Dhruvanand Swami. When the group was ready to leave for Ahmedabad, Lord Shree Swaminarayan took Shree Dhruvanand Swami to His abode. At that moment there was a shower of sandalwood paste. Many people in the group collected the sandalwood paste and formed it into lozenge shapes. In this manner, the group experienced a truly memorable occasion. From there, the group arrived in Ahmedabad.

After having the *darshan* of the Lord in the Temple, Jeevanpran Bapashree went to meet Sadguru Shree Nirgundasji Swami. Jeevanpran Bapashree and Sadguru Shree Nirgundasji Swami embraced each other. Jeevanpran Bapashree said, "Swami! It has been a long time since I last had your *darshan.*"

Sadguru Shree Nirgundasji Swami replied, "Bapa! I came (in a divine form) to Vrushpur to take the disciple Anda to Akshardham when he died. You were sitting next to him. Your nephew disciple Govind became frightened by seeing the mass of lustre. You assured him and explained that it was the lustre of Shreejimaharaj and His *Muktas.* We then took the disciple Anda to the abode. That was only two months ago. So why are you saying that it has been a long time since we met? We are always together." At this, Bapashree gently smiled.

Jeevanpran Bapashree and Sadguru Shree Nirgundasji Swami used to take many souls to Akshardham.

In Samvat 1944, Sadguru Shree Nirgundasji Swami had gone to Muli for the *Chatur-mas* discourses. Jeevanpran Bapashree also went there with a group of devotees from Kutch. One day, at 3 o'clock in the afternoon, the chief of the village Maliya, Modji Darbar, Purani Shreekrishnadasji and other *sants* and devotees had gathered before Jeevanpran Bapashree and Sadguru Shree Nirgundasji Swami. Sadguru Shree Nirgundasji Swami asked Jeevanpran Bapashree, "At the present time, is there anyone who, whilst sitting here (on this Earth) can immerse souls into the bliss of Shreejimaharaj's *Murti*?"

Jeevanpran Bapashree replied, "Yes! Amongst the ascetics, he is the one who is seated beside me (referring to Sadguru Shree Nirgundasji Swami), and amongst the *gruhasths*, he is the one who is sitting beside you (referring to himself, Jeevanpran Bapashree)."

Hearing this conversation, the *sants* and disciples recognised the greatness of Jeevanpran Bapashree and Sadguru Shree Nirgundasji Swami and bowed down to them in reverence.

Sankalp-swaroop
The physical embodiment of the thoughts of Lord Swaminarayan, i.e. those who give darshan upon this Earth by the will of the Lord; they are synonymous with the Lord Himself

Such an immensely powerful Sadguru Shree Nirgundasji Swami used to say to all the *sants* and disciples who came to him, "You should remain in the association of Jeevanpran Bapashree. He is a unique personage. There is no-one else as majestic as him. He gives *darshan* by the will of Shreejimaharaj. He is my Jeevanpran. Just as the life of a fish depends on water, my life and soul is Jeevanpran Bapashree."

If a great personage such as Sadguru Shree Nirgundasji Swami considered Jeevanpran Bapashree to be his life and soul, how great could this Jeevanpran Bapashree be! Such is the grandeur and divinity of the Sankalp-swaroops of Shreejimaharaj!

Jeevanpran Bapashree explains the true supremacy of Lord Shree Swaminarayan and His Sankalp–swaroops

Chapter 28

Nidar Siddhantvadi
Sadguru Shree Ishwarcharandasji Swami

The eminence of Sadguru Shree Gopalanand Swami was inherent within Shree Nirgundasji Swami, who was my guru. He brought this Ishwar Bapa to me and revealed his greatness. You can look through the entire universe; still, you will not find a sant like him anywhere. The darshan of this sant is infinitely precious. If one recalls the darshan of this sant, the Murti of the Lord is also remembered.

Bapashree ni Vato Part 2 Varta 14

Bapashree replied, "There will be a storm at sea during those days. Therefore, you must go now. You will not face any trouble at sea. I too wish to come with you, but due to my illness, I am not able to accompany you. So you all go, and convey my 'Jay Shree Swaminarayan' to Swamishree. You will not be able to have the *darshan* of such a great *sant* later on."

The *sants* and disciples reached Ahmedabad. After having the *darshan* of the Lord (*Thakorji*) in the temple, they went where Swamishree was presiding and prostrated in reverence to him. Swamishree asked, "So many of you *sants* and disciples have come, but why has my Jeevanpran Bapashree not come with you?" Vashrambhai of Rampur replied, "Swami! He is so ill that he is unable to turn himself without help. That is why he was unable to come himself. However, he has sent us all and has conveyed his 'Jay Shree Swaminarayan' to you." Swamishree said, "He will come here tomorrow afternoon."

The next day, the *sants* prepared the meal and called Swamishree to dine. Swamishree said, "I will wait until Jeevanpran Bapashree arrives and dine with him."

Swamishree also announced in the assembly, "Jeevanpran Bapashree will definitely come here today. Therefore, whoever wishes to go and greet him should go to the station."

Accordingly, many devotees went to the railway station and greeted Jeevanpran Bapashree as he stepped off the coach. The disciples said, "Swamishree had told us in the assembly that you would be arriving today."

Jeevanpran Bapashree and the disciples came to the temple. Having performed the Lord's *darshan* in the temple, Jeevanpran Bapashree went where Swamishree was presiding. Sadguru Shree Nirgundasji Swami stood up and lovingly embraced Jeevanpran Bapashree. They both asked about each other's illnesses.

Then Sadguru Shree Nirgundasji Swami said to the *sants* and devotees, "Look! Jeevanpran Bapashree did come. Perform *darshan* to him."

Everyone performed *darshan* to Jeevanpran Bapashree and Swamishree. A devotee asked Jeevanpran Bapashree, "You were very ill. How did you

manage to come here?" Jeevanpran Bapashree replied, "After you left, I thought that I too should go for *darshan*. With this thought, I dismissed the illness and came here." In this manner, Jeevanpran Bapashree and Swamishree revealed the unity between them.

The following day, after the discourses, Jeevanpran Bapashree and Sadguru Nirgundasji Swami were presiding in their seats. It was lunchtime and all the *sants* and disciples had gone to dine. At that time, Swamishree said to Jeevanpran Bapashree, "I am unable to have your *darshan* properly. Come a little closer and grant me your *darshan*."

Jeevanpran Bapashree moved closer. Swamishree put on his spectacles and said, "I still cannot see you properly. Remove your *angadi*."

Jeevanpran Bapashree removed his *angadi*. Immediately, a mass of lustre emerged from within him and pervaded everywhere.

Angadi
Long jacket like, upper body garment

A mass of lustre emanates from the divine Murti of Jeevanpran Bapashree

Shree Balkrishnadasji Swami
A leading sant of the Swaminarayan temple in Muli who had great respect for Jeevapran Bapashree

Seeing this, Swamishree exclaimed, "Oh! You are the divine lustrous *Murti*. You consist only of divine lustre." Jeevanpran Bapashree replied, "You are equally as divine and lustrous as I am." Saying this, he concealed the lustre and put on the *angadi*.

Shree Balkrishnadasji Swami of Muli was fasting that day. So he was also sitting there. He heard the conversation between both of them and asked Bapashree to show him the lustre. However, Bapashree did not show it to him. When the other *sants* and devotees had finished their meal and came back, he told them all about what had happened. All the *sants* and disciples became extremely delighted and prostrated in reverence to Jeevanpran Bapashree and Sadguru Shree Nirgundasji Swami.

Sadguru Shree Nirgundasji Swami then called Sadguru Shree Ishwarcharandasji Swami to Jeevanpran Bapashree. This was the first time that Jeevanpran Bapashree and Sadguru Shree Ishwarcharandasji Swami had met.

The meeting between Jeevanpran Bapashree and Sadguru Shree Ishwarcharandasji Swami was wonderful and unprecedented. Jeevanpran Bapashree was gently smiling. Sadguru Swamishree stared lovingly at him and bowed down.

Sadguru Shree Nirgundasji Swami places the hand of Shree Ishwarcharandasji Swami in that of Jeevanpran Bapashree

Sadguru Shree Nirgundasji Swami took Sadguru Shree Ishwarcharandasji Swami's hand and placed it in the hands of Jeevanpran Bapashree and said, "Oh Jeevanpran! I entrust him to you."

Jeevanpran Bapashree replied, "Swami! He is already mine. He is extremely great and powerful. Like you, he gives *darshan* here by the will of Shreejimaharaj. Just as you have looked after the Karan Satsang, he too will take great care of it. Through him, many great tasks will be accomplished in the *Satsang*. He is just as able and powerful as Sadguru Shree Gopalanand Swami. He will perform great deeds as Sadguru Shree Gopalanand Swami did."

Saying these words, Jeevanpran Bapashree placed his hand on Sadguru Shree Ishwarcharandasji Swami's head and became immensely pleased.

Nidar Siddhantvadi Sadguru Shree Ishwarcharandasji Swami knew who Jeevanpran Bapashree was and why he had manifested. Therefore, he used to go to Jeevanpran Bapashree, and in solitude, adorn him with sandalwood paste, garland him with flowers, embrace him, pray to him, bow and prostrate in reverence before him, and please Jeevanpran Bapashree. He would go to where Jeevanpran Bapashree was resting, and even though Bapashree forbade him, he would humbly pray to him and remain in Bapashree's service as his personal attendant.

One day, Jeevanpran Bapashree complained to Sadguru Shree Nirgundasji Swami, "Sadguru Shree Ishwarcharandasji Swami knows my glory, and remains in my service. Tell him not to do so."

Sadguru Shree Nirgundasji Swami called Nidar Siddhantvadi Sadguru Shree Ishwarcharandasji Swami to him and said, "From today, I command you to understand the true unparalleled greatness of this divine personage and serve him well. He is the divine *Murti*. There is no equal to him. You are well aware of all this and recognise who he is. Still, I must say to you that he is your and my Jeevanpran. Remain under his guidance and take care of the Karan Satsang."

Sadguru Shree Nirgundasji Swami then turned to Jeevanpran Bapashree and prayed, "Oh Jeevanpran Bapa! You have manifested out of sheer mercy. Shower your divine grace upon all souls. Do not remain hidden. Propagate the supreme *upasana* and glory throughout the entire *Satsang*. This Swami

Karan Satsang
True association with Lord Swaminarayan. See Chapter 1

Satsang
Fellowship, associated with the Swaminarayan religion

Upasana
Correct understanding of the Lord. See Appendix

185

Sampraday
Holy fellowship

Ishwarcharandasji will remain with you. As the spiritual heir and leader of the Karan Satsang, he will perform great deeds. However, you must remain the doer of all his deeds and reveal to the *Satsang* the true nature of the spiritual knowledge."

Jeevanpran Bapashree replied, "Swami! Do not worry. The Karan Satsang, Shree Swaminarayan *Sampraday* will remain flourishing with the supreme *upasana* and supreme glory. The spiritual knowledge and glory will flourish in a unique new form. Sadguru Shree Gopalanand Swami had told you in secret that through the fourth in his spiritual succession, a great revelation would occur in the *Sampraday*. You are well aware of this."

Saying this, Jeevanpran Bapashree smiled gently. Sadguru Shree Nirgundasji Swami knew what hidden secret Jeevanpran Bapashree was referring to by those words, and so he also smiled gently.

Then Jeevanpran Bapashree prepared to leave for Kutch. In the assembly, Sadguru Shree Nirgundasji Swami pointed to Jeevanpran Bapashree and said, "*Sants* and devotees! This divine personage is unique. Do not mistakenly understand him to be a mere mortal. He is an extraordinary divine *Murti*. Understand his true greatness and remain associated with him but do not let the arrogance of your higher caste or class hinder you. If you will remain under his guidance and serve him well and attain his favour, he will bestow his divine grace on you and take you to Akshardham. Then, you will enjoy the bliss of the *Murti*."

Swamishree then pointed to Sadguru Shree Ishwarcharandasji Swami and addressed the *sants* and disciples, "From today, this Swami is in my place. Sadguru Shree Gopalanand Swami entrusted the responsibility of the Karan Satsang to me. From today I entrust that responsibility to this Swami. He, with the grace of Lord Shree Swaminarayan and Jeevanpran Bapashree, will take care of the *Satsang*. You must all obey his wishes and remain in the service of Jeevanpran Bapashree. If you act accordingly, Lord Shree Swaminarayan will definitely enable you all to enjoy the bliss of His *Murti*. This Swami is an independent (*swatantra*) entity and gives *darshan* here by the will of Shreeji. Sincerely believe all his words to be the truth and please him well."

Swamishree then turned to Sadguru Shree Ishwarcharandasji Swami and said, "Remain with Jeevanpran Bapashree. Serve him well and remaining under his guidance, take care of all. Explain the supreme *upasana* and glory of Lord Shree Swaminarayan to all and ensure that all abide by the religious decree and devotion. This is my final command to you all."

All the *sants* and devotees prayed and bowed in reverence and pleased Jeevanpran Bapashree, Sadguru Shree Nirgundasji Swami and Sadguru Shree Ishwarcharandasji Swami.

In Samvat 1948 Aso Sud 1, Sadguru Shree Nirgundasji Swami withdrew his human *darshan*.

Jeevanpran Shree Abji Bapashree and Sadguru Swamishree give darshan with Shree Ghanshyamjeevandasji Swami, and devotees

Chapter 29

The Immense Prowess of Jeevanpran Bapashree

Jeevanpran Bapashree and Nidar Siddhantvadi Sadguru Shree Ishwarcharandasji Swami were renowned within the *Satsang*. Many *sants* and disciples experienced that the key to eternal salvation (*aatyantik-moksh*) exists with them and therefore, those who wish to attain salvation whilst in this very life, should resort to their shelter.

Once, Sadguru Shree Ishwarcharandasji Swami went to Kapadvanj where he met Chunilal, the son of the Modh *Brahmin* named Shrikrishna. By the *darshan* of the powerful and charismatic Sadguru Swamishree, Chunilal attained spiritual enlightenment. Sadguru Swamishree preached to him about the supreme glory of Purna Purushottam Lord Shree Swaminarayan and said, "Lord Shree Swaminarayan gives *darshan* today through Jeevanpran Bapashree." Chunilal asked, "Swami! Take me for his *darshan* right away." Sadguru Swamishree replied, "I have just come from him, so it's not appropriate to return immediately without his permission. However, when I do go back to him, I will definitely take you with me." Chunilal immediately gave Sadguru Swamishree his address in Mumbai and said, "Swami! When you go again to meet Bapashree, do let me know. I will certainly come for his *darshan*."

When Sadguru Swamishree was going to Kutch again, he wrote a letter to Chunilal and said, "I am going to Kutch so you may also come."

In Mumbai, Chunilal read the letter and promptly sent another letter in reply, in which he said, "At the moment, my exams are going on. I have completed half the papers but half are still remaining. So let me know which route I should take to Kutch." Sadguru Swamishree gave the letter to Bapashree to read. Bapashree said, "Swami! Write to him and tell him that he should first go home and then come here."

According to Bapashree's command, Sadguru Swamishree wrote a letter. Chunilal received the letter. He completed his examinations and first went home. There, he fell ill. Three days later, Chunilal had the divine lustrous *darshan* of Jeevanpran Bapashree and Sadguru Swamishree. Jeevanpran Bapashree said to Chunilal, "Come to Akshardham." Chunilal said to his father and other relatives, "Bapashree of Kutch has come to take me. Therefore, I am going to Akshardham." His father asked, "You have never had his *darshan*, so how did you recognise him?" Chunilal replied, "The one who introduced me to him, Sadguru Swamishree, enabled me to recognise him. Sadguru Swamishree is also giving *darshan* with Bapashree. He is just as lustrous and magnificent as Jeevanpran Bapashree. If you want salvation, resort to their shelter and remain associated with them." Saying this, he left his mortal body.

Such is the divine prowess of Jeevanpran Bapashree and Sadguru Shree Ishwarcharandasji Swami.

Once, Sadguru Swamishree went to the village of Roha in the Kutch district. The chief minister for the king of the village, Kunverjibhai, was a very pious man. He was in search of God. He had taken a vow that he would become the disciple of any *sant* who defeated his current guru in a debate.

On Sadguru Swamishree's arrival, many people went for his *darshan*. Someone said, "Kunverjibhai! Come to the temple. Lord Shree Swaminarayan's chief *sant* has arrived there."

That evening, Kunverjibhai attended the discourses. After hearing Sadguru Swamishree's striking discourses, delivered in a charismatic manner, he became extremely delighted. Then, a disciple said to Kunverjibhai, "Honourable Minister! Accept Swamishree as your guru. He is so powerful that he can

Jeevanpran
Life and soul

Nidar Siddhantvadi
Fearless, principle proclaimer

Sadguru
Status of eminent ascetics (sants)

Satsang
Fellowship, associated with the Swaminarayan religion

Sants
Ascetics, the closest Western equivalent being monks

Modh
A class of the Brahmin caste. See Chapter 1

Brahmin
Category of the Hindu caste system (see Chapter 1) – those who are contemplative, philosophical, impart knowledge and perform religious rites

Darshan
The visualisation of the Lord. Also the act of looking with reverence and devotion at the image or deity in the shrine, sometimes of seeing a holy person

Purna Purushottam
Almighty, Supreme Lord of Lords

Akshardham
The divine abode of Lord Shree Swaminarayan

Murti
Divine image or form of the Lord

Sadhu
An ascetic

Tilak-chandlo
A mark applied on the forehead, as part of one's morning worship. The Swaminarayan mark is of a U shape made of yellow sandalwood paste (chandan) with a circle of sacred red powder (kanku) in the middle.
See Appendix

Vachanamrut
The words of Lord Shree Swaminarayan compiled as a scripture. See Appendix

elevate you to Akshardham (bestow eternal salvation)." Informing Sadguru Swamishree about his vow, Kunverjibhai said, "Oh Swami! I accept as my guru, he who defeats my present guru in a debate." Sadguru Swamishree replied, "Call your guru." The minister said, "My guru has gone away from the village and will return in three days." Sadguru Swamishree said, "I will be leaving tomorrow."

The next day, Sadguru Swamishree left Roha and went to another village. However, the charismatic *Murti* of Sadguru Swamishree and his discourses had become so embedded in the heart of Kunverjibhai that he could not forget him even if he tried, because Kunverjibhai was a true aspirant of salvation and Sadguru Swamishree was the true donor of salvation.

After three days, his guru returned. Kunverjibhai said to him, "Lord Swaminarayan's chief *sant* had come here and you were supposed to debate with him." Immediately, the guru replied, "I never debate with a *sadhu* of Shree Swaminarayan. They are deceivers. They use deception to misguide people." To deceive the minister, the guru then tried to illustrate his argument with a fabled story about a buffalo.

> **Buffalo Story:** On one occasion, a devotee gave consecrated food of Shreejimaharaj to a person who was not a devotee of the Lord. He had doubts and thought that if he ate the blessed food, he would become mad. So he threw it in the manger of his buffalo. The buffalo ate the blessed food, so the buffalo became mad.

The minister said, "Guruji! There is no difference between the buffalo and you." Saying this, he left the guru.

Some time later, Kunverjibhai went to the village of West Sukhpur where he met the disciple Laxman. He recognised the *tilak-chandlo* on his forehead and asked, "Are there any scriptures about your religion?" The disciple replied, "Yes, the Vachanamrut." The minister asked, "If you have it, will you give it to me to read?" The disciple Laxman gave Kunverjibhai a copy of the Vachanamrut.

Kunverjibhai was deeply dedicated to seeking salvation. So he immediately sat down to read the Vachanamrut. He was so interested in the sacred scripture

that he completed the reading of the Vachanamrut in a single sitting. He became so engrossed in it, he started to read it again. This time he completed the reading in three days. To gain a better understanding about it, he started to read it for a third time. This recital lasted seven days. He realised that this scripture contained an unsurpassed level of spiritual knowledge and was superior to any other scripture.

Kunverjibhai then went to Bhuj and stayed at the temple. Meanwhile Sadguru Swamishree also arrived there. He saw Kunverjibhai and said to him, "Kunverjibhai! What made you to come here?" Kunverjibhai immediately recognised Sadguru Swamishree as the *sant* who had come to his village. He got up and bowed down at Sadguru Swamishree's lotus feet. He joined both hands and humbly prayed, "Oh Swami! I want you to be my guru. I am now resorting to your shelter. Shower your mercy on me so that I can visualise the *Murti* of Lord Shree Swaminarayan."

Sadguru Swamishree performed the *vartman* ceremony to Kunverjibhai and explained the supreme *upasana* and glory of Lord Shree Swaminarayan. He also instructed him about meditation and said;

निजात्मानं ब्रह्मरूपं देहत्रयविलक्षणम् ।
विभाव्य तेन कर्तव्या भक्तिः कृष्णस्य सर्वदा ॥

Nijaatmaanam Brahmaroopam deh-traya-vilakshanam,
Vibhaavya ten kartavyaa bhaktih Krushnasya sarvadaa.

Shikshapatri, Slok 116

Separate yourself from the three states of the body and think of yourself as being *Brahma-roop*. Sit in the *swastikasan*. Keep your attention focussed on the tip of your nose (*nasikagra-vruti*). Recite the name 'Swaminarayan' within your mind, in time with your breathing. Without thinking about anything else, meditate upon Lord Shree Swaminarayan.

Through associating with Sadguru Swamishree, Kunverjibhai learnt the process of performing *pratilom* meditation and started to master the process.

As he was a chief minister, he had never sat cross-legged. Therefore, when he sat in the *swastikasan*, his thighs remained high off the ground. To correct this

Vartman
An oath taken when an aspirant joins the faith, to abide by the five sacred vows, Chapter 3

Upasana
Correct understanding of the Lord. See Appendix

The three states of the body
Physical, invisible and causal

Brahma-roop
In the form of the lustre of the Lord

Swastikasan
Cross-legged posture wherein the feet are interlocked between the thighs of the opposite legs which forms the sign of the Swastik

Pratilom
When one believes the Lord is not separate and in front of him, and is merged within the Lord

posture, he placed the two heavy stones from a grinding mill on his knees. In this manner, he perfected the posture. Through his diligence and the grace of his guru, after twelve months of practice, he succeeded in meditating for two and a half hours continuously, without any other thoughts entering his mind.

Kunverjibhai and Sadguru Swamishree met again. Kunverjibhai said, "Swami! By your mercy, I have managed to meditate for two and a half hours continuously. However, after two and a half hours, thoughts arise so I get up."

Sadguru Swamishree said, "Come! I will let you have the *darshan* of such a divine personage; he will relieve you from all your thoughts."

Sadguru Swamishree took Kunverjibhai to Vrushpur. As they entered the outskirts of the village, all of Kunjverjibhai's thoughts subsided and he experienced an extraordinary peace.

Just as the merchant from the Sindh region experienced divine peace and tranquillity when he entered the village of Piplana and his thoughts and volitions all subsided (see Chapter 9), Kunverjibhai's thoughts were also vanquished when he entered Vrushpur. What an extraordinary prowess of Lord Shree Swaminarayan and Jeevanpran Bapashree!

As Kunverjibhai and Sadguru Swamishree climbed the steps of Vrushpur temple, they met Jeevanpran Bapashree who said, "Well Kunverjibhai! Did all your thoughts cease?"

In their very first encounter, Jeevanpran Bapashree revealed his powers of omniscience. Kunverjibhai was amazed and fell at Bapashree's lotus feet and prostrated in reverence to him.

By the grace of Jeevanpran Bapashree, Kunverjibhai experienced the bliss of the *Murti* despite the obstacle of his material body. What an extraordinary divine grace! What an unsurpassed divine prowess!

Once, Jeevanpran Bapashree was touring Gujarat with a group of pilgrims. Sadguru Shree Ishwarcharandasji Swami was also accompanying them. They travelled from village to village, attracting many souls who were aspiring for

salvation and bestowed their bliss to them all. Wherever they stopped, they preached about the supreme *upasana* and supreme glory. Everyone would perform adoration to Jeevanpran Bapashree, apply sandalwood paste to his forehead, perform *aarti* to him and pronounce acclamations.

The group reached Vadtal and commenced their routine of chanting, singing hymns and holding discourses. As a result, many souls were drawn to Jeevanpran Bapashree.

By the grace of Sadguru Shree Nirgundasji Swami, Gopallalbhai from Thasara was able to visualise the *Murti* of Lord Shree Swaminarayan Himself. Once, Gopallalbhai went to Sadguru Shree Nirgundasji Swami for *darshan*. Swamishree said to him, "Gopallalbhai! If, by the grace of the Lord, you become a district magistrate, you must ensure a temple is built in Kadi." Gopallalbhai replied, "Swami! I have made an application, but I am ninth in the order of preference." Swamishree replied, "Do not worry about that." Gopallalbhai said, "Swami! You are my guru and I am your servant. Whether I get a promotion or not, if you command me, I will have a temple built in Kadi. Shower your auspicious blessings on me." Sadguru Shree Nirgundasji Swami exclaimed, "Go! The Lord's blessings are with you."

By the blessings of Sadguru Shree Nirgundasji Swami, he became district magistrate of Kadi. He inspired many people to give donations, with which he built a temple.

Whenever he had to adjudicate in a trial, and the lawyers presented their arguments and confused him, he would close his eyes and recall the *Murti* of Lord Shree Swaminarayan. Then, Lord Shree Swaminarayan Himself would come and tell him the truth and reveal which side was at fault. He would then give his verdict accordingly. Such was the high status that Gopallalbhai had achieved by the grace of Sadguru Shree Nirgundasji Swami.

Lord Shree Swaminarayan gave *darshan* to Gopallalbhai at night and said, "My Sankalp-swaroop Bapashree has arrived in Vadtal with a group of disciples. Go there for his *darshan*. Perform adoration to him and perform *aarti* to him. In this manner, experience the bliss of serving Me in person."

Aarti
Ritual ceremony. See Appendix

Sankalp-swaroop
The physical embodiment of the thoughts of Lord Swaminarayan, i.e. those who give darshan upon this earth by the will of the Lord; they are synonymous with the Lord Himself

Varniji
Referring to Shree Nirgunanand Brahmchari who wrote the Purushottam Leelamrut Sukhsagar, which contains a narrative of Lord Shree Swaminarayan's divine episodes (predominantly in Kutch). It is written in the form of a poem, and contains the supreme upasana and glory of Lord Shree Swaminarayan. It also contains a narrative of Jeevanpran Bapashree's true identity

When Jeevanpran Bapashree went to Saraspur, Sadguru Swamishree showed him the scriptures. Seeing the Vachanamrut compiled with the commentary Rahasyarth Pradeepika Tika (Rahasyarth Pradeepika Tika sah Vachanamrut), Jeevanpran Bapashree became extremely pleased and said, "Swami! A great task has been accomplished. The sacred source of eternal salvation (*aatyantik-moksh*) has been created." Seeing Jeevanpran Bapashree so pleased, Sadguru Shree Ishwarcharandasji Swami performed the task of a caring mother and asked for his blessings. He said, "Bapa! Give your blessings on this Vachanamrut scripture." Jeevanpran Bapashree proclaimed, "Those who read this Vachanamrut scripture along with its commentary, will attain eternal salvation during their present life." Sadguru Swamishree then asked, "What if someone is illiterate?" Jeevanpran Bapashree replied, "Whosoever listens to the recital of this Vachanamrut with the commentary and understands its glory, will attain the same salvation." Again, Sadguru Swamishree requested, "Bapa! But what if someone is illiterate and deaf?" Jeevanpran Bapashree replied, "It is my great fortune to be granted the *darshan* of this Vachanamrut that contains such a commentary! Anyone who performs *darshan* to it and lovingly embraces it, while understanding its glory, will also attain the same salvation." Once again, Sadguru Swamishree asked, "What if someone is illiterate, deaf and blind?" Jeevanpran Bapashree replied, "Whoever understands the glory of this Vachanamrut and takes it in hands, touches it to their eyes and chest, will attain the same salvation."

It is said

શ્રીજીની ઇચ્છા થકી જ પ્રગટ્યા, બાપા દયા દિલ ધરી
વચનામૃત સુગૂઢ કેરી વ્હાલે, રહસ્યાર્થ ટીકા કરી
મૂર્તિમાં રસબસ જનોને કરવા, બે ભાગ વાતો થઇ
પુરુષોત્તમ લીલામૃત ગ્રંથ કર્યો, વર્ણીજી દ્વાર લઇ

Shreeji-nee eechhaa thakee ja pragatyaa, Bapa dayaa dil dharee
Vachanamrut sugoodh keree vahaale, Rahasyarth tikaa karee
Murti-maa rasabas jano-ne karvaa, be bhaag vaato thaee
Purushottam Leelamrut granth karyo, Varniji dvaar laee

By the will of Shreeji, Bapa (Jeevanpran Bapashree) mercifully manifested on this earth to enable souls to become united with the *Murti*,

Brahmachari
Bhramin who is initiated as
a tyagi (renouncer) into the
Swaminarayan fellowship
they explain the meanings of the
mythological scriptures.

Sadguru Brahmachari Shree Nirgunanandji
Swami. Author of the scripture Purushottam
Leelamrut Sukhsagar

He graciously bestowed the Rahasyarth Tika to clarify the hidden meanings
in the Vachanamrut. He also bestowed the sermons (*vato*) in two volumes.
And inspired the Varni, to inscribe the Purushottam Leelamrut scripture.

Whoever seeks salvation and listens to these divine scriptures;
recites them with affection; performs *darshan* to them;
understands their glory and touches them; will attain great bliss.
Such immensely benevolent blessings he mercifully bestowed.
With great exuberance, proclaim the acclamations of Shreeji and Bapa.

Sadguru Swamishree travelled extensively with Jeevanpran Bapashree
throughout Kutch and Gujarat, preaching the supreme glory. He never
tolerated even a slight breach of the Lord's commands and would fearlessly and
unreservedly explain the errors to the individuals concerned. Irrespective of
how learned a person was, Sadguru Swamishree would explain the supreme

Shree Krishnavallabhacharya of Junagadh was an eminent scholar and philosopher, who
has written commentaries to 24 of the great Sanskrut scriptures. Such a skilled and highly
regarded literary genius was amazed when he read the Vachanamrut with the Rahasyarth
Pradeepika Tika. He confessed that even he could never produce such a magnificent
commentary and said, "Whoever has written this commentary (*tika*) is definitely a divine
entity who has descended from Akshardham. In addition, he who has thought of the
questions, must also have come from the divine abode. Others would not be able to think
of such questions. No-one other than the Lord Himself can ask such questions and answer
them in this manner."

Swami Narayansevakdasji
An eminent ascetic (sant)

Baniya
Those belonging to the vaishya caste, who are engaged in trade, banking and commerce

Jeevanpran Bapashree describes the immense glory of Sadguru Swamishree and says, "You may search through the entire universe. Still, you will not find a sant as great as this"

The true Acharya is he who personifies the heritage of Shree Swaminarayan Gadi. Therefore, Sadguru Swamishree is the true Acharya.

Once, Swami Narayansevakdasji asked Jeevanpran Bapashree, "A lot of harm has come to the *Satsang*. Why would Shreejimaharaj be allowing it to happen?" Jeevanpran Bapashree replied, "Lord Swaminarayan never reacts immediately to anything. He is like a *Baniya*. Slowly but surely, He will stabilise everything. One day, He will remove all the defects that have arisen and reveal His true intention."

Jeevanpran Bapashree often uttered such mysterious words and indicated that the flourishing of the Karan Satsang would occur in a remarkable manner, which would bring about a new transformation to the *Sampraday*.

Jeevanpran Bapashree predicated that a headquarters of the Karan Satsang will shortly be established, where the true supremacy of Lord Swaminarayan will be understood and from where His divine bliss will be disseminated to all sincere adherents of the faith.

Sadguru Swamishree was travelling in Gujarat when Jeevanpran Bapashree, by his own will, withdrew his human *darshan* in Samvat 1984 Ashadh Sud 5 (Friday 22nd June 1928). Intense sorrow was inflicted on the Karan Satsang. Hearing the news, Sadguru Swamishree arrived in Kutch. Jeevanpran Bapashree was the life and soul for Sadguru Swamishree. How could he endure

the pain of this grief? Sadguru Swamishree sat in meditation and started to pray to Jeevanpran Bapashree, "Bapa! My guru, Sadguru Shree Nirgundasji Swami placed my hands in yours and entrusted me to you to look after. You gave your word that you would take care of me. Yet Bapa! You have left me alone and gone!" Just then, Jeevanpran Bapashree gave his lustrous divine *darshan* to Sadguru Swamishree and said, "Swami! I have not gone. I am still in the *Satsang* and I am with you. Do not forget the purpose for which we have manifested. The true principles have been disseminated. Ensure that they remain alive for all eternity. You know the wishes of Shreejimaharaj. Therefore, you must prepare the platform to allow its fruition. We are always together." Saying this, Jeevanpran Bapashree withdrew his *darshan*.

When Jeevanpran Bapashree's relatives and many ardent followers came for his *darshan*, Sadguru Swamishree consoled and comforted them and said, "Bapashree has done as he wished. Do not grieve. If you had not performed the final cremation ceremony, I would have definitely called Bapashree once again. However, what has happened is to be accepted." This indicates the unity of Jeevanpran Bapashree and Sadguru Swamishree!

Then, Sadguru Swamishree gathered all the followers and performed the scripture recital and other ceremonies to please Jeevanpran Bapashree. Again, he comforted everyone. He then departed for Gujarat.

> During His divine ordination in Akshardham Lord Shree Swaminarayan revealed to His *Muktas* that he would give *darshan* upon this earth for 125 years. However, after giving *darshan* for just over 49 years, He withdrew His human *darshan*.
>
> By manifesting as Jeevanpran Bapashree, Lord Shree Swaminarayan fulfilled His intention to give *darshan* for 125 years.

As soon as Jeevanpran Bapashree left, the activities of the opponents in Kutch surfaced, which resulted in a dire situation for the disciples. Through the power and influence of Jeevanpran Bapashree's presence, they had been suppressed from voicing their opposition. However, as soon as Jeevanpran Bapashree withdrew his human *darshan*, they started to cause havoc.

Shreeji-sankalp-murti
The physical embodiment of the thoughts of Lord Swaminarayan, i.e. those who give darshan upon this earth by the will of the Lord; they are synonymous with the Lord Himself

Seeing the opposition from all directions, one disciple asked Sadguru Swamishree, "Swami! When you are no longer around, will the magnificence and splendour of the Karan Satsang cease to exist?"

Sadguru Swamishree replied, "Do not worry."

આન ભી રહેશે શાન ભી રહેશે, કીર્તિ કથા વધતી જાશે
દુશ્મન જલતા બળતા રહેશે, ધર્મ-ધ્જા લહેરાઈ જશે ....

Aan-bhi rahese shaan-bhi rahese, kirti kathaa vadhatee jaashe;
Dushman jaltaa baltaa rahese, dharma-dhajaa laheraai jashe.

The glory will remain, the magnificence will remain and its power and significance will continue to flourish. The opponents may continue to smoulder and blaze, but the flag of the faith will always fly proudly.
Shree Harirasamrut Kavya

"I will give you such a great divine personage that the Karan Satsang will flourish throughout the world and the principles of Jeevanpran Bapashree will echo everywhere."

A little while after this conversation, Shreeji-sankalp-murti Shree Muktajeevan Swamibapa arrived in the presence of Sadguru Swamishree.

Sadguru Swamishree
announces the imminent
arrival of Jeevanpran Swamibapa

Chapter 31

Jeevanpran Swamibapa

I only have one desire within My heart; when I relinquish this body, even though there is no reason for Me to take birth again, I wish to reappear in the midst of sants.

Lord Shree Swaminarayan, Vachanamrut Gadhada Middle Section 48

Accordingly, the Lord manifested again in the form of Jeevanpran Shree Muktajeevan Swamibapa.

They (Shreeji-sankalp-murti) incessantly remain within the Murti.
By the will of Shreeji, they appear here.
By performing adoration to them, Hari (the Lord) has been revered.
By harassing them, the Lord has been pained.

Shree Harignanamrut Kavya

श्रीजीबापा   स्वामीबापा

श्रीजीसंकल्पमूर्ति विश्वधर्मचूडामणि वेदशास्त्रसंरक्षक
भारतभास्कर विशिष्टाद्वैतशिरोमणि महामंडलेश्वर
सनातनधर्मसम्राट् धर्मधुरंधर आद्य आचार्यप्रवर
धर्मप्राण १००८ श्री मुक्तजीवन स्वामीबापा संस्थापित

ॐ श्री स्वामिनारायण गादी ॐ

Manifestation to Initiation

Muljibhai Patel lived in the village of Kheda, on the banks of the River Vatrak. His affiliation to the *Satsang* was admirable. Each day, without fail, he would attend the morning and evening discourses in the temple. His wife Ichchhaba was also a devout, loving disciple of the supreme Lord Shree Ghanshyam. She had an unfaltering faith and a true understanding about the Lord's supremacy. The life of the couple was filled with religion and devotion.

A Yogi arrives at the home of Muljibhai and Ichchhaba and forecasts the arrival of the Lord's Sankalp-swaroop. Jeevanpran Swamibapa

Muljibhai Patel was a government revenue official. His office was in the village of Mahij. Once, whilst Ichchhaba was engaged in her house-work at their home in Mahij, a strange *Yogi* arrived. He had a fascinating, inspiring appearance. Ichchhaba welcomed the *Yogi* and offered him a seat. She made arrangements for him to dine. By then, it was evening and Muljibhai returned home. The *Yogi* completed his meal and sat, satiated. Ichchhaba asked if he required anything else and requested him to remain there for the night. The *Yogi* became extremely pleased to hear her respectful and humble words and showered blessings on her, "Lady! You are extremely fortunate. The Lord's Sankalp-swaroop will manifest at your home. He will bestow salvation (*moksh*) to innumerable souls and will spread the religion all around the world." The couple became extremely pleased to hear these words and once again,

Jeevanpran
Life and soul

Sants
Ascetic, the closest Western equivalent being a monk

Vachanamrut
The words of Lord Shree Swaminarayan compiled as a scripture. See Appendix

Shreeji-sankalp-murti
The physical embodiment of the thoughts of Lord Shree Swaminarayan i.e. those who give darshan upon this Earth by the will of the Lord; they are synonymous to the Lord Himself

Murti
Divine image or form of the Lord

Shree Harignanamrut Kavya
Compilation of devotional songs written by Jeevanpran Swamibapa

Satsang
Fellowship, associated with the Swaminarayan religion

Yogi
One who has accomplished the virtues of the Yog philosophy

Sankalp-swaroops
Thoughts of the Lord that take physical form, i.e. the Lord gives darshan through the personification of his thoughts

requested the *Yogi* to stay at their home for the night. However, the *Yogi* said, "I will spend the night in the village refuge." Saying this, he left the house. Muljibhai went after him to make arrangements but as soon as he reached the end of their street, the *Yogi* disappeared. Muljibhai watched in amazement.

In Samvat 1963 Bhadarva Vad Amas (Monday 7th October 1907), the Adya Acharya-pravar of Shree Swaminarayan Gadi, Dharma-dhurandhar, Sanatan-dharma-samrat Shree Muktajeevan Swamibapa manifested at the home of Muljibhai. His name prior to initiation as a *sant* was Purushottambhai

> The literal meaning of Purushottam is God - the almighty being. This reveals the true identity of Jeevanpran Swamibapa.
>
> Fifteen years after Sadguru Shree Nirgundasji Swami withdrew his human *darshan* Jeevanpran Swamibapa manifested upon this Earth. Such a 15 years gap is seen throughout our Guru-parampara.

Amas
Last day of the lunar month when there is no moon visible

Adya Acharya-pravar
Pioneer and chief spiritual preceptor of the throne

Dharma-dhurandhar
Chief or head of religion

Sanatan-dharma-samrat
The protector of the eternal religion, Sanatan Dharma

Sant
Ascetic, the closest Western equivalent being a monk

Darshan
The visualisation of the Lord. Also the act of looking with reverence and devotion at the image or deity in the shrine, sometimes of seeing a holy person

Guru-parampara
Spritiual heritage; holy and pious lineage

Pooja
An act of adoration, also performed as part of one's daily worship

Lord Shree Swaminarayan gives darshan to Ichchhaba and then assumes the form of the delightful baby Swamibapa

Swamibapa soon started to walk, run and play, purifying the land on which he placed his divine feet. He used to play divine games with his friends and please them all. As part of his daily routine, he would bathe in the river Vatrak, perform *pooja*, and then go for *darshan* in the temple and sit in the discourses.

211

Bhaktachintamani
Biographical scripture of Lord Shree Swaminarayan written by Shree Nishkulanand Swami. It consists of 8527 verses organised in 164 chapters and portrays the life and diviine episodes of Lord Shree Swaminarayan in chronological order

Villagers bring gifts for the new baby, Jeevanpran Swamibapa

Whilst playing on the banks of the River Vatrak with his friends, Jeevanpran Swamibapa would build a temple of sand and make a large heap of sand opposite to it. Swamibapa would install a *Murti* in the temple and the friends would seat Swamibapa on the heap of sand. They would offer a garland to Swamibapa and sit before him, and listen to his discourses.

Even in his youth, Jeevanpran Swamibapa revealed the purpose of his manifestation; To establish temples around the world and impart spiritual knowledge to his disciples.

Jeevanpran Swamibapa constructing a temple of sand (left) and teaching meditation to his friends (right) at the bank of the River Vatrak

Swamibapa would go to the temple and recite his favourite scripture, the Bhaktachintamani. His voice was sweet and he had an extraordinary flair for reciting the scripture. Therefore, everyone decided that he should recite the scriptures in the temple each day. All the disciples, both young and old, would attend and devoutly listen to his discourse.

212

Bapashree ni Vato
The discourses of Jeevanpran Abji Bapashree

Jeevanpran Swamibapa narrating the Bhaktachintamani scripture in the temple

After some time, Jeevanpran Swamibapa, by his own will, firstly sent his mother, then later, his father, to enjoy the bliss of Shreejimaharaj's *Murti*. He then looked after his younger brother Govind. He would recite the scripture Bhaktachintamani to him, cook for him and play with him. Through all this, Swamibapa bestowed his divine bliss to his younger brother and made him worthy of salvation. Soon, he too was sent to enjoy the ecstasy of the *Murti*.

For further studies, Swamibapa then went to Ahmedabad. From there, he went to Mumbai to work. There too, he attended the temple and listened to the discourses. This was his daily routine.

It was there that he met Khimjibhai Darji of Rampara and Jagjeevanbhai of Sayla. They said to Swamibapa, "We are ardent followers of Bapashree. We get together and hold discourses. If you come there, you too can enjoy them." Swamibapa took the address and went there the following day. In the discourse, a hand-written manuscript of Bapashree ni Vato was read. In accordance with the normal practice, everyone in turn recalled a passage from the reading. Swamibapa's turn came to speak. To everyone's amazement, he recited the entire chapter. After this, the responsibility of reading during these discourses was given to Swamibapa.

213

Sadguru
Status of eminent ascetics (sants)

Jeevanpran Swamibapa recites the entire chapter of Bapashree ni Vato at the assembly in Mumbai

Swamibapa asked about the author of the sermons of Bapashree and was told that it had been written by Sadguru Shree Ishwarcharandasji Swami. An intense desire developed for Sadguru Shree Ishwarcharandasji Swami's *darshan* and Jeevanpran Swamibapa decided to go to Saraspur in Ahmedabad for his *darshan*. That very same day in Saraspur temple, disciples asked Sadguru Swamishree a question, "Swami! At present, you are giving *darshan* and bestowing bliss to all. However, after you, who will ably protect, preach and flourish the divine principles of Bapashree?" Hearing this question, Sadguru Swamishree (Shree Ishwarcharandasji Swami) immediately sat up and said to

Sadguru Swamishree announces the imminent arrival of Jeevanpran Swamibapa

Karan Satsang
True association with Lord
Swaminarayan. See Chapter 1

Jeevanpran Swamibapa
before his initiation as a sant

everyone, "Do not worry. Bapashree will strengthen his principles in such a manner, that you all will be surprised. A divine personage is on his way. Through him, the Karan Satsang will be given a novel form. Bapashree's principles will be propagated all over the world in their original form."

All the disciples became pleased to hear these words and sat gazing at the divine lustre radiating from Sadguru Swamishree's lotus face.

Soon after, Swamibapa arrived in Saraspur Temple. At that time, Sadguru Swamishree was presiding on his seat writing a letter. Swamibapa prostrated in reverence to the Lord in the temple and then to Sadguru Swamishree. As soon as Sadguru Swamishree's gaze fell on Swamibapa, Sadguru Swamishree stood up and lovingly embraced him. Sadguru Swamishree gently smiled and said, "You have arrived just in time."

He then asked about Swamibapa's health and sat him down to dine. In the afternoon, when everyone else had gone to rest, Sadguru Swamishree made

215

Swamibapa sit beside him and asked about his father's name, home etc. Swamibapa gave all the details of his past. Sadguru Swamishree said, "He (your father) was also mine, and you too are mine. However, tell me. What are your plans for the future?"

Swamibapa replied, "I am thinking of going to Africa." Sadguru Swamishree gently smiled and said, "There will be many occasions for you to visit Africa, but when are you coming here (to join the *sant* fraternity)?" Swamibapa replied, "Whenever you command me." Sadguru Swamishree said, "Come right now." Swamibapa replied, "I am ready," and remained there.

Three days later, in Samvat 1986 Kartik Sud 11 (Wednesday 13th November 1929), Sadguru Shree Ishwarcharandasji Swami gave Swamibapa initiation as a *sant* and named him Shree Muktajeevandasji Swami.

Sadguru Swamishree initiates Jeevanpran Swamibapa into the sant fraternity

Lord Shree Swaminarayan was sometimes referred to as the Jeevan-Mukta - the one who bestows salvation to souls. This same name (Mukta-jeevan) was given to Jeevanpran Swamibapa, indicating his true identity.

Guardian of Bapashree's Disciples and Principles

When Jeevanpran Swamibapa was initiated as a *sant*, Jeevanpran Bapashree had already withdrawn his human *darshan*. Sadguru Swamishree was also showing signs of old age. However, he still had tremendous willpower and his invincible divine miraculous personality was glowing as bright as the Sun. Just as bats are unable to look towards the Sun, so they hang upside-down on the branches of a tamarind tree; those who had envious motives were unable to voice their opposing opinions in the presence of Sadguru Swamishree.

However, after Jeevanpran Bapashree withdrew his human *darshan* in Kutch, arrogant and envious heretics, who had been kept silent by the might and charismatic personality of Jeevanpran Bapashree, came out to harass his ardent devotees, like insects of the night that crawl out from beneath their rocks when darkness falls. Their harassment was not tame but aggressive and violent. Whenever Jeevanpran Bapashree's followers came out of their houses, they were attacked and battered with clubs. Due to the heretics' jealousy, they would throw away their food if they even came into contact with one of Jeevanpran Bapashree's followers.

Jeevanpran Bapashree's sons could not even enter the village. In fear of violent repercussions, they had to remain hidden on the farms. However, just as the Sun rises to remove the darkness of the night, Jeevanpran Swamibapa graced the land of Kutch to comfort Bapashree's ardent followers and revealed his own might.

What a young ascetic personage Jeevanpran Swamibapa was! His mode of walking was like an arrow in flight. His speech was like the strum from the bowstring of Gandiv, threatening the enemies. His gaze was like the lustre of the Sudarshan-chakra, burning the devils and providing peace and tranquillity to devotees. Such a great personage, Swamibapa, in the disguise of a young ascetic, treading the land of Kutch reached Vrushpur and went to the Chhatri of Jeevanpran Bapashree. This was the very site where Lord Shree Swaminarayan had given His divine lustrous *darshan* to Devuba and granted her with her boon. It was the site where Jeevanpran Swamibapa arrived to ease the suffering of Jeevanpran Bapashree's followers and to revitalise the supreme principles of Lord Shree Swaminarayan that Jeevanpran Bapashree had expounded.

Jeevanpran
Life and soul

Sant
Ascetic, the closest Western equivalent being a monk

Darshan
The visualisation of the Lord. Also the act of looking with reverence and devotion at the image or deity in the shrine, sometimes of seeing a holy person

Sadguru
Status of eminent ascetics (sants)

Gandiv
The bow of Arjun (a disciple of Shree Krishna)

Sudarshan-chakra
A luminous disc–like weapon used by Shree Krishna to kill demons

Chhatri
Umbrella shaped monument. See Chapter 29

The *sants* and disciples of the Satsang Mahasabha - those who sided with the Lord, loudly hailed victory and began to praise Sadguru Swamishree and Swamibapa.

Bhagwad Geeta
Religious scripture

Kashi
Renowned as a gathering place for learned scholars, and regarded as a holy city. It is situated on the banks of the river Ganges. It is also known as Varanasi and Banaras

Vishishtadwait
Philosophy of the Swaminarayan faith. See Appendix

Jeevanpran Swamibapa explaining the true interpretations of the scriptures at the assembly of scholars, thus protecting the teachings of Jeevanpran Bapashree

It is said in the Bhagwad Geeta:

विषयान् ध्यायतः पुंसः संगस्तेषूपजायते ।
संगात् संजायते कामः कामात् क्रोधोऽभिजायते ।।
क्रोधाद् भवति संमोहः संमोहात् स्मृतिविभ्रमः ।
स्मृतिभ्रंशाद् बुद्धिनाशो बुद्धिनाशात् प्रणश्यति ।।

Vishayaan dhyaayatah punsah sangas-teshoo-pajaayate
Sangaat sanjaayate kaamah kaamaat krodho-bhijaayate
Krodhaad bhavati sammohah sammohaat smruti-vibhramah
Smruti-bhranshaad buddhi-naasho buddhi-naashaat pranashyati

The more that one associates with the five senses (sound, touch, sight, taste and smell), by contemplating about them, the deeper and deeper one falls. From desire grows anger and from anger stems ignorance. The ignorance results in loss of judgement. From this, one loses balance of mind. The ultimate consequence is self-destruction.

At the age of eight, Lord Shree Swaminarayan attended the debate of scholars in Kashi, and explained His Vishishtadwait philosophy. Just over eight years after receiving initiation as a *sant*, Jeevanpran Swamibapa debated in this assembly and expounded the true supremacy and principles of Lord Shree Swaminarayan.

Kadi Incident

The opponents thought that after Sadguru Swamishree (Shree Ishwarcharandasji Swami), there was no-one who could protect the Karan Satsang and so, they would succeed in fulfilling their illicit motives. However, from the debate of scholars, it was evident that their aspirations would not be fulfilled.

The heretics became angry. From anger arises delusion. As a result of this, one's intellect becomes totally corrupted. Consequently, the Kadi incident was contrived.

> The Kadi incident refers to a secret plan to defame Jeevanpran Swamibapa by insinuating that he was contravening his vow of celibacy.

By the command of Sadguru Swamishree, Jeevanpran Swamibapa resided at Shree Swaminarayan Temple in Kadi (Since Samvat 1990 Bhadrva Sud 4, Wednesday 12th September 1934). The opponents conspired and made an effort to defame him with false accusations. Even in this, they were unsuccessful.

That day, Shree Ghanshyam Maharaj Himself gave *darshan* to Jeevanpran Swamibapa, awoke him and said, "Are you serving Me or am I in your service?" Jeevanpran Swamibapa replied, "My dear Lord! You are our parents. What service can a mere child offer to his parents? With their sentiments of love and compassion, the parents look after their child in all respects."

Hearing these words, Lord Shree Ghanshyam became extremely pleased, lovingly embraced Swamibapa and then said, "Don't worry. Some people had tried to defame you but I have ensured that all their efforts are in vain. You are well aware of all this. You give *darshan* through My will and are an independent entity."

After saying these words, Lord Shree Ghanshyam showed His immense pleasure over Jeevanpran Swamibapa and then returned to His place of rest – the *sinhasan*.

Sadguru
Status of eminent ascetics (sants)

Karan Satsang
True association with Lord Swaminarayan. See Chapter 1

Jeevanpran
Life and soul

Darshan
The visualisation of the Lord. Also the act of looking with reverence and devotion at the image or deity in the shrine, sometimes of seeing a holy person

Sinhasan
Ornately decorated shrine where the idols of the Lord are installed

221

Shree Satsang Mahasabha
The trust established by Jeevanpran Abji Bapashree to save the principles and doctrines of the supreme Swaminarayan Sampraday from corruption and to reform the adminstration of the religious association

Sants
Ascetics, the closest Western equivalent being monks

Parshad / Palas / Bhagat
The first stage of initiation into ascetic life; ascetics who wear white clothing

Mangla aarti
Ritual ceremony, conducted before dawn.

Aarti
Ritual ceremony. See Appendix

Satsang
Fellowship associated with the Swaminarayan religion

Some time later (in Samvat 1996 Aaso Sud 5, Sunday 6th October 1940) a general meeting of the Shree Satsang Mahasabha was called in Joravarnagar. All of Jeevanpran Bapashree's ardent followers and *sants*, young and old, assembled in Joravarnagar.

Only one *sant*, a *parshad* and three or four devotees remained with Swamibapa in Kadi. Seeing an opportunity to strike again, the opponents secretly entered Kadi temple accompanied by armed bandits. They created chaos in the temple whilst the *mangla aarti* was being performed. They snatched away the *aarti* and insulted the sanctity of Lord Shree Ghanshyam and Bapashree.

They harassed Jeevanpran Swamibapa and insulted him, thereby committing a great sin. Thereafter, they all remained in the temple for six hours before they were arrested and taken to jail.

In the court, an appeal was lodged for the possession of the temple. However, the courts gave a ruling that the rights to the temple belonged to the disciples of the village. All the ardent disciples of Bapashree who lived in Kadi requested Jeevanpran Swamibapa to stay in the temple.

As a result of this event, one thing was gained: A precedent was set for the entire *Satsang* that all the village temples belong to the disciples of that particular village; however, no-one else has any rights to the property or its wealth.

Jeevanpran Swamibapa then created a trust to run Kadi temple and through this trust, the temple administration continues to function effectively to this very day.

The Might of Jeevanpran Swamibapa

Once, Sadguru Shree Ishwarcharandasji Swami and Sadguru Shree Vrundavandasji Swami were touring to preach about the faith in the Bhal-Nalkantha region of Gujarat. At that time, Jeevanpran Swamibapa arrived in Gujarat after having toured Kutch to preach about the faith. He had an intense desire for the *darshan* of Sadguru Swamishree. So he went to the Nalkantha region. Travelling from one village to the another, he passed through seven or eight villages and walked for about 20 miles, until he reached Nanodara. There he was told that the Sadgurus would be arriving there shortly, and so remained there.

After a short while, both the Sadgurus also arrived in the village of Nanodara and presided on the *gadi-takiya* in the temple. Jeevanpran Swamibapa prostrated in reverence to them and then approached them for *darshan*. As he came close, both the Sadgurus lovingly held each of his hands and sat him down in-between them. They asked Swamibapa about the situation in Kutch and showing their great pleasure, they placed their hands on his head. They did not allow him to get up until the discourses had concluded. What an explicit ordination!

By the command of Sadguru Swamishree, Jeevanpran Swamibapa went to Visnagar to deliver the Chatur-mas discourses. Two to three other *sants* were already there. They said, "Disciples come here for *darshan* but leave immediately. To whom will you preach?" Swamibapa replied, "If there is no-one else, these pillars will listen to the discourses." This stunned the *sadhus* into silence.

Just then, an elderly disciple arrived. He had heard that Sadguru Swamishree's *sant* had arrived, so he came for *darshan*. He lifted his lantern with one hand and placed his other hand over his eyebrows to make a canopy so that he could clearly look at Swamibapa. He stared at Swamibapa and then said, "This *sant* is very noble. He is truly lustrous." He then continued, "Swami! At night, only Tarachand and I come here (to hear the discourse). In the morning, Bhaichand, Keshavlal and I come here." Swamibapa replied, "Why worry about others. You will come to the discourses, won't you?" The devotee said, "Yes Swami!"

Jeevanpran
Life and soul

Sadguru
Status of eminent ascetics (sants)

Sadguru Shree Vrundavandasji Swami
Head (mahant) of the Swaminarayan Temple at Dholka. A highly respected sant who had a deep affection for Jeevanpran Bapashree

Darshan
The visualisation of the Lord. Also the act of looking with reverence and devotion at the image or deity in the shrine, sometimes of seeing a holy person

Gadi-takiya
Symbolic seating mat and cushion indicating the elevated status of sadgurus

Chatur-mas
The four month period between Ashadh Sud 11 and Kartik Sud 11, usually between July and October. This is a kind of Lent for Hindus. At the start of Chatur-mas, certain vows are taken such as: fasting, daily recitation of scriptures (parayan), meditation and various other religious observances

Sants
Ascetics, the closest Western equivalent being monks

Sadhus
Ascetics

223

Diwali
Last day of the Lunar year;
the festival of lights

Bapashree ni Vato
The discourses of Jeevanpran
Abji Bapashree

Bapji
An affectionate term
for an ascetic (sant)

Jeevanpran Swamibapa
delivering the Chatur–mas
discourses in Visnagar

The discourses commenced. On the first day, the assembly numbered only four. On the second day there were six and on the third day there were eight disciples in the congregation. When these eight people began to praise Swamibapa's discourses, on the fourth day, the assembly numbered 20 and on the fifth day there were 50 disciples. Soon the temple became too small to accommodate the number of people. Seeing all this, the elderly disciple remarked, "Swami! This number of people do not even gather here on the festival day of Diwali, but you have attracted everyone to you." During that period, Jeevanpran Swamibapa stayed in the temple attic. Until late into the night, he would sit reading the scripture Bapashree ni Vato.

After a month, Swamibapa concluded the discourses and prepared to leave for Ahmedabad. However, the disciples of the village surrounded him and said, "Bapji! Please stay here for the entire monsoon season and deliver your discourses. We will all come here regularly to listen." Swamibapa replied, "I have to go to another village now." Still, the devotees persisted. Jeevanpran Swamibapa accepted their affectionate requests and remained there for an extra week. From there, Swamibapa went to another village and then returned to Ahmedabad.

The following year, some other *sadhus* went to Visnagar to preach. They also stayed in the same temple attic where Jeevanpran Swamibapa stayed. At night, just as they were getting ready to sleep, they saw a ghost in the rafter above them. The ghost had hooked its legs on the beam and was hanging upside down. It squealed, "May I come? May I come?" The *sadhus* became frightened. The ghost spoke again, "Why have you come here? I was unable to go near the one who came here last year. I started to burn even if I thought to go near him. However, I will definitely come to haunt you."

The *sadhus* screamed and fled from the attic. They barely gathered their belongings and hurried back to Ahmedabad.

What a difference between Jeevanpran Swamibapa and these other *sadhus*! Lord Shree Swaminarayan has said that ghosts and spirits can never come close to those who have the strength of faith about the Lord's form and have chaste devotion towards Him. How can such cowardly *sadhus*, those who fear ghosts and spirits, grant salvation to others?

Both Sadgurus, Sadguru Shree Ishwarcharandasji Swami and Sadguru Shree Vrundavandasji Swami, stayed together. Whenever anyone went to Sadguru Shree Vrundavandasji Swami and asked a question, he would reply, "Ask Sadguru Shree Ishwarcharandasji Swami. He is the engine. I am merely a carriage. Whatever he says is the truth."

Sadguru Shree Vrundavandasji Swami had attained a high status. Consequently, he knew about Jeevanpran Swamibapa's greatness. Whenever any of his disciples asked him about the future, and asked about whom they should associate with, he would point to Swamibapa and command them all to unite with him. At that time, some would ask again, "Swami! You are showing us one of Sadguru Shree Ishwarcharandasji Swami's *sants*. Why are you not showing us one of your own *sants*?" Sadguru Shree Vrundavandasji replied, "Only those who are great should be recognised as being great. I can only show you him, to whom Lord Shree Swaminarayan has entrusted the key to salvation (*moksh*). You regard me as your guru, so I am commanding you to remain associated with him (Jeevanpran Swamibapa)."

Jeevanpran Swamibapa presented these three *kirtans* at Sadguru Swamishree's lotus feet and melodiously sang them to him. Sadguru Swamishree became delighted to hear these *kirtans*, which described the true precepts of Jeevanpran Bapashree. Sadguru Swamishree became immensely pleased with him and repeatedly embraced Swamibapa. He commanded Swamibapa to compose at least a hundred such *kirtans*, which explained the true philosophy of the Lord. Jeevanpran Swamibapa obeyed Sadguru Swamishree's command and wrote over 100 such *kirtans*. He compiled them into the Harignanamrut Kavya scripture, and presented it to the entire Karan Satsang.

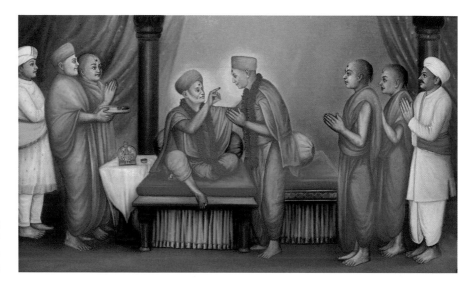

Sadguru Swamishree entrusting the sovereignty of Shree Swaminarayan Gadi to Jeevanpran Swamibapa

(In Samvat 1998 Aaso Vad 11, Tuesday 3rd November 1942) An assembly of *sants* and devotees had gathered in the presence of Sadguru Swamishree. He called Jeevanpran Swamibapa to him and then addressed the entire assembly, "*Sants* and devotees! From today, this Swami Muktajeevandasji is in my place. The helm of the Karan Satsang, which Sadguru Shree Nirgundasji Swami had entrusted to me, I am now handing to him. You all must remain under his command. Support him, with your body, mind and wealth, in all that he does for the propagation of Bapashree's tenets and do as he says and serve him well. The ultimate favour of Lord Shree Swaminarayan and Jeevanpran Bapashree lies in it. And also your salvation lies within it. This is my command. You all must act according to this decree."

Murti
Divine image or form of the Lord

Sinhasan
Ornately decorated shrine where the idols of the Lord are installed

Sadhus
Ascetics

After saying these words, Sadguru Swamishree seated Jeevanpran Swamibapa beside him, took off the garland from his neck and garlanded him. Then he said, "The spiritual heritage of the Karan Satsang that Sadguru Shree Nirgundasji Swami entrusted to me, I now entrust to you. Take good care of it. Spread the precepts of Bapashree and the Karan Satsang around the entire world and ensure that all adhere to the religious decree."

The third revolutionary step taken by Sadguru Swamishree, in the establishment of the headquarters of the Karan Satsang, was that he commanded Swamibapa, "Come with me. Let us install a *Murti* of Bapashree in every temple." Without hesitation, Jeevanpran Swamibapa replied, "Let's go!" Sadguru Swamishree became delighted to hear these unquestioning words and said, "I am extremely pleased with you. I command you to install the *Murti* of Jeevanpran Bapashree in the main *sinhasan*, alongside Lord Shree Swaminarayan, in every temple that you build." Jeevanpran Swamibapa promised Sadguru Swamishree that he would obey this command.

Sadguru Swamishree said to Jeevanpran Swamibapa, "In doing this, you will not get any cooperation from any *sadhus*. Presently, all those who call themselves the *sadhus* of the Mahasabha are concerned with material issues and are selfish. When the time comes, they will all move aside. Only some devotees will remain with you. However, Lord Shree Swaminarayan, Jeevanpran Bapashree and I are always with you. Therefore, you must remain alert in performing the task of spreading the principles of Bapashree."

Jeevanpran Swamibapa replied, "Swami! Your words are the commands of the Lord to me. I will implicitly obey your every command and will never allow even a slight deviation from them. I am not concerned whether others are with me or not. You are with me, that is all I need." Sadguru Swamishree became immensely pleased at these words and exclaimed, "Bless you! Bless you! I need a true disciple just like you. Now I have no worries. The true tenets and principles of Jeevanpran Bapashree will flourish everywhere and the glory and *upasana* of Lord Shree Swaminarayan will be sung throughout the entire world." Sadguru Swamishree showered these blessings on Jeevanpran Swamibapa.

Disappearance of Sadguru Swamishree's Human Darshan

A short time later, in Samvat 1998 Aso Vad Amas at night (Sunday 8th November 1942 at 11 p.m.), the Diwali festival, Sadguru Swamishree (Shree Ishwarcharandasji Swami) withdrew his human *darshan*. At that moment, a divine lustre illuminated and pervaded throughout the temple. The Sankalp-swaroop of Purna Purushottam Lord Shree Swaminarayan, Sadguru Swamishree, withdrew his human *darshan*.

The instigator of the Karan Satsang, the pioneer of the Satsang Mahasabha, Nidar Siddhantvadi Sadguru Swamishree had withdrawn his human form, yet he is always present amongst us all.

Still, how could his loving disciples tolerate the grief of his departure? They had experienced bliss by his *darshan*. Under his shelter, they remained fearless and as a result of his glory, they attained divine strength. His departure naturally submerged them all into mourning. 'He is an independent (*swatantra*) entity and is always present amongst us. He does not take birth and die like ordinary human beings.' Such spiritual knowledge may ease the pain of the grief, but does not completely eliminate it.

A palanquin was prepared (Samvat 1999 Kartik Sud 1, Monday 9th November 1942). Jeevanpran Swamibapa bathed Sadguru Swamishree, dressed him and tied a turban on his head. When he began to fold his legs in a *padmasan*, his hand touched a bandage that was wrapped around Sadguru Swamishree's leg. Jeevanpran Swamibapa moved back in shock and thought, "It may have pained my beloved Sadguru Swamishree." This shows that Jeevanpran Swamibapa still considered Sadguru Swamishree to be giving *darshan*.

In the morning, Sadguru Swamishree was seated on the palanquin. Jeevanpran Swamibapa and the other *sants* carried the palanquin on their shoulders. Many of *sants* and disciples began to sing *kirtans* and some started chanting the Lord's name as they walked alongside. Sadguru Swamishree's final procession passed through Ahmedabad city, going through Gandhi Road, Ratanpol, Nar-Narayan Temple Square, Dubgarwad and Delhi Gate. At that time, due

to the Second World War, the city of Ahmedabad was occupied by the American military. All along the funeral route, the soldiers stood with their guns downward and saluted in reverence to Sadguru Swamishree as the palanquin went past. The procession finally reached Dudheshwar, by the banks of the River Sabarmati, where Jeevanpran Swamibapa bathed Sadguru Swamishree and performed the funeral ceremony.

After the ceremonial ablutions, everyone went back to the temple. That night, Jeevanpran Swamibapa returned to Kadi. For him, it was as if his entire life had gone. His grief took the form of an illness, which started during the train journey to Kadi. He took a vow of silence and began to reminisce about Sadguru Swamishree's divine episodes. Tears rolled from his lotus eyes. Whilst remembering Sadguru Swamishree's *Murti*, Jeevanpran Swamibapa began to pray to him. This prayer took the form of a *kirtan* that he had spontaneously composed.

Commemoration

હે સદ્ગુરુજી! જેમ કહેશો તેમ કરશું જોડી હાથજી
હે કૃપાનિધિ! કૃપા કરીને રાખો અમને સાથજી ....

He Sadguruji! Jem kahesho tem karshu, jodi haathji.
He krupanidhi! krupa kari-ne raakho amane saathji

Oh Sadguru! We will do as you command, with joined hands.
Oh epitome of mercy! Have mercy on us all and keep us with you.

This prayer is still sung to this day on Amas (the last day of lunar month) i.e. the Sadguru-din commemorations, in memory of Sadguru Swamishree.

Jeevanpran Swamibapa arrived in Kadi. Sadguru Swamishree, whom he considered to be his entire life and dearer than anything else, had withdrawn his human *darshan*. He stopped drinking milk and minimised his diet. He took on an illness, in the form of a severe fever.

On the night of Labh Pancham (Kartik Sud 5), Jeevanpran Swamibapa was sleeping in Kadi temple. All of a sudden, the entire temple was filled with divine lustre. Amongst the lustre were divine *sants*. All the *sants* were young, identical and charming in appearance. All were wearing the same divine

Kirtans
Devotional songs, praising the Lord

Jeevanpran
Life and soul

Sants
Ascetics, the closest Western equivalent being monks

Murti
Divine image or form of the Lord

Sadguru-din
Held on the last day of each lunar month (Amas). In commemoration of Sadguru Shree Ishwarcharandasji Swami and Sadguru Shree Vrundavandasji Swami, Who withdrew his human form on Aaso Vad Amas and Kartik Vad Amas respectively

Labh Pancham
The final festival during the Diwali period – the fifth day of the Hindu new year

233

Acharya
Preceptor

Rahasyarth Pradeepika Tika
Accompanying commentary to
the Vachanamrut. See Appendix

Vachanamrut
The words of Lord Shree
Swaminarayan compiled as
a scripture. See Appendix

Bapashree ni Vato
The discourses of Jeevanpran
Abji Bapashree

**Purushottam Leelamrut
Sukhsagar**
Scripture written by Nirgunanand
Brahmachari detailing the divine
episodes of the Lord (while He
resided in Kutch)

Sadhus
Ascetics

lustrous clothing. The entire temple was filled with these *sants*. Amongst them, the *sant* sitting first in line and directly opposite Swamibapa, had a bandage on his leg. Swamibapa recognised that this was his guru, Sadguru Swamishree. Just then, Sadguru Swamishree said, "Yes. I am showing you this bandage so that you can recognise me. When you were folding my legs into a *padmasan*, you thought it would hurt me and you hesitated. But, look! It is nothing." Saying this, he moved his hand over the bandage and it immediately disappeared. Sadguru Swamishree continued, "This is how divine and lustrous I am. Look at all these *sants*. Lord Shree Swaminarayan, Jeevanpran Bapashree, I, and all these *sants* are with you. You are not alone. Do not worry in the slightest. I have not gone. I am always present. You have stopped drinking milk. However, it is my command that you start taking it again." After saying these words, Sadguru Swamishree lovingly placed his hands over Jeevanpran Swamibapa's head and withdrew his *darshan* along with all the divine *sants*.

After Sadguru Swamishree had withdrawn his human *darshan*, the other *sants* abandoned the Satsang Mahasabha and became affiliated to the opposing side, who promoted allegiance to the Acharya (of Nar-Narayan Gadi), rather than allegiance to the Lord.

The great tasks and sacred sources of eternal salvation (*aatyantik-moksh*) that Sadguru Swamishree had established were the Rahasyarth Pradeepika Tika of the Vachanamrut scripture, Bapashree ni Vato and Purushottam Leelamrut Sukhsagar. He also received the blessings from Jeevanpran Bapashree that whoever reads and contemplates about these scriptures, will attain the bliss of the *Murti*.

Except for Jeevanpran Swamibapa and his group of *sants*, all the other *sadhus* signed a 'declaration of slavery', in which they stated that they would no longer read or recite the Vachanamrut with the Rahasyarth Pradeepika Tika, Bapashree ni Vato, etc. They also stated that they would no longer believe, follow or preach the principles of Lord Shree Swaminarayan that Jeevanpran Bapashree had explained. The words of Sadguru Swamishree came true; "All these other *sadhus* are concerned with material issues and are selfish. None of them care at all for the principles. Therefore, none of them will give you any support in your work."

Despite signing such a declaration, in order to fulfil their self-interest, many still promoted themselves as the followers of Bapashree. One cannot ever hope to gain salvation from such selfish hypocrites, who are purely concerned with filling their stomachs.

The time came to hold a commemorative scripture recital (*parayan*) in honour of Sadguru Swamishree. It was decided to hold the recital at Saraspur temple, where Sadguru Swamishree mainly resided. The devoted *gruhasth* disciples of the Satsang Mahasabha decided that it was only right that in memory of Sadguru Swamishree, the recital should be of the Vachanamrut with the Rahasyarth Pradeepika Tika. However, the *sadhus* could not agree to this because they had signed the 'declaration of slavery'. It was therefore decided to hold a recital of the Shikshapatri Bhashya scripture instead.

As soon as Jeevanpran Swamibapa came to know about this fact, he immediately announced, "It does not matter if they do not conduct a recital of the Vachanamrut scripture. We will hold its recital here, in Kadi. Sadguru Swamishree devoted his whole life to the preparation of the commentary - Rahasyarth Pradeepika Tika on the Vachanamrut scripture, in which he had clearly explained the route to dwell in the Lord's *Murti* and the supreme *upasana* of Lord Shree Swaminarayan. Being his disciples, it is our duty to conduct a recital of this Vachanamrut in commemoration of Sadguru Swamishree. Whoever wishes to please Jeevanpran Bapashree and Sadguru Swamishree may come here and participate in the recital." Jeevanpran Swamibapa inspired a devotee from Surat to donate the expenses for holding the recital. He then held a recital lasting seven days (Samvat 1999 Kartak Sud 12, Thursday 19th November 1942). Thousands of devotees rushed to Kadi and eagerly commemorated the occasion.

In this manner, the recital of the Vachanamrut with the Rahasyarth Pradeepika Tika was held in Kadi. Jeevanpran Swamibapa alone recited the scripture. In addition, he had allowed an illness to remain in his body. Whenever Swamibapa presided on the dais, the fever would immediately leave his body and sit amongst the congregation to hear the discourses. As soon as Jeevanpran Swamibapa stepped down from the stage, the fever would return. Swamibapa would recite continuously for three hours without any intermission. Such a session was held twice each day. What immense prowess!

Gruhasth
Those with family associations

Shikshapatri Bhashya
Scripture written by Shree Shatanand Swami which elucidates each verse of the Shikshapatri (the holy commandments of Lord Swaminarayan)

Upasana
Correct understanding of the Lord. See Appendix

Sant
Ascetic, the closest Western equivalent being a monk

Khichadi
A very basic meal of rice with green mung beans

Thal
Meals offered to the Lord.

Aarti
Ritual ceremony. See Appendix

On the auspicious day of Samvat 1999 Shravan Vad 5 (Friday 20th August 1943), Jeevanpran Swamibapa arrived at Maninagar and stayed in one of the three small rooms which stood in the Northern section of the main building. There were no cooking utensils. He had to make a saucepan by cutting an empty kerosene tin. A *sant* went to get some coal to fuel the fire. As he opened the sack, a line of scorpions emerged from it and climbed on to his hand. The scorpions did not sting him. The *sant* shook them off and immediately they fell to the ground, and walked away in a straight line. Jeevanpran Swamibapa said, "Look! These are not ordinary scorpions. They represent the abundant, overflowing wealth that will arise from here."

Khichadi being cooked in an empty kerosene tin

They then made *khichadi* in the kerosene tin. Jeevanpran Swamibapa sent for a *Murti* of Shree Sahajanand Swami Maharaj from the home of Shree Chandrashankarbhai Dwivedi and a *Murti* of Shree Abji Bapashree from the home of Shree Baldevbhai Sheth. He then installed these two *Murtis* in the temple room, offered *thal* and performed *aarti* to the Lord. By the divine lustre of these *Murtis*, the supreme precepts of Lord Shree Swaminarayan, propounded by Jeevanpran Bapashree, are alive today, and have been spread all over the world to enlighten all with the divinity of this spiritual knowledge.

Darshan
The visualisation of the Lord. Also the act of looking with reverence and devotion at the image or deity in the shrine, sometimes of seeing a holy person

Shree Vrundavandasji Swami
Head (mahant) of the Swaminarayan Temple at Dholka. A highly respected sant who had a deep affection for Jeevanpran Bapashree

The *Murtis* of Jeevanpran Bapashree and Lord Shree Swaminarayan - Shree Sahajanand Swami Maharaj, which were first installed in Shree Swaminarayan Temple Maninagar. These two *Murtis* still give *darshan* in the main temple at Maninagar, behind the beautiful *Murti* of Shree Sahajanand Swami Maharaj.

Jeevanpran Swamibapa now began preparations for the installation of the divine *Murti* of Shree Ghanshyam Maharaj.

Sadguru Shree Vrundavandasji Swami was residing in the temple at Kalupur in Ahmedabad and was ill. Swamibapa informed him about the installation of the *Murtis*. He sent the message to Jeevanpran Swamibapa in which he said, "By the command of Sadguru Swamishree, you are making preparations to install the *Murti* of Shree Ghanshayam Maharaj. By this deed, Shree Ghanshyam Maharaj and Bapashree have become extremely pleased. From the headquarters in Maninagar, the Karan Satsang will prosper and flourish immensely. Whatever you are doing, is indeed extremely good. Install the *Murtis* with great joy and enthusiasm. If my health would have been better, I too would have been present there. However, you must consider me as being with you."

The invitation cards for the *Murti* installation ceremony of Shree Ghanshyam Maharaj were distributed. The ardent followers of Jeevanpran Bapashree and the Karan Satsang came with great zeal to Shree Swaminarayan Temple,

241

Diwali
Last day of the Lunar year;
the festival of lights

Sharad-poonam
Aso Sud Poonam (day of the
full moon). This day is considered
to be a sacred day on which
moonlight is exceedingly bright

In Samvat 2005, during the month of Bhadarva, just before the Diwali festival, Jeevanpran Swamibapa adopted an illness and remained in hospital until the Sharad-poonam festival. He then returned to the temple in Maninagar. There, Jeevanpran Bapashree gave his divine lustrous *darshan* and said to Swamibapa, "Now celebrate the festival with great joy and fervour." After saying these words, Jeevanpran Bapashree withdrew his *darshan*. Jeevanpran Swamibapa immediately bid farewell to the illness and went to Kutch.

In Samvat 2006 Kartik Sud 11 to 15 (Tuesday 1st to Saturday 5th November 1949), Jeevanpran Swamibapa held the Centenary Celebration of Jeevanpran Bapashree in Kutch at the Chhatri site in Vrushpur. Devotees from Kutch, Gujarat and Saurashtra assembled and took part in the festivities. They were all impressed by the organisation and arrangements of this festival. The religious discourses and cultural programmes were all based on the supreme tenets. This was the first time in Kutch that an electric sound system and electric lighting had been used, so everyone became astonished by this all. Everyone experienced the same bliss and joy at this festival as they did during Jeevanpran Bapashree's grand festivals. Jeevanpran Swamibapa inspired young devotees to perform drama productions based on religious themes and thereby started a novel method of conveying and propagating the messages of the faith.

An assembly held during the
Jeevanpran Bapashree
Centenary Festival

In Samvat 2007 (C.E. 1951), Jeevanpran Swamibapa sat in continuous meditation for thirteen days at Shree Swaminarayan Temple, Kadi.

Miraculous Swamibapa

Jeevanpran Swamibapa travelled from village to village throughout Kutch and Gujarat, enlightening all to the spiritual knowledge and principles of Jeevanpran Bapashree. He also performed many extraordinary miracles and revealed his great prowess.

Once, Jeevanpran Swamibapa went to the Ganga of Rampur in Kutch with many of his devotees. He ceremonially bathed Shree Harikrishna Maharaj with milk and yoghurt. Everyone then took the opportunity to demonstrate their devotion towards Jeevanpran Swamibapa and performed *aarti* to him. Thereafter everyone played *raas*. They sang the *kirtan*:

આજે તો શ્રીજી પ્રગટ ભગવાન, દે છે આત્યંતિક મોક્ષનું દાન

Aaje to Shreeji pragat Bhagwan, de chhe aatyantik moksh-nu daan

Today, the supreme Lord Shreeji is present before us,
bestowing eternal salvation to all.

It was late into the evening when the dancing concluded. Everyone had danced with such enthusiasm and energy to the rhythm of the *dokad* that they were extremely hungry. But, how could they find food in the forest? However, the one who provides auspicious delight everywhere, even in a forest, Jeevanpran Swamibapa, was with them. The *sants* had a half-filled, small tin of *magaj*, for offering to the Lord. Jeevanpran Swamibapa offered this to Shree Harikrishna Maharaj and then said everybody, "Everyone form a queue to receive *prasad*." There were all about 300 to 400 devotees and there was only a half filled tin of *prasad*. So they prayed, "Swamibapa! You and the *sants* eat. We will be satisfied by that." Jeevanpran Swamibapa replied, "We all will take *prasad*." According to Swamibapa's command, everyone came and held out their hands to receive the *prasad*. Jeevanpran Swamibapa started serving handfuls of *magaj* to each devotee. The line of devotees ended, but the tin of *prasad* remained just as full it was! Jeevanpran Swamibapa then asked, "If there is anyone left, come and take *prasad*." Who would remain without receiving such divine *prasad*? Jeevanpran Swamibapa asked again, "If anyone wishes to have *prasad* again, let them come." However, the devotees were fully satisfied, and replied, "Swamibapa! We have all had enough to eat."

Jeevanpran
Life and soul

Ganga
A site outside the village of Rampur where a spring of water emerges from the ground. This spring is regarded as the sacred waters of the River Ganges. Lord Shree Swaminarayan and Jeevanpran Bapashree had visited this site on many occasions and held assemblies here. It is therefore regarded as being a sacred site of pilgrimage

Shree Harikrishna Maharaj
Small golden Murti of Lord Shree Swaminarayan carried by the sants (ascetics) for offering adoration and performing daily religious observances or practices to while travelling

Aarti
Ritual ceremony. See Appendix

Raas
Communal dance where participants circumambulate around the Lord

Kirtan
Devotional song, praising the Lord

Dokad
Musical instrument

Sants
Ascetics, the closest Western equivalent being monks

Magaj
Indian sweet delicacy

Prasad
Consecrated offerings; food or other articles that have been blessed by the Lord

it would take him three days. So he set off by car. It was raining heavily. He left the main road and took a short cut. However, this road was rough and muddy. He came across a river with a temporary bridge over it. Whilst crossing the river, the car slipped off the bridge and fell into the river. There was not much water in the river. The car had overturned. All four wheels were turning in the air. Bhimjibhai became frightened.

All of a sudden, he heard Jeevanpran Swamibapa's gentle voice, "Bhimjibhai! Do not be scared. Nothing has happened to the car. Open the left-hand side door and come out of the car." Encouraged by this voice, Bhimjibhai opened the left-hand side door and came out of the car. He stood in the river, looking at the car. There was no way he could turn the car upright on his own. Just then, a Mwanzan police van arrived. They saw Bhimjibhai and the car and helped to turn the car over and then dragged it out of the river onto the road. As soon as they turned the ignition, the engine started. The police inspector tested the car to make sure it was safe and then handed it over to Bhimjibhai to continue his journey. From there, Bhimjibhai reached Tabora from where he took a train. He arrived at Dar-es-Salaam station early the next morning. Jadvabhai Murjibhai and others had come to receive him. Bhimjibhai was amazed at this. He had not informed anyone of the train he was going to take. So how did the devotees know when to go to meet him? He asked Jadvabhai, "Without any message, how did you come to know about my arrival?" Jadvabhai replied, "Jeevanpran Swamibapa told us to go to the station as you were coming. So we did."

From the station, Bhimjibhai arrived before Jeevanpran Swamibapa and prostrated in reverence to him. Jeevanpran Swamibapa said 'Jay Swaminarayan' to him and asked, "You have not been hurt too much, have you?" Bhimjibhai fell at Jeevanpran Swamibapa's divine feet and said, "Bapa! You are my protector. How can I come to any harm?"

In this manner, Jeevanpran Swamibapa protects and rescues his devotees. To his loving devotees, nothing is dearer than Jeevanpran Swamibapa. All the devotees who have served and are serving Lord Shree Swaminarayan, Jeevanpran Bapashree and Jeevanpran Swamibapa during the festivals, with their mind, body and wealth, enjoy the Lord's bliss during their current life and thereafter. By the divine grace of Jeevanpran Swamibapa, the economic, social and spiritual status of his devotees progresses day by day.

Dharampur, Shree Swaminarayan Palli, Vaghjipur, Karjisan, Vadodara, Delhi and many other places. According to the command of Sadguru Swamishree (Shree Ishwarcharandasji Swami), the *Murtis* of Purna Purushottam Lord Shree Swaminarayan, Shreeji-sankalp-swaroop Jeevanpran Bapashree and other Sankalp-swaroop were installed in these temples. The Karan Satsang was truly blooming.

Sadguru
Status of eminent ascetics (sants)

Murti
Divine image or form of the Lord

Purna Purushottam
Almighty, supreme Lord of Lords

Shreeji–sankalp–swaroop
The physical embodiment of the thoughts of Lord Swaminarayan, i.e. those who give darshan upon this Earth by the will of the Lord; they are synonymous with the Lord Himself

Karan Satsang
True association with Lord Swaminarayan. See Chapter 1

Shashtipurti
Sixtieth Anniversary

Kirtan
Devotional songs praising the Lord

The magnificent procession held during the Shashtipurti Platinum Tula Mahotsav, through the main streets of Ahmedabad

In this manner, Jeevanpran Swamibapa fulfilled the promises he had made to Sadguru Swamishree. Describing all these, Jeevanpran Swamibapa composed a *kirtan*.

The words to this *kirtan* are:

સંદેશ કહું બીજો સારો રે, બંધવા સંદેશ કહું બીજો સારો
ગુરુ રાજિપા માટે ન્યારો રે, બંધવા સંદેશ કહું બીજો સારો ....

Sandesh kahu beejo saaro re, bandhavaa sandesh kahu beejo saaro
Guru raajipaa maate nyaaro re, bandhavaa sandesh kahu beejo saaro

I have wonderful news to tell you all, which will attain the guru's pleasure.

Shree Swaminarayan Temples that Jeevanpran Swamibapa constructed in the Panchmahal district are exceptionally worthy of note. The rural people of this undeveloped district were completely engrossed in superstition, spells, spirits, curses and blind faith. Jeevanpran Swamibapa relieved them from their blind beliefs, taught them about the true religious decree and made them disciples of Lord Shree Swaminarayan. Even those who performed spells and evoked incantations became followers and started chanting the name of Shree Swaminarayan in the temple.

In Samvat 2025 Maha Vad Amas to Fagan Sud 3 (Sunday 16th Febraury to Wednesday 19th February 1969), the Rajat Pratishtha Mahotsav was celebrated on the auspicious occasion of the 25th anniversary of the *Murti* installation of Shree Ghanshyam Maharaj at Shree Swaminarayan Temple, Maninagar.

In Samvat 2026 Kartik Sud 11 to Kartik Sud 15 (Thursday 20th November to Sunday 23rd November 1969), the Jeevanpran Bapashree Shat Rajat Jayanti Mahotsav was held to celebrate the 125th anniversary of Jeevanpran Bapashree's manifestation on the Earth. Concurrently, the Jeevanpran Swamibapa 40th Diksha Jayanti Mahotsav was also celebrated to acknowledge the completion of forty years since Jeevanpran Swamibapa was initiated as a *sant*. Thousands of devotees gathered to experience the divinity of these extraordinary festivals.

Rajat Pratishtha Mahotsav
Silver Jubilee Festival

Diksha
Initiation into the ascetic fraternity

Jayanti
Anniversary

Mahotsav
Festival

Sants
Ascetics, the closest Western equivalent being monks

Acharya Swamishree offers adoration to Jeevanpran Swamibapa during the Diksha Jayanti Mahotsav

International Tour

In Samvat 2026 (commencing on Bhadarva Sud 5, Sunday 6th September 1970), Jeevanpran Swamibapa, together with 50 *sants* and disciples, embarked on an international tour for the propagation of the faith. During the tour, he visited Nairobi, Mombasa, Dar-es-Salaam, Zanzibar, Arusha, Kampala, Entebe and various other places in Africa. Wherever Jeevanpran Swamibapa went, he brought joy to all and bestowed divine ecstasy on all the local inhabitants and devotees.

Jeevanpran
Life and soul

Sant
Ascetic, the closest Western equivalent being a monk

Jeevanpran Swamibapa being garlanded by the Mayor of Bradford, Mr E. B. Singleton, during his tour of the UK

Jeevanpran Swamibapa also went to England and visited London, Bradford, Loughborough, Manchester, Oldham, Bolton, Brighton and many other towns and cities. In all these places, he held general assemblies during which religious drama productions, religious ceremonies and other cultural events were performed. It was autumn and the seasons were changing. The sky always remained covered with dark clouds. The wind blew and the rain poured everyday. The Sun rarely emerged from amongst the clouds and it was constantly foggy. However, wherever Lord Shree Swaminarayan, Jeevanpran Bapashree and Jeevanpran Swamibapa preside, spring is always in bloom. On 17th October 1970, a grand procession, in honour of Lord Shree Swaminarayan and Jeevanpran Swamibapa, was to be held through the streets of Central London. On the day before, the weather forecasts on television and radio had said that the 17th would remain cloudy and windy, and it would rain all day.

267

The devotees were disheartened by this. If it rains and the sky remains overcast, how could the procession be a joyous occasion? Leading disciples approached Jeevanpran Swamibapa and prayed for the sky to remain clear and for the Sun to shine, so that they could enjoy the procession. Jeevanpran Swamibapa said, "Do not worry! Shree Ghanshyam Maharaj has reserved the date of the 17th for you. Regardless of what anyone else says, the sky will be clear and the weather will remain pleasant. You will not face any problems."

The next day, just as Jeevanpran Swamibapa had said, the clouds vanished and the sky remained clear all day. On 17th October 1970, a magnificent procession was held, with great enthusiasm, in Central London. The procession concluded in Trafalgar Square, where a public assembly was held. Jeevanpran Swamibapa addressed the gathered vast crowds and the *sants* performed cultural folk dances (*raas*).

In the same manner, Jeevanpran Swamibapa toured the United States of America, where he visited New York, New Jersey, Chicago, Washington DC, Buffalo, Seattle, and various other places, and also crossed the border to Niagara in Canada. Wherever Jeevanpran Swamibapa visited, he held religious and cultural programmes, including grand assemblies, through which he professed the fundamentals of the religious decree to the masses.

Jeevanpran Swamibapa gives darshan at Trafalgar Square

As a part of the tour, Jeevanpran Swamibapa also visited Europe with the *sants* and devotees. He travelled to Paris - France, Rome - Italy, and Jersey, amongst other prominent places. Jeevanpran Swamibapa attracted innumerable souls who were seeking salvation, to the faith and out of his sheer grace, made them all worthy of salvation. Many expatriate Indians residing in those countries, witnessed the various programmes held throughout the tour and proclaimed, "Jeevanpran Swamibapa has brought India to us here." In this manner, Jeevanpran Swamibapa lit the flame of Indian culture among the Indians living abroad and enabled them to experience the ecstasy of their motherland.

When Jeevanpran Swamibapa returned to India after this tour, he was warmly welcomed at Mumbai and a grand welcoming reception was held in the prestigious Bharatiya Vidya Bhavan (Samvat 2027 Maha Vad 10 Saturday 20th February 1971). Representatives of various cultural, educational and industrial institutions showed their appreciation of him and garlanded Jeevanpran Swamibapa and offered adoration to him. A religious opera, 'Sadguru Praudh Pratap' was performed during this assembly.

Jeevanpran Swamibapa being welcomed back to India by Mumbai's prominent dignitaries including Shree Naval Tata

Jeevanpran Swamibapa then arrived in Ahmedabad. A large number of devotees had gathered at Ahmedabad airport to greet Jeevanpran Swamibapa and a grand procession was led through the streets of Ahmedabad (Samvat 2027 Maha Vad Amas Thursday 25th February 1971). An unprecedented greeting festival was

Sanatan-dharma-samrat
Emperor of the eternal
Vedic religion

held in the grounds of Shree Swaminarayan Temple, Maninagar (Samvat 2027 Fagan Sud 1 Friday 26th February 1971) during which famous scholars commended Jeevanpran Swamibapa with an honorary title 'Sanatan-dharma-samrat'. Jeevanpran Swamibapa then visited the various villages and towns of Gujarat and Kutch. Everywhere he went, processions and welcoming assemblies were held. In this manner, Jeevanpran Swamibapa alleviates his devotees from their troubles and tensions, and ensures they experience bliss during this life and thereafter.

Sixty-one Days
Continuous Meditation

Once, when Jeevanpran Swamibapa was presiding with *sants* and disciples, he announced, "I want to sit in meditation." Everyone thought he must be speaking of his normal routine of meditating so continued in what they were doing. However, Swamibapa continued, "It is not certain when I will awaken from the meditation." Everyone was amazed and puzzled about what Swamibapa had intended to do. Everyone collectively prayed to Swamibapa, so at the time, he conceded and said, "Well, I will see."

After a month, Jeevanpran Swamibapa reiterated his wish and revealed his firm determination to sit in meditation. The *sants* and disciples humbly prayed, "Swamibapa! You are the almighty, independent (*swatantra*) personage. You have manifested to bring joy to our lives. Have mercy on us and continue to give your *darshan* just as you are." Seeing his *sants* and devotees so emotional, Swamibapa remained silent and at that time, he made them all forget about his intentions. However, the *sants* and devotees knew that Jeevanpran Swamibapa had already made up his mind.

Approximately 15 days later, Jeevanpran Swamibapa once again spoke about sitting in meditation. The *sants* and disciples again prayed to him. Jeevanpran Swamibapa remained silent and sat with his eyes closed. One minute, two minutes, ten minutes passed. Swamibapa opened his eyes and signalled for some paper and a pen. He wrote something on the paper and said, "Tell me! Shall I listen to you or to Shree Ghanshyam Maharaj? I have received instructions from Shree Ghanshyam Maharaj." Everyone put their hands together and humbly requested, "Bapa! Have mercy and tell us the instructions you have received." Jeevanpran Swamibapa handed over the piece of paper. Everyone was curious and eager to know what was written on the paper. The writing on the letter was set vertically.

Jeevanpran
Life and soul

Sants
Ascetics, the closest Western equivalent being monks

Darshan
The visualisation of the Lord. Also the act of looking with reverence and devotion at the image or deity in the shrine, sometimes of seeing a holy person

Murti
Divine image or form of the Lord

Swastikasan
Cross-legged posture where the feet are interlocked between the thighs of the opposite legs which forms the sign of the Swastik

The command that Jeevanpran Swamibapa received from Lord Shree Swaminarayan

Dhyey	Aim
Aadarsh-ne	Ideal
Paamvaa	To attain
Maun	Silence
Tap	Austere
Ekant-ne	Solitude
Sevo	Undergo
Ordaa-maj	Only in room
Raho	Remain
Anya	Another
Aadesh	Command
Male-j	Receive, only then
Bahaar	Outside
Aavo	Come
Amal	Abide by
Karo	Do

To attain the ideal aim, take an austere vow of silence.
Observe solitude in this room. Come outside only after you
receive further commands. Abide by these instructions.

After reading Lord Ghanshyam Maharaj's instructions to His Holiness almighty Jeevanpran Swamibapa, everyone became speechless. They did not like the fact that their beloved Jeevanpran Swamibapa would sit in continuous meditation without taking any food or drink. On the other hand, it was the command of Shree Ghanshyam Maharaj. Everyone was stunned into silence and merely stared at Jeevanpran Swamibapa. Jeevanpran Swamibapa said, "We must remain just as the Lord keeps us and see whatever He reveals. Wait and see what the Lord wishes to show us." Everyone remained silent, and gave full respect to Swamibapa's words.

The very next day (Samvat 2028 Posh Sud 2, Sunday 19th December 1971), Jeevanpran Swamibapa sat in continuous meditation in his room, situated in Shree Muktajeevan Ashram. His divine *Murti* was seated upright in the *Swastikasan*, with his lotus eyes closed. The days began to pass. Ten days, fifteen days, one month passed. Still, Jeevanpran Swamibapa did not come out of meditation. The beloved devotees started to pray. Whenever they went to

Satsang
Fellowship, associated with
the Swaminarayan religion

Jeevanpran Swamibapa
meditating continuously
for 61 days

the temple they would pray to Shree Ghanshyam Maharaj. They would prostrate and pray outside Swamibapa's room with tears of love rolling from their eyes. The news spread swiftly throughout the entire *Satsang*. Prayers came by letter, telegram and telephone, from all over the world. Everyone had the same sentiments in their hearts, "Swamibapa! Have mercy on us all and come out quickly from the meditation."

Shree Vasantbhai composed his emotional prayer into a kirtan and sang:

સ્વામીબાપા આવોને, દર્શન આપોને
છૂપાયા છો શાને? આવું કાંઈ ના ચાલે ....

Swamibapa aavo-ne, darshan aapo-ne
chhoopaayaa chho shaane? aavu kai na chaale

Swamibapa, come and give darshan.
Why are you hiding yourself? This is unbearable.

273

Panchamrut-snan
Ceremonial bathing using the five nectars: Milk, yoghurt, clarified butter, honey and saffron water

Aarti
Ritual ceremony. See Appendix

Patotsav Ceremony
Vedic ceremony performed to mark the anniversary of the installation of idols (Murtis) in temples

Kirtans
Devotional songs, praising the Lord

Six weeks had passed since Jeevanpran Swamibapa began his meditation. Still, there were no indications about when he would awaken. The anniversary day (*patotsav*) of the installation of the *Murti* of Shree Ghanshyam Maharaj in Maninagar, Fagan Sud 3, had nearly arrived. Every year, this auspicious day had been celebrated in the divine presence of Jeevanpran Swamibapa. Everyone is usually given the golden opportunity of witnessing Jeevanpran Swamibapa performing the Panchamrut-snan Ceremony to Shree Ghanshyam Maharaj. Will Swamibapa grant everyone such *darshan* this year or will he remain in continuous meditation? No-one was able to predict what would happen.

People from all over the country and from around the world were frantically asking for news about when Swamibapa would give *darshan* again. Nobody could answer their questions. Fagan Sud 3 was coming nearer and nearer. Just then, a note was sent from the room, in which it was written, "I will come out after the 61st day." Within the blink of an eyelid, this joyous news spread everywhere. Everyone had an uncontrollable eagerness for Swamibapa's *darshan*. A large marquee was erected and a festival was organised. On Fagan Sud 3 (Samvat 2028, Thursday 17th February 1972), after 61 days, Jeevanpran Swamibapa bestowed his *darshan* to all. As soon as he emerged from his room, devotees offered *aarti* to him. Jeevanpran Swamibapa then went to the temple where he performed the *darshan* of the supreme Lord Shree Ghanshyam Maharaj. All the *sants* and devotees were overjoyed to have the *darshan* of Jeevanpran Swamibapa and cheered in acclamation. Jeevanpran Swamibapa performed *aarti* to Shree Ghanshyam Maharaj and prayed to Him. He then ceremonially bathed Shree Ghanshyam Maharaj with milk, yoghurt, clarified butter, honey, sugar, saffron water and fresh water. He sprinkled the consecrated water over everyone and granted them all the immense bliss of this auspicious *darshan*. Again he offered *aarti* to the Lord, and then the devotees too, had the unique opportunity to perform *aarti*. In this manner, Jeevanpran Swamibapa performed the annual Patotsav Ceremony. He performed *darshan* to the Lord and proceeded to go to the ladies' temple to perform the *Murti* installation ceremony. As he reached the main doors of the temple, devotees offered *aarti* to him. He presided on a palanquin and was carried to the ladies' temple, accompanied by *sants* and devotees who were singing *kirtans*. Jeevanpran Swamibapa performed the *Murti* installation ceremony at the ladies' temple and was then taken to the temple forecourt, where a large marquee had been erected to hold the vast assembly. Everyone cheered in delight. Jeevanpran Swamibapa

Jeevanpran Swamibapa performs
the Panchamrut–snan Ceremony
to Shree Ghanshyam Maharaj

Vyas-pith
One of the incarnations of God
incarnated in the form of a sage
named Vyas. The extremely
learned Vyas subsequently
authored several of the great
Hindu scriptures including the
Mahabharat and the Bhagwad
Geeta. Pith means elevated seat,
usually from which sermons are
delivered. A Vyas-pith is therefore
an elevated seat reserved for
extremely knowledgeable, learned
and revered scholars to
deliver sermons

Yogi
One who has accomplished the
virtues of the Yog philosophy

Muktas
Liberated souls

graced the stage and presided on the *Vyas-pith.* Everyone performed *darshan* to
Jeevanpran Swamibapa. His *Murti* was like that of an ascetic. He had a long
beard, like that of a *Yogi.* His lotus face was glistening with divine lustre and
his divine lotus eyes were bright and lustrous. Recently, it had been impossible
to have the enchanting *darshan* of Jeevanpran Swamibapa's *Murti,* but today,
by his mercy, it had become possible. Jeevanpran Swamibapa presided on the
Vyas-pith with his eyes closed. Occasionally, he opened his lotus eyes, gazed
mercifully at the devotees and then closed them again. Listening to the prayers
of everyone, he was gently smiling at the *sants* and disciples and was showing
immense affection towards them all.

Everyone then filed past Jeevanpran Swamibapa, and offered adoration and
aarti to him. Everyone was careful so that he would not experience any kind
of discomfort. Everyone humbly prayed, "Oh Swamibapa! Make us happy by

275

Everyone moved closer to Jeevanpran Swamibapa. He then mercifully announced, "Whilst I was in meditation, Shree Ghanshyam Maharaj gave me His divine lustrous *darshan* and placed His hand on my head. His servant (Swamibapa), immediately stood up and embraced Shree Ghanshyam Maharaj and humbly prayed to Him, 'Maharaj! What is your command?'

"Shree Ghanshyam Maharaj – Lord Shree Swaminarayan patted me on my cheek and commanded me, 'From the time I entrusted the helm of the *Satsang* to Sadguru Shree Gopalanand Swami, Shree Swaminarayan Gadi has been established. Now the time has come to give it a physical embodiment. Give it a physical form and name it Shree Swaminarayan Gadi. The *sants* and devotees of this, My Gadi, will progress day by day, achieve salvation and will attain the divine ecstasy of My *Murti*. Such are My divine blessings.'

"When Shree Ghanashyam Maharaj said these words to me, I replied, 'Maharaj, I accept Your command.' Shree Ghanashyam Maharaj continued, 'The key to eternal salvation lies with this Gadi. I will take, whosoever becomes a devotee of Shree Swaminarayan Gadi, to Akshardham. Only those who resort to Shree Swaminarayan Gadi will attain eternal salvation (*aatyantik-moksh*).' Once again Shree Ghanshyam Maharaj embraced me and said, 'Now make preparations.' These were His words."

After revealing the command, Jeevanpran Swamibapa turned to the assembled *sants* and devotees and asked, "Tell me. What shall we do?" The *sants* and devotees replied, "Now, with pleasure and zeal, we will start preparing." Jeevanpran Swamibapa said, "Very well. Proceed with the preparations."

By the command of Jeevanpran Swamibapa, everyone enthusiastically started making preparations. Invitation cards were printed, a marquee was erected, and all the surroundings were beautifully decorated. With their mind, body and wealth, everyone offered their services during the festival. Everyone was eager to please Jeevanpran Swamibapa and became engrossed in the preparations.

In this manner, Jeevanpran Swamibapa Suvarna Jayanti Smruti Mahotsav commenced. Devotees came from all over the world to take part in the festivities and enjoy the various programmes. A grand procession was held through the streets of Ahmedabad city.

The Physical Embodiment of Shree Swaminarayan Gadi

The auspicious morning of Samvat 2028 Bhadarva Vad Amas (Saturday 7th October 1972), Jeevanpran Swamibapa's manifestation day arrived. After completing their daily routines, the devotees congregated in the temple for the *darshan* of Shree Ghanshyam Maharaj during the *shangar aarti*. When Jeevanpran Swamibapa arrived in the temple, all the devotees hailed in acclamation. Jeevanpran Swamibapa then performed *aarti* to Shree Ghanshyam Maharaj.

> The English date for Jeevanpran Swamibapa's manifestation on this Earth and the physical embodiment of Shree Swaminarayan Gadi were both 7th October. This reveals further the purpose of Jeevanpran Swamibapa's manifestation; to give a physical form to the supreme Lord's eternal Gadi.

Purna Purushottam Lord Shree Swaminarayan – Shree Ghanshyam Maharaj was granting His radiant *darshan* to all. He was adorned with a golden crown upon His head, golden *kundal* on His ears and golden robes. In one hand, He carried a sword. In the other, He was holding a rifle and a silk handkerchief. An ornate gold waist-band was adorned around His waist and He was wearing golden anklets. In this manner, Lord Shree Swaminarayan – Shree Ghanshyam Maharaj was showering the entire assembly with His blissful salvation-granting *darshan*, by which everyone became delighted. When this temple was first established, there was nothing here. Subsequently, by the grace of Lord Shree Swaminarayan, Jeevanpran Bapashree and Jeevanpran Swamibapa, a large complex had been created. Jeevanpran Swamibapa has shown many miraculous events and saved innumerable devotees from their adversities. At the end of their life, he has granted his devotees his divine *darshan* and taken them to Akshardham. On many occasions, Jeevanpran Swamibapa revealed beads of perspiration emerging from his *Murti*, and in this manner, revealed to all that his *Murti* in an idol form (*pratima*) and he, are the same.

The *sants* and devotees prayed to Jeevanpran Swamibapa to install his *Murtis* in the temple. Two *Murtis*, one of Jeevanpran Swamibapa seated in the Tula (in remembrance of the various Tula ceremonies) and the other of Jeevanpran Swamibapa presiding on an elephant during a grand procession, were

Jeevanpran
Life and soul

Darshan
The visualisation of the Lord

Shangar aarti
Second of the five daily aartis performed after the Lord is adorned in full regalia See Appendix

Aarti
Ritual ceremony. See Appendix

Purna Purushottam
Almighty, supreme Lord of Lords

Kundal
Ornate jewellery worn on the ears usually shaped like a fish or a peacock

The Lord's regalia
On Amas days, the Lord is seen carrying items of weaponry such as a sword, rifle, dagger etc. These articles are symbolic of the fact that the Lord is constantly protecting His devotees from their internal enemies of lust, anger, arrogance etc. and defending them from worldly influences

Akshardham
The divine abode of Lord Shree Swaminarayan

Murti
Divine image or form of the Lord

Sants
Ascetics, the closest western equivalent being monks

Tula
Ancient and auspicious weighing ceremony

279

ceremonially installed, to much acclamation, in the presence of Jeevanpran Swamibapa. *Thal* was offered and *aarti* was performed. The devotees also offered *aarti* with great pleasure. After performing *darshan* in the temple, everyone came down to where the office is currently situated. Beside the office is the room in which Jeevanpran Swamibapa sat in continuous meditation for 31 days in Samvat 2001. He had also meditated in that room on numerous other occasions. As an eternal memorial to Swamibapa's episodes of continuous meditation, a seated *Murti* of Swamibapa giving his salvation-granting *darshan* to all, was ceremoniously installed there according to Vedic traditions. The *sants* and devotees hailed in acclamation, bowed and prostrated, and offered *aarti*.

The Murti of Jeevanpran Swamibapa installed to commemorate his numerous episodes of continuous meditation

Then Jeevanpran Swamibapa along with the *sants* and devotees proceeded to the Suvarna Tula Smruti Bhavan (Shree Swaminarayan Tower). The *sants* and devotees sang *kirtans* and chanted the Swaminarayan name as they walked behind Jeevanpran Swamibapa. At the Tower, verses from the Vedas were being recited. As soon as Jeevanpran Swamibapa arrived, everyone hailed in acclamation.

Jeevanpran Swamibapa then ceremonially installed the *Murtis* of Purna Purushottam Lord Shree Swaminarayan, Shreeji-sankalp-murti Jeevanpran Bapashree, Shreeji-sankalp-murti Shree Gopalanand Swami, Shreeji-sankalp-murti Shree Nirgundasji Swami and Shreeji-sankalp-murti Shree Ishwarcharandasji Swami, and then perfomed *aarti*. In remembrance of Jeevanpran Swamibapa's Golden Jubilee, a *Murti* of Jeevanpran Swamibapa

Thal
Food offerings to the Lord

Vedic
From the ancient Hindu scriptures the Vedas

Kirtan
Devotional song, praising the Lord

Vedas
Ancient Hindu scriptures.

Purna Purushottam
Almighty, supreme Lord of Lords

Shreeji-sankalp-murti
The physical embodiment of the thoughts of Lord Swaminarayan, i.e. those who give darshan upon this Earth by the will of the Lord; they are synonymous with the Lord Himself

Shree Swaminarayan Tower

Sankalp-swaroops
The physical embodiment of the thoughts of Lord Swaminarayan, i.e. those who give darshan upon this Earth by the will of the Lord; they are synonymous with the Lord Himself

Karan Satsang
True association with Lord Swaminarayan. See Chapter 1

seated on the Tula was ceremonially installed with Vedic ceremonies and then *aartis* were performed. In this manner, Purna Purushottam Lord Shree Swaminarayan along with His Sankalp-swaroops, the guardians of the Karan Satsang presided here. Purna Purushottam Lord Shree Swaminarayan took His divine seat magnificently presiding alongside His Sankalp-swaroops, through whom He has liberated innumerable souls, given *darshan* to them in the final moments of their lives and led them to Akshardham. What an extraordinary, divine event!

The divine Murtis of Lord Shree Swaminarayan and His Sankalp–swaroops that give darshan at Shree Swaminarayan Tower. In commemoration of Jeevanpran Swamibapa's Golden Jubilee, he is seated in the original Tula that was used during his Golden Tula in 1957

281

The eminent scholars then performed Swamibapa's coronation ceremony by reciting verses from the Vedas. And then performed the Tilakaayat Ceremony by applying sandalwood paste to his forehead. Jeevanpran Swamibapa gave his glorious *darshan* enthroned on Shree Swaminarayan Gadi, surrounded by the royal symbols; the ceremonial umbrella, *chammar*, mace and *abdagiri*. With great enthusiasm the *sants* and devotees offered *aarti*.

Acharya Swamishree and leading disciples performing the panchamrut snan ceremony to the lotus feet of Jeevanpran Swamibapa

In this manner, Shree Swaminarayan Gadi was given a physical embodiment. The auspicious divine will of Purna Purushottam Lord Shree Swaminarayan had been fulfilled. The prophecy of the *Nand-padvi sants*, who had passed this forecast to other *sants*, had today become reality. The divine words of Jeevanpran Bapashree, 'Shreejimaharaj is like a Baniya. Slowly but surely, He will take everything and one day, He will ensure everything is set right' had come true. Shree Swaminarayan *Sampraday* had been revealed in its true, pure and real form; the true religious decree, discipline and obedience, the supreme *upasana* and glory.

Adya Acharya-pravar
Pioneer and Chief Spiritual
Preceptor of the throne

Presiding upon Shree Swaminarayan Gadi, the Adya Acharya-pravar of Shree Swaminarayan Gadi Jeevanpran Swamibapa delivered his first blessings and said,

"*Sants* and devotees, the beloved children of Lord Shree Swaminarayan and Jeevanpran Bapashree, and disciples of Shree Swaminarayan Gadi! I, as your guru, spiritual teacher and Acharya, along with my divine blessings say 'Jay Shree Swaminarayan' to you all. I want to share my experience with you all. I am sure that you are all eager to hear about this. The command from that experience has now taken a physical form. The result of that command has been echoed from all your hearts and has reached me. This clearly shows that the act performed today has occurred through the resolute will of Lord Shree Swaminarayan - Shree Ghanshyam Maharaj.

"As you all know, after I returned from the international spiritual tour, I sat in continuous meditation for 61 days. By the mercy of Lord Shree Swaminarayan - Shree Ghanshyam Maharaj, I was granted the bliss of becoming one with Him. The ecstasy of this unity cannot be expressed in words. That pleasure can only be experienced. To experience union with Lord Shree Swaminarayan – Shree Ghanshyam Maharaj is truly enchanting. I wish to tell you about one occasion that occurred whilst I was unified with the Lord. You all have total faith in me and are devoted to me as your guru. Therefore, you accept my words as the commands of Lord Shree Swaminarayan and abide by them. The command I wish to give you today is a direct decree from Lord Shree Swaminarayan - Shree Ghanshyam Maharaj. This loving ordination was given to me by Lord Shree Swaminarayan - Shree Ghanshyam Maharaj whilst I was united with Him. I wish to convey that command to you all. I have no doubt that you will willingly accept and abide by it. You must firmly realise that this is the ordination of our merciful Lord Shree Swaminarayan – Shree Ghanshyam Maharaj.

"Before I reveal the ordination, I must clarify one issue. Lord Shree Swaminarayan – Shree Ghanshyam Maharaj gave me this command. The attainment that you have all received by the execution of this command, was also bestowed by Him. As a consequence of His inspiration, the devotees, living here and abroad, have offered their prayers. What a wonderful sequence of events!

"I am now revealing this directive to you all."

289

श्रीजीसंकल्प...भूत विश्व...पू...भणि ...स्त्रसंरक्षक
भारतभास्कर विशिष्टाद्वैतशिरोमणि महामंडलेश्वर
सनातनधर्मसम्राट् धर्मधुरंधर आद्य आचार्यप्रवर
धर्मप्राण १००८ श्री मुक्तजीवन स्वामीबापा संस्थापित
॥ श्री स्वामिनारायण गादी ॥

The Lord's Command

Purna Purushottam Lord Shree Swaminarayan declared, "From the time I entrusted the helm of the entire *Satsang* to Sadguru Shrce Gopalanand Swami, I have established Shree Swaminarayan Gadi. Now the time has come to give it a physical embodiment and name it Shree Swaminarayan Gadi. The *sants* and devotees of this, My Gadi, will progress day by day and will attain the divine ecstasy of My *Murti* and achieve salvation. Such are My divine blessings."

Jeevanpran Swamibapa conveys the command of Lord Shree Swaminarayan

Jeevanpran Swamibapa continued, "According to this command, I have formally established Shree Swaminarayan Gadi. From today, you all are disciples of Shree Swaminarayan Gadi. I command you all to always abide by the directives you receive from Shree Swaminarayan Gadi. You must have the utmost of faith that Lord Shree Swaminarayan – Shree Ghanshyam Maharaj Himself has established Shree Swaminarayan Gadi. That very same supreme Shree Sahajanand Swami – Lord Shree Swaminarayan is bestowing His divine blessings and saying that all those who seek salvation and are, or will become disciples of Shree Swaminarayan Gadi, will attain eternal salvation (*aatyantik-moksh*). Instil these words of Lord Shree Swaminarayan – Shree Ghanshyam Maharaj within your heart and ensure that you abide by them with your mind, deeds and words. Those who have love and faith and believe in the principles and tenets of the Shree Satsang Mahasabha, Shree Swaminarayan Siddhant Uttejak Trust (the trust for the encouragement of the principles of Lord Shree Swaminarayan), Shree Suvarna Jayanti Mahotsav Smarak Trust (the

Purna Purushottam
Almighty, supreme Lord of Lords

Satsang
Fellowship associated with the Swaminarayan religion

Sadguru
Status of eminent ascetics (sants)

Sants
Ascetics, the closest Western equivalent being monks

Murti
Divine image or form of the Lord

Jeevanpran
Life and soul

Shree Satsang Mahasabha
The trust established by Jeevanpran Abji Bapashree to save the principles and doctrines of the supreme Swaminarayan Sampraday from corruption and to reform the adminstration of the religious association

291

Adya Pithadhishwar
First holder of the throne

Sanatan-dharma-samrat
Emperor of the eternal
Vedic religion

Dharma-dhurandhar
Protector of the religion

Shreeji-sankalp-murti
The physical embodiment of the
thoughts of Lord Swaminarayan,
i.e. those who give darshan upon
this Earth by the will of the Lord;
they are synonymous with the
Lord Himself

Sadguru
Status of eminent
ascetics (sants)

Param Kalyan-kari
Ultimate bestower of salvation

Darshan
The visualisation of the Lord

Satsang
Fellowship associated with
the Swaminarayan religion

Parshads
The first stage of initiation into
ascetic life; ascetics who wear
white clothing

Acharya
Preceptor

Gruhasths
Those with family associations

trust in memory of the Golden Jubilee of Jeevanpran Swamibapa) and Shree Swaminarayan Siddhant Sajivan Mandals (the associations to sustain and propogate the true principles of Lord Shree Swaminarayan) are disciples of Shree Swaminarayan Gadi. You all must not have even a shadow of doubt about these words and blessings of Lord Shree Swaminarayan – Shree Ghanshyam Maharaj. Be immersed in these divine blessings of Lord Shree Swaminarayan – Shree Ghanshyam Maharaj, and remain rejoicing. And have firm faith that you have already attained eternal salvation. Make others, who are also seeking salvation, disciples of Shree Swaminarayan Gadi, and gain the divine favour of Lord Shree Swaminarayan – Shree Ghanshyam Maharaj. There is absolutely no doubt that Lord Shree Swaminarayan – Shree Ghanshyam Maharaj becomes immensely pleased with those who become disciples of Shree Swaminarayan Gadi."

Hearing these divine, nectar-filled words of the Adya Pithadhishwar of Shree Swaminarayan Gadi, Sanatan-dharma-samrat, Dharma-dhurandhar 1008 Shree Jeevanpran Swamibapa, the entire assembly enthusiastically hailed in acclamation, "Hail to Shree Ghanshyam Maharaj, hail to Shree Harikrishna Maharaj, hail to Shree Sahajanand Swami Maharaj, hail to Shree Swaminarayan Bhagwan, hail to Shreeji-sankalp-murti Bapashree, hail to Sadguru Shree, hail to Sanatan-dharma-samrat Param Kalyan-kari Jeevanpran Swamibapa."

From the divine words of Jeevanpran Swamibapa, all the *sants* and devotees understood that Purna Purushottam Lord Shree Swaminarayan – Shree Ghanshyam Maharaj Himself, had given *darshan* to him and commanded him to reveal Shree Swaminarayan Gadi to all. Accordingly, Jeevanpran Swamibapa established the Gadi. However, this Gadi had already been established from the time Lord Shree Swaminarayan entrusted the entire *Satsang* to Sadguru Shree Gopalanand Swami and made him the head of all the *sants, parshads, Acharyas* and *gruhasths*. This Gadi is the Gadi of the ascetics. It has been handed down through Sadguru Shree Gopalanand Swami's lineage of spiritual successors and has been given a physical embodiment by the fourth in Sadguru Shree Gopalanand Swami's succession. This Shree Swaminarayan Gadi is the supreme, paramount, eternal, original Gadi. Eternal salvation is attained by resorting to this Gadi.

Take resort at Shree Swaminarayan Gadi. Without doubt, the reward of eternal salvation will be attained.

Divine Miracles

Purna Purushottam Lord Shree Swaminarayan introduced extraordinary and divinely miraculous ways of granting salvation. These same extraordinary processes are continued today through the Adya Acharya of Shree Swaminarayan Gadi, Jeevanpran Swamibapa.

During their final moments, he grants his divine lustrous *darshan* to disciples and takes them to the abode. To some, he gives *darshan* and tells them to be ready on a particular day, and accordingly returns to take them to the divine abode. He sometimes gives *darshan* to relatives of disciples who live far away, and tells them that he has taken their relatives to the abode. Such extraordinary, divine and miraculous events still occur at Shree Swaminarayan Gadi, through Jeevanpran Swamibapa. There are numerous such miraculous events but only a few have been cited here.

In the village of Kera in Kutch, there lived a disciple of Shree Swaminarayan Gadi, Shree Naranbhai Valjibhai Khokhrai. Shreemad-acharya-pravar Jeevanpran Swamibapa gave *darshan* to him and said, "Four days from today, I will take you to the abode." He happily replied, "I am ready Swamibapa." Shree Naranbhai then completed all his outstanding financial and domestic issues and explained everything to his family. His wife asked, "Are you going away?" Naranbhai replied, "Swamibapa will come to our village and a great celebration will be held. Then, I will be going with him." His wife asked again, "But Swamibapa will be in Madhapur on Sharad Poonam. Will he also be coming to our village?" Naranbhai replied, "Before that, he will come here and grant his *darshan*." Everyone became pleased to hear this news.

On the fourth day, Lord Shree Swaminarayan, Jeevanpran Bapashree and Shreemad-acharya-pravar Jeevanpran Swamibapa gave their divine *darshan* together with a group of *sants*. They had arrived on a motor coach to take Shree Naranbhai.

At that time, the people of the village saw Jeevanpran Swamibapa entering Kera in a coach. The coach stopped outside Naranbhai's house. *Sants* were seen leaving and then boarding the coach. Naranbhai arrived, performed *darshan* to Swamibapa and then sat in the coach. The coach departed.

Murti
Divine image or form of the Lord

This was witnessed by many people of the village, who informed devotees of Shree Swaminarayan Gadi, "Your Swamibapa has come and gone to Naranbhai's house. Why have you not gone for *darshan*?" Hearing this news, the devotees hurried towards Naranbhai's house for Jeevanpran Swamibapa's *darshan*. However, whilst on the way, they received the news, "Naranbhai had left his physical body." Everyone understood what had happened. Jeevanpran Swamibapa had come to collect Naranbhai and take him to the abode. What a divine miracle! Such miracles occur only at Shree Swaminarayan Gadi.

A disciple of Shree Swaminarayan Gadi, Shree Bhalabhai Bapubhai Patel lived in the village of Kanbha. He was seriously ill. One of his close relatives, Shree Ratilalbhai was on his way to Ahmedabad. When he came near the town of Rakhiyal, he had the *darshan* of Jeevanpran Swamibapa sitting in a car. The car stopped, so he got off from his bicycle and went for *darshan*. Shreemad-acharya-pravar Jeevanpran Swamibapa said to him, "Return to Kanbha. I am going there to take Bhalabhai." Ratibhai replied, "Very well Bapa, but how will I possibly get there in time by bicycle?" Swamibapa said, "I will wait until you reach there." Swamibapa's car accelerated away. When Ratibhai reached Kanbha, the final rites were being performed. He said, 'Jay Shree Swaminarayan' to Bhalabhai and informed everyone what had happened. As soon as he finished speaking, Bhalabhai departed from his material body.

The key to eternal salvation (*aatyantik-moksh*) resides at Shree Swaminarayan Gadi in Maninagar. Therefore, salvation can only be attained by resorting to Shree Swaminarayan Gadi.

A disciple of Shree Swaminarayan Gadi, Karsan Bhagat, lived in the village of Salal. He was going to America. Before he left, he came to Shree Swaminarayan Temple in Maninagar for *darshan*. However, Jeevanpran Swamibapa was away at the time. Karsanbhai prayed to the *Murti* of Purna Purushottam Lord Shree Swaminarayan and Jeevanpran Swamibapa, to remain with him. He prostrated in reverence to Shree Swaminarayan Gadi and lovingly touched it. He then departed for America. One night, Jeevanpran Swamibapa gave *darshan* to Karsan Bhagat and said, "You came to Maninagar but I was away. You intended to ask me to perform a scripture recital on behalf of an old lady. Today, I have taken her to the abode." Jeevanpran Swamibapa then informed Karsan Bhagat of the exact time of this occurrence and then

withdrew his *darshan*. The following morning, Karsan Bhagat told all his relatives what happened that night. A few days later, a letter reached America from Salal, informing them all that the old lady had been taken to the abode. The day and the time stated in the letter were exactly the same as Jeevanpran Swamibapa had told Karsan Bhagat.

Eternal salvation can only be attained through the Adya Acharya-pravar of Shree Swaminarayan Gadi. Therefore, in every respect, Shree Swaminarayan Gadi is the essential resort for those who seek salvation.

Jeevanpran Swamibapa is always present everywhere. Through his idol-form (*pratima murti*), he remains ever-present. He has revealed this fact through many miraculous and amazing occurrences. In Viramgam, at the home of Manubhai; in Bavla, at the home of Mafatbhai; in Vadodara, at the home of Shankarbhai; in Nandanagar-Ahmedabad, at the home of Prabhudasbhai; and at many other places, Jeevanpran Swamibapa has revealed beads of perspiration emerging from his *Murti*. Such *darshan* has occurred on many occasions and has been witnessed by numerous people.

Many disciples of Shree Swaminarayan Gadi live in London, U.K. By the divine grace of Jeevanpran Swamibapa, Shree Swaminarayan Siddhant Sajivan Mandal has been established there. Under the auspices of this Mandal, a Shree Swaminarayan Temple has been built there. The divine *Murtis* of Purna Purushottam Lord Shree Swaminarayan, Shreeji-sankalp-swaroop Jeevanpran Bapashree, the Sadgurus and Jeevanpran Swamibapa have been installed in the Temple. Once, on the auspicious day of Guru-poonam, the followers gathered at the Temple to offer adoration to their guru. The guru of them all, Jeevanpran Swamibapa was presiding in Maninagar at the time. There too, the festival of Guru-poonam was being celebrated.

With their deep conviction and faith about the omnipresence of the Lord, the devotees at London lovingly placed the *Murtis* of Purna Purushottam Lord Shree Swaminarayan, Jeevanpran Bapashree and Jeevanpran Swamibapa on an elaborate stage and commenced their adoration. They offered garlands, bracelets, fruits, garments etc. to the Lord and then offered *aarti*. They began to praise the glory and greatness of their guru. Suddenly, a divine and pleasant sound, like that of a sitar was heard. This melodious sound resonated through

Shree Swaminarayan Siddhant Sajivan Mandal
The association to sustain and propogate the true principles of Lord Shree Swaminarayan

Shreeji-sankalp-swaroop
The physical embodiment of the thoughts of Lord Swaminarayan, i.e. those who give darshan upon this Earth by the will of the Lord; they are synonymous with the Lord Himself

Sadguru
Status of eminent ascetics (sants)

Guru-poonam
A day dedicated to honour and offer adoration to one's Guru. Ashadh Sud Poonam

Aarti
Ritual ceremony. See Appendix

295

Sinhasan
Ornately decorated shrine where the idols of the Lord are installed

Sampraday
Holy fellowship

the entire assembly. Everyone was astonished and began to look around. They looked towards the *sinhasan*. It was swaying to the rhythm of the melodious sound. At this instant, the divine *Murtis* of Shree Ghanshyam Maharaj, Jeevanpran Bapashree and Shreemad-acharya-pravar Jeevanpran Swamibapa installed in the *sinhasan* emitted a divine lustre and gently smiled as they swayed with the melody and showered their graceful gaze upon all. Everyone was captivated by this divine *darshan*. The *Murti* of Jeevanpran Swamibapa giving *darshan* in a resting position had been installed in the top section of the *sinhasan*. Jeevanpran Swamibapa himself appeared through this *Murti* and was seen gently smiling and by raising both his hands was blessing the assembly. Everyone became entranced by the divine *darshan*. To provide the bliss of the Guru-poonam festival to all his disciples and fulfil their spiritual desires, Jeevanpran Swamibapa gave *darshan* in this divine form. Such is the greatness of the beloved saviour of millions, the Adya Acharya-pravar of Shree Swaminarayan Gadi, Jeevanpran Swamibapa.

Shreemad-acharya-pravar Jeevanpran Swamibapa grants *darshan* to innumerable devotees and takes them to the abode. Accepting the prayers of his devotees, he also allows them to remain in this world, even if their intended life-span has come to an end.

There are innumerable such divine and extraordinary miracles of the Adya Acharya-pravar of Shree Swaminarayan Gadi Jeevanpran Swamibapa. If they were all to be described, numerous volumes would be compiled.

To become free from the bondage of the cycle of birth and death and attain eternal salvation, one must resort to Shree Swaminarayan Gadi. This characteristic is exclusive to the Swaminarayan *Sampraday*.

Salvation-Granting Pilgrimage

In Samvat 2029 Fagan Sud 3, the annual installation anniversary of Shree Ghanshyam Maharaj at Shree Swaminarayan Temple, Maninagar was celebrated. Shreemad-acharya-pravar Jeevanpran Swamibapa then led a group of disciples on a salvation-granting pilgrimage (Moksh-dayi-yatra) of Northern India Samvat 2029 from Fagan Sud 5 to Fagan Vad 13 (Friday 9th March to Sunday 1st April 1973). The pilgrimage entourage left Maninagar by coach. There were twenty coaches for the devotees and two coaches for the *sants*.

After leaving Maninagar, the group first went to the village of Todla, the manifestation site of Shreeji-sankalp Sadguru Shree Gopalanand Swami. From there, they went to Shamlaji, Udaipur, Nathdwara, Kakroli, Ajmer, Pushkarrai, Jaipur, Agra and eventually reached Mathura. In Mathura, the temple Chief Priest, Chobeji, held a grand procession through the city of Mathura to honour Shreemad-acharya-pravar Jeevanpran Swamibapa. The entire city began to recite the Swaminarayan name and sing the glory of the Adya Acharya-pravar of Shree Swaminarayan Gadi Jeevanpran Swamibapa. At various places during the procession, the citizens of Mathura honoured Jeevanpran Swamibapa. The procession finally reached Vishram-ghat, the banks of the sacred river Jamuna, where an assembly was held. Shreemad-acharya-pravar Jeevanpran Swamibapa showered his divine blessings over all.

Shreemad-acharya-pravar
Pioneer and chief spiritual preceptor of the throne

Jeevanpran
Life and soul

Sants
An Ascetic, the closest Western equivalent being monks

Shreeji-sankalp
The physical embodiment of the thoughts of Lord Swaminarayan, i.e. those who give darshan upon this Earth by the will of the Lord; they are synonymous with the Lord Himself

Sadguru
Status of eminent ascetics (sants)

Adya Acharya-pravar
Pioneer and chief spiritual preceptor of the throne

The great scholars of the Vedas performing the Vasant Pooja to honour Jeevanpran Swamibapa in Kashi (Banaras) They also presented Jeevanpran Swamibapa with two honorary titles, 'Ved-shastra-sanrakshak' and Vishwa-dharma-chudamani'.

297

Ved-shastra-sanrakshak
Protector of the eternal
scriptures, the Vedas

Vishwa-dharma-chudamani
Crown jewel of the
worldwide religion

The pilgrimage proceeded to Vrundavan, Gokul and Govardhan-giri. The next day, they left Mathura and proceeded to Delhi. During this journey, due to the intense fog, the Number Three coach overturned. However, Shreemad-acharya-pravar Jeevanpran Swamibapa was their protector, so no-one was hurt. One by one, each passenger emerged from the coach, totally unharmed. A one and a half year old boy was sleeping when the accident occurred. Luggage had fallen all around him and had entrapped him. However, when the luggage was moved, the boy was found to be still sleeping peacefully, unaffected by the accident. Nobody was harmed. The immensely powerful Shreemad-acharya-pravar Jeevanpran Swamibapa was with them. Why should anyone have any worries or fears?

The pilgrimage proceeded to Modinagar, Hardwar, Rushikesh, Luknow, Ayodhya, and reached Chhapaiya and then arrived in Kashi, where an unprecedented event took place. The eminent scholars of Kashi held a special assembly in honour of Jeevanpran Swamibapa. During this extraordinary assembly, the Mayor of Banaras, Shree Puranchandra Pathak presented the City Award to Jeevanpran Swamibapa. The scholars presented Jeevanpran Swamibapa with two honorary titles, 'Ved-shastra-sanrakshak' and 'Vishwa-dharma-chudamani' (Samvat 2029 Fagan Vad 5, Saturday 24th March 1973).

The Mayor of Banaras
presenting Jeevanpran
Swamibapa with the City Award

Then, the great scholars of the Vedas performed the Vasant Pooja to honour Jeevanpran Swamibapa whilst singing verses from the Sam-ved. Shreemad-acharya-pravar Jeevanpran Swamibapa then delivered a lecture about the Sam-ved scripture, in the Sanskrut language.

A magnificent procession was held through the streets of Kashi – Banaras, with Shreemad-acharya-pravar Jeevanpran Swamibapa presiding on an elephant (Samvat 2029 Fagan Vad 6, Sunday 25th March 1973). Everywhere, the people of the city honoured Swamibapa and showered flowers over him. The pilgrimage then proceeded to Allahbad, Prayag (Triveni-sangam), Chitrakut, Ujjain, Dakor and Bavla, before returning to Maninagar.

Throughout the pilgrimage, Shreemad-acharya-pravar Jeevanpran Swamibapa was warmly welcomed and honoured at each place. Thousands of people warmly greeted him. Such is Jeevanpran Swamibapa, the beloved father of all.

Vedas
Ancient Hindu scriptures

Vasant Pooja
Ancient ceremony traditionally performed during spring-time

Sam-Ved
There are four Vedas namely Rug-Ved, Yajur-Ved, Sam-Ved, Atharva-Ved. Of these the Samved is specified for Sarvariya Brahmin. Dharmadev, the father of Lord Swaminarayanwas Sarvariya Brahmin. Therefore verses of Sam-Ved were chanted to honour Jeevanpran Swamibapa

Panchamrut-snan
Ceremonial bathing using the five nectars: Milk, yoghurt, clarified butter, honey and saffron water

Sants and devotees perform the panchamrut–snan ceremony to Jeevanpran Swamibapa in the River Ganges at Haridwar

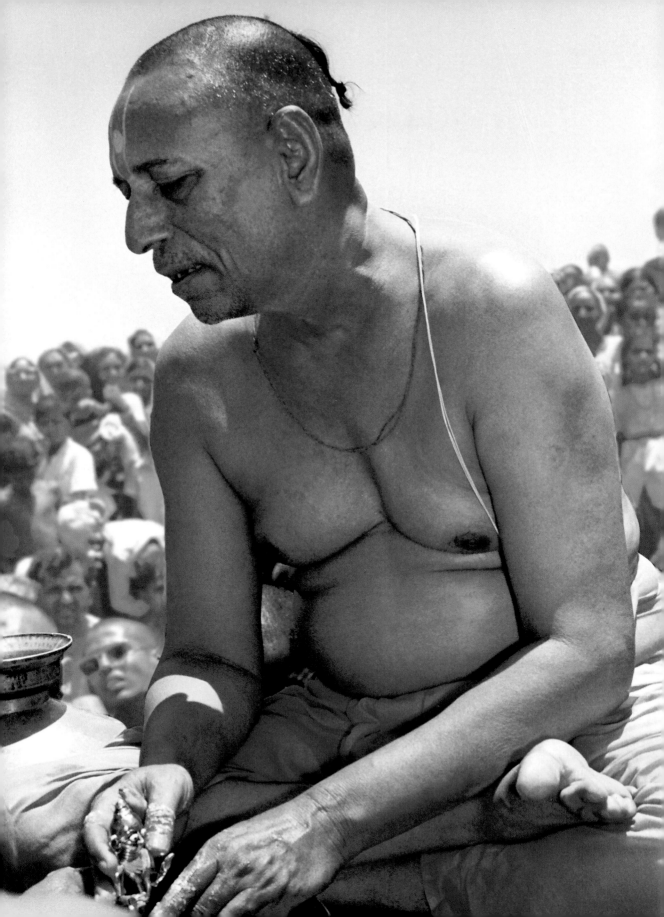

Shree Swaminarayan Gadi

In accordance with the command given by Purna Purushottam Lord Shree Swaminarayan to Jeevanpran Swamibapa:

- Shree Swaminarayan Gadi has been established by Purna Purushottam Lord Shree Swaminarayan Himself.
- Shree Swaminarayan Gadi had been established from the time when the helm of the entire *Sampraday* was entrusted to Sadguru Shree Gopalanand Swami.
- The foundations of this *Sampraday* were created by Sadguru Shree Ramanand Swami, who was an ascetic. He entrusted the throne of the *Sampraday* to Nilkanthvarni – Shree Sahajanand Swami – Lord Shree Swaminarayan.
- Lord Shree Swaminarayan handed over the responsibility of the entire religion and Shree Swaminarayan Gadi to Sadguru Shree Gopalanand Swami. This Shree Swaminarayan Gadi remained in a concealed form until it was revealed by the fourth in the spiritual lineage, Jeevanpran Swamibapa, in accordance with the command of Lord Shree Swaminarayan Himself.
- Shree Swaminarayan Gadi is the supreme, paramount Gadi because, according to the spiritual knowledge of the *Vishishtadwait* philosophy explained by Lord Shree Swaminarayan, the status of *Anadi-mukta* is disseminated from Shree Swaminarayan Gadi.
- The principles of the supreme *upasana*, chaste devotion, having the strength of faith about the form of the Lord, etc. are preached and practised only at Shree Swaminarayan Gadi. Lord Shree Swaminarayan Himself works through the spiritual sovereigns of Shree Swaminarayan Gadi; Sadguru Shree Gopalanand Swami, Sadguru Shree Nirgundasji Swami, Sadguru Shree Ishwarcharandasji Swami and Shree Jeevanpran Swamibapa. Through them, He remains ever-present and performs miraculous deeds. He will continue in this manner, through this heritage.

Purna Purushottam
Almighty, supreme Lord of Lords

Jeevanpran
Life and soul

Sampraday
Holy fellowship

Sadguru
Status of eminent ascetics (sants)

Vishishtadwait
Philosophy of the Swaminarayan faith. See Appendix

Anadi-mukta
Highest state of a liberated soul. See Chapter 1

Upasana
Correct understanding of the Lord. See Appendix

301

■ There is not even an iota of difference between the divine form (*dham-nu-swaroop*) of Lord Shree Swaminarayan that resides in Akshardham, His human form (*manushya-swaroop*) that manifested in Samvat 1837 in Chhapaiya, and the idol-form (*pratima-swaroop*) of Shree Ghanshyam Maharaj etc. that are installed in the supreme temples.

■ The ever-presence and omnipresence of Purna Purushottam Lord Shree Swaminarayan can only be, and will forever be, experienced at this Gadi.

Those who seek salvation, take resort at Shree Swaminarayan Gadi.

In the scriptures of the *Sampraday*, Lord Shree Swaminarayan had described His own glory in an indirect manner, in accordance with the situation at that time. However, His supreme *upasana*, glory, unsurpassed spiritual knowledge and His true, heartfelt intentions were not stated in clear, categorical terms in the scriptures of the time and therefore details of the true spiritual knowledge and principles were not fully revealed. However, the dissemination and preaching of this supreme spiritual knowledge remained alive through the verbal preachings of His spiritual successors. The *sants* and *sadgurus* who were associated with Jeevanpran Bapashree, such as Purani Dharmakishordasji and Shree Shwetvaikunthdasji Swami of Muli, and many others were fortunate to hear about this true, supreme, spiritual knowledge, and talked about it in assemblies on many occasions. The message of the true, supreme spiritual knowledge and glory has been passed down through the lineage of the Lord's spiritual heirs. Lord Shree Swaminarayan works through Sadguru Shree Gopalanand Swami, Sadguru Shree Nirgundasji Swami, Sadguru Shree Ishwarcharandasji Swami and Jeevanpran Swamibapa. Examples of how Lord Shree Swaminarayan has worked through them have been depicted in this scripture. These events and miracles are well known throughout the entire *Satsang*. Those who sincerely seek salvation, have total faith in the supremacy of Lord Shree Swaminarayan as narrated by His spiritual heirs, and become disciples of Shree Swaminarayan Gadi. They faithfully pray to Lord Shree Swaminarayan each day, and remain associated with Jeevanpran Swamibapa. Their faith shall be fulfilled and they will attain eternal salvation (*aatyantik-moksh*) during their present life.

Finally, a prayer to Purna Purushottam Lord Shree Swaminarayan, Jeevanpran Bapashree, the Sadgurus and Shreemad-acharya-pravar Jeevanpran Swamibapa.

'Enlighten the flame of faith in the hearts of all. May that light abolish the darkness of ignorance, so that all become disciples of Shree Swaminarayan Gadi, attain the status of *Anadi-mukta* and live pious lives in the service of the *Satsang*. This is our humble prayer.'

निजाश्रितानां सकलार्तिहन्ता सधर्मभक्तेरवनं विधाता ।
दाता सुखानां मनसेप्सितानां तनोतु कृष्णोऽखिलमङ्गलं नः ।।

Nijaashritaanaam sakalaartihantaa
Sadharmabhakte-ravanam vidhaataa
Daataa sukhaanaam manasepsitaanaam
Tanotu Krushno-khilamangalam naha

May such a merciful Lord (Lord Shree Swaminarayan)
who destroys all the pains of His disciples
fulfils their wishes, and who protects the faith
bestow His divinity upon us all
(Shikshapatri, Slok 212)

This concludes the English translation of the scripture,
Shree Swaminarayan Gadi

Created by
His Divine Holiness Acharya Swamishree Purushottampriyadasji Maharaj

Jay Shree Swaminarayan

Shreemad-acharya-pravar
Pioneer and chief spiritual preceptor of the throne

Shikshapatri
Scripture containing the holy commandments of Lord Swaminarayan.
See Appendix

Appendix

Supreme Upasana

Understanding the glory of Lord Shree Swaminarayan to be as great and supreme as it truly is, and having faith in Him accordingly, is called having upasana to him.

The word upasana is derived from;
Up, meaning near, and Asan, meaning to remain with an unfaltering status.

Therefore, the definition of upasana is to remain in the vicinity of Lord Shree Swaminarayan with a firm status. This perfectly describes the status of Anadi-mukta, who exist in the same form as the supreme Lord (Purushottam-roop) and are merged into His Murti. They always remain in the Murti of Lord Shree Swaminarayan and constantly enjoy His supreme bliss.

The four fundamental pillars, which are the foundations of supreme upasana that must be categorically understood are;

1   Lord Shree Swaminarayan is the supreme, incarnator of all incarnations (Sarvavatari) God.

2   Lord Shree Swaminarayan is divine and always exists with a human-like form. He is not just a light or a mass of energy.

3   Lord Shree Swaminarayan is always present everywhere.

4   Lord Shree Swaminarayan is omniscient and knows about everyone's innermost thoughts. Therefore, each of His commands must be faithfully obeyed.

If such upasana for Lord Shree Swaminarayan is understood, and put into practice then eternal salvation (aatyantik-moksh), the status of Anadi-mukta can be attained. Such understanding can only truly be gained through remaining associated with the Acharya of Shree Swaminarayan Gadi.

Hindu Calendar

The reference point that is used as the starting point of the most widely used calendar in Hinduism, is the coronation year of King Vikramaditya of Ujjain, in Central India. The Vikram Era, or the Vikram Samvat (Samvat or V.S.) commenced in 57 BC.

According to the Hindu calendar, the months are based around the lunar cycle, the seasons are based on the solar cycle and the days are based around both. Each solar year is divided into 12 lunar months. Each month is further divided into two equal halves. The first half (Sud) is referred to as the bright half and this corresponds to the 15 days from when there is a new moon to when a full moon is visible (Poonam), i.e. when the moon is waxing. The dark half (Vad) refers to when the moon is waning, i.e. the 15 days from the full moon to when there is none (Amas).

Each lunar day is called a Tithi. These are calculated using the difference of the longitudinal angle between the position of the Sun and Moon. As a result, Tithis vary in length and on certain days, they may not have changed by sunrise. Consequently, there can be occasions when a Tithi is omitted or two consecutive days have the same Tithi.

The lunar months correspond to the following solar months, and make up the six seasons (rutu).

Kartik	October - November	Sharad rutu (autumn)
Magshar	November – December	
Posh	December – January	Hemant rutu (1st half of winter)
Maha	January – February	
Fagan	February – March	Shishir rutu (2nd half of winter)
Chaitra	March – April	
Vaishakh	April – May	Vasant rutu (spring)
Jeth	May – June	
Ashadh	June – July	Greeshma rutu (summer)
Shravan	July – August	
Bhadarva	August – September	Varsha rutu (monsoon)
Aaso	September – October	

Ekadashi

The eleventh day of each half of the lunar month is called ekadashi (literally translated as 11) and is observed by devotees as a day of fasting. This fasting does not refer just to food but also restrictions on the five senses, their organs and also the mind. These eleven (i.e. the five senses, the five organs of the senses and the mind) are deprived of enjoyments to worldly afflictions and are instead concentrated on the Lord.

Prabodhini Ekadashi

Kartik Sud 11, also known as Prabodhini ekadashi, is when the four month fasting season (chatur-mas) comes to an end. It is the first ekadashi after the Diwali festival. Prabodh means to awaken. This is the day that the Lord (Dev) is said to arise from his four-month sleep.

For disciples of Shree Swaminarayan Gadi, this day has an even greater significance as six great historical events occurred on this day:

- In the year Samvat 1796, Lord Swaminarayan's father, Dharmadev was born in the village of Itar.
- In the year Samvat 1857 in the village of Piplana, Sadguru Shree Ramanand Swami initiated Shree Nilkanthvarni, Lord Swaminarayan as a sant.
- In Samvat 1858, Sadguru Shree Ramanand Swami handed over the entire helm of the religion to Shree Sahajanand Swami Maharaj, Lord Swaminarayan.
- From the moment He took control of the religion, Lord Swaminarayan also became seated upon His divine throne, Shree Swaminarayan Gadi.
- Jeevanpran Shree Abji Bapashree gave darshan upon this earth today in the year Samvat 1901 in the village of Vrushpur, Kutch, Gujarat.
- Jeevanpran Shree Muktajeevan Swamibapa took initiation as a sant from His gurudev Sadguru Shree Ishwarcharandasji Swami on this day in the year Samvat 1986 in Saraspur, Ahmedabad.

Due to the significance of this day, a 24-hour continuous dhoon (chanting of the Lord's name) is held at the headquarters of the Karan Satsang, Shree Swaminarayan Temple, Maninagar.

Adhik Mas

Every three years, an adjustment is made in the calendar (synonymous to the Western leap year). An extra month is added to the year. This is called the Adhik (extra), or Purushottam Mas (the month of the Lord). The extra month carries the name of its subsequent month. The Adhik month is considered very auspicious and extra observances (vrat) are taken during it's duration.

Theological Ages

In Hinduism, there are four theological ages of time (Yug) in which the life of the universe is divided. They are based around the age of Brahma, the deity of creation. Each age is graced with the appearance of an incarnation of God.

Sat-yug is the first of the four ages and is the largest, lasting 1,728,000 (432,000 x 4) years. This age is regarded as the ideal golden age of truth, morality, religion, bliss, prosperity and perfection. Lord Dattatreya incarnated during this age.

Treta-yug is the second of the four ages, lasting 1,296,000 (432,000 x 3) years, with Maryada Purushottam – Lord Ramchandraji, preaching observance to the principles of behaviour according to the Vedic scriptures.

Dwapar-yug is the third of the four ages, lasting 864,000 (432,000 x 2) years with Leela Purushottam – Lord Krishna giving affection through his divine episodes.

Kali-yug is the fourth, lasting 432,000 years. This is regarded as the age of immorality and sin, which leads to the ultimate destruction of the universe. It is in this age that the supreme, Purna Purushottam Lord Swaminarayan manifested upon this Earth.

Vishishtadwait Philosophy

There are five schools of thought and ideology in Hindu philosophy; Adwait, Dwait-dwait, Dwait, Shuddhadwait and Vishishtadwait. They are all very complex and are concerned with the distinction between the Lord, humans, and the nature of the cosmos. The Vishishtadwait philosphy was founded by Shree Ramanujacharya, an eminent philosopher who lived in the 11th

Century CE. His philosophy described three ultimate realities; the Lord, souls and matter (the creations of Maya). Of these, only the Lord is the independent reality and the other two are dependent upon Him. The soul and the matter are thus distinct from the Lord and not separate from Him. According to Shree Ramanujacharya, the Lord is the creator, preserver and the destroyer of the world. Liberation is not absorption with the Lord, but union with Him.

Lord Swaminarayan accepted the basics of this ideology, but added His own specific distinctions. He revealed that there are five, not three, eternal and real entities; Jeev, Maya, Ishwar, Brahm and Parabhrahm. The Parabrahm refers to the supreme Lord. The other four entities are dependent on, and are obedient to Him. These four entities remain distinct, but not separate from the Lord. They are two real and identical entities; the master and the devotee. When the two merge, they appear as one, the master. Yet in reality they remain distinct in their nature and their attributes, with the Lord remaining the master and the soul forever the mastered.

Tilak-chandlo and Kanthi

The mark of the tilak-chandlo distinguishes a follower of Lord Swaminarayan from all others. The sight of it will prompt others to utter the name Swaminarayan, or for those who do not know, to urge them to enquire about its significance and thereby, they too will become introduced to Lord Swaminarayan, through His devotees, as a result of this mark.

The tilak is made of sandalwood paste (chandan). This has a cool, soothing effect and the fragrance helps to maintain a pure and clear mind. The chandlo is made of red kanku (potash nitrate). The tilak-chandlo is impressed daily by all male devotees of Lord Swaminarayan as part of their morning worship (pooja). It is impressed on the forehead (to ensure one's thoughts remain pious and moral), on both upper arms (giving the strength to do virtuous deeds) and on the chest (to ensure spiritual emotions of the heart). The female devotees apply a red chandlo of kanku on their forehead. This mark, according to Hindu belief signifies "akhand suhag", eternal union, which comes with the marriage of a woman to man. This mark of the Swaminarayan religion signifies the marriage of the devotee to God and one's chaste devotion for the Lord.

The kanthi is a double stranded necklace made of wooden beads, usually the sacred tulsi plant. When disciples place a kanthi around their neck, they take the vows of the religion and swear by their own necks to abide by them.

The tilak-chandlo and kanthi are unique to the Swaminarayan religion. They symbolise the Vishishtadwait philosophy of Lord Swaminarayan. The tilak represents the Lord and the chandlo represents the Muktas that reside within Him. Once the Muktas enter the Murti, they eternally remain there. There is a union between them, i.e. they appear as one, but there is a distinction, the master and the devotee. When the two merge, they appear as one - the master (just like the tilak-chandlo is one symbol, and the kanthi is one necklace), but in reality they remain distinct in their nature and their attributes, with God remaining the master and the soul forever remaining the servant. Similarly, the kanthi appears as one unit but in reality it is composed of two identical strands.

The Vachanamrut Scripture

This is the principal scripture of the Swaminarayan Sampraday. It contains a collation of the divine discourses of Lord Shree Swaminarayan Himself. Vachan means speech and Amrut means nectar. Therefore, the Vachanamrut scripture contains the sweet words of Lord Swaminarayan, i.e. they are the explicit words of the Lord.

The scripture contains 273 Vachanamruts divided into separate sections, named after the town in which the discourse was held, i.e. Gadhada, Sarangpur, Kariyani, Loya, Panchala, Ahmedabad, Aslali and Vadtal. The discourses held in Gadhada are further divided into 3 parts, Gadhada First Section, Gadhada Middle Section, and Gadhada Last Section.

This narrative of the Lord was compiled into this great scripture by Sadguru Shree Gopalanand Swami, Shree Muktanand Swami, Shree Nityanand Swami, Shree Brahmanand Swami and Shree Shukanand Swami. The words are written in exactly the same manner as they were spoken, in a question and answer form. The start of each Vachanamrut mentions the date, the place and even the divine garments that the Lord had adorned on that day.

The Vachanamrut is a comprehensive, philosophical scripture containing the true essence of all the previous Hindu scriptures. The complex issues discussed in the Vachanamrut are difficult to understand without guidance. Only those who give darshan on behalf of the Lord can elucidate on the meanings of the Lord's words. So that everyone can understand the true meanings of the Vachanamrut scripture, Sadguru Shree Ishwarcharandasji Swami collated questions about various apparent contradictions within the text. Jeevanpran Shree Bapashree mercifully explained their true meanings. This glorious, explanatory text was compiled as a commentary to the Vachanamrut, called Shree Rahasyarth Pradeepika Tika. The remarkable aspect of this commentary is that Jeevanpran Bapashree answered each question by referring to another Vachanamrut; no other scripture has been used as a justification. Consequently, the meanings of the Vachanamrut have been explained according to the Vachanamrut itself.

Shikshapatri

This divine scripture was written by the supreme Lord Swaminarayan Himself. The essence of 354 Scriptures is comprised in 212 sloks. They contain the values that Lord Swaminarayan so mercifully advocates and describe the fundamental rules that one should abide by, in order to lead an honest and moral life. The Shikshapatri is an important text for all, whether they are of the Swaminarayan faith or not. It is just as relevant today as it was when the divine scripture was written. The merciful Lord Swaminarayan has given guidance on various issues that affect everyone's lives, such as one's ethics, the ideology of non-violence (ahinsa), guidance about the standards that must be adopted in one's daily life, the restrictions about food and drink, social and professional etiquette, guidance for the rulers of society, tolerance, devotion etc.

Aarti

This devotional ceremony involves the waving of lighted wicks in front of the Murti of the Lord. In ancient times when there was no electricity, this form of light was used to attract the attention of devotees to the Murti of God. The lighted wicks are waved in clockwise motion so that the whole Murti can be seen. A small bell is also rung during the ceremony and a drum beat is sounded to attract and inform people that the aarti ceremony is being performed, so that they can come for darshan.